'This wide-ranging collection of essays has much to offer students of fantasy, children's literature, film, illustration, and anyone who has a deep interest in Tolkien's writings.' – **Susan Hancock**, *University of Roehampton*

J. R. R. Tolkien is arguably the most influential and popular of all fantasy writers. Although his position and status have long been controversial, his popularity has not faded. His best-loved works, *The Hobbit* and *The Lord of the Rings*, have sold millions of copies around the world and continue to enthral readers young and old.

This lively collection of original essays examines *The Hobbit* and *The Lord of the Rings* in the light of children's literature theory and approaches, as well as from adult and fantasy literature perspectives. Exploring issues such as gender, language, worldbuilding, and ecocriticism, the volume also places Tolkien's works in the context of a range of visual media, including Peter Jackson's film adaptations.

Peter Hunt is Professor Emeritus at Cardiff University where he was the first specialist in Children's Literature to be appointed full Professor of English in a British university.

This latest series of *New Casebooks* consists of brand new critical essays specially commissioned to provide students with fresh thinking about key texts and writers. Like the original series, the volumes embrace a range of approaches designed to illuminate the rich interchange between critical theory and critical practice.

D1145391

New Casebooks
Collections of all new critical essays

CHILDREN'S LITERATURE

MELVIN BURGESS
Edited by Alison Waller

ROBERT CORMIER
Edited by Adrienne E. Gavin

ROALD DAHL
Edited by Ann Alston & Catherine Butler

C. S. LEWIS: *THE CHRONICLES OF NARNIA*
Edited by Michelle Ann Abate & Lance Weldy

J. K. ROWLING: *HARRY POTTER*
Edited by Cynthia J. Hallett & Peggy J. Huey

J. R. R. TOLKIEN: *THE HOBBIT* AND *THE LORD OF THE RINGS*
Edited by Peter Hunt

NOVELS AND PROSE

JOHN FOWLES
Edited by James Acheson

FURTHER TITLES ARE CURRENTLY IN PREPARATION

For a full list of published titles in the past format of the New Casebooks series, visit the series page at www.palgrave.com

---

New Casebooks Series

Series Standing Order
ISBN   978-0-333-71702-8   hardcover
ISBN   978-0-333-69345-2   paperback
(Outside North America only)

You can receive future titles in this series as they are published by placing a standing order. Please contact your bookseller or, in case of difficulty, write to us at the address below with your name and address, the title of the series and the ISBN quoted above.

Customer Services Department, Macmillan Distribution Ltd, Houndmills, Basingstoke, Hampshire, RG21 6XS, UK

New Casebooks

J. R. R. TOLKIEN
THE HOBBIT AND
THE LORD OF THE RINGS

Edited by

PETER HUNT

palgrave
macmillan

First published 2013 by
PALGRAVE MACMILLAN

Palgrave Macmillan in the UK is an imprint of Macmillan Publishers Limited, registered in England, company number 785998, of Houndmills, Basingstoke, Hampshire RG21 6XS.

Palgrave Macmillan in the US is a division of St Martin's Press LLC, 175 Fifth Avenue, New York, NY 10010.

Palgrave Macmillan is the global academic imprint of the above companies and has companies and representatives throughout the world.

Palgrave® and Macmillan® are registered trademarks in the United States, the United Kingdom, Europe and other countries.

ISBN 978–1–137–26400–8   hardback
ISBN 978–1–137–26399–5   paperback

This book is printed on paper suitable for recycling and made from fully managed and sustained forest sources. Logging, pulping and manufacturing processes are expected to conform to the environmental regulations of the country of origin.

A catalogue record for this book is available from the British Library.

A catalog record for this book is available from the Library of Congress.

Typeset by MPS Limited, Chennai, India.

Contents

Contents

Series Editor's Preface

Welcome to the latest series of New Casebooks.

Each volume now presents brand new essays specially written for university and other students. Like the original series, the new-look New Casebooks embrace a range of recent critical approaches to the debates and issues that characterize the current discussion of literature.

Each editor has been asked to commission a sequence of original essays which will introduce the reader to the innovative critical approaches to the text or texts being discussed in the collection. The intention is to illuminate the rich interchange between critical theory and critical practice that today underpins so much writing about literature.

Editors have also been asked to supply an introduction to each volume that sets the scene for the essays that follow, together with a list of further reading which will enable readers to follow up issues raised by the essays in the collection.

The purpose of this new-look series, then, is to provide students with fresh thinking about key texts and writers while encouraging them to extend their own ideas and responses to the texts they are studying.

Martin Coyle

Acknowledgements

A shorter version of C. W. Sullivan III's essay was presented at the 2012 International Conference of the Fantastic in the Arts, Orlando, Florida. Some of the material therein is briefly paraphrased or quoted from two of his previously published articles: 'J. R. R. Tolkien and the Rediscovery of the North', and 'J. R. R. Tolkien and the Telling of a Traditional Narrative'. The editor and publishers are grateful for the permission of Donald E. Morse for the Hungarian Society for the Study of English, and Brian Attebery, Editor of *Journal of the Fantastic in the Arts*, for permission to use this material.

The editor would like to acknowledge the help of Robin Rudd, St Leo University, Atlanta, in researching on-line writing, creative writing, and Tolkien's influence.

Notes on Contributors

Hazel Sheeky Bird was the recipient of an AHRC Collaborative Doctoral Award; her doctoral thesis was on British interwar camping and tramping fiction. Her current research concentrates on constructions of national identity in children's British and American naval fiction during the period 1890–1945.

Catherine Butler is Associate Professor in English at the University of the West of England. Her critical work has appeared in, among other places, *Children's Literature in Education* and *Children's Literature Association Quarterly*, and has been honoured with a ChLA Article Honor Award, and a Mythopoeic Scholarship Award for *Four British Fantasists* (Scarecrow Press, 2006). Catherine was co-author with Hallie O'Donovan of *Reading History in Children's Books* (Palgrave Macmillan, 2012), and co-editor with Ann Alston of *Roald Dahl: a New Casebook* (Palgrave Macmillan, 2012). Catherine has so far produced six novels for children and teenagers, as well as some shorter works.

Jane Suzanne Carroll's research interests include children's literature, landscape, Vikings, and textiles in literature. She has published a monograph, *Landscape in Children's Literature* (Routledge, 2012), as well as articles on twentieth-century ghost stories and children's fantasy. She lectures in English Literature in the Department of English and Creative Writing at the University of Roehampton.

Maria Sachiko Cecire is an Assistant Professor of Literature at Bard College, New York, where she teaches courses on children's literature, medieval literature and its reception, media studies, and cultural studies. She has published in each of these areas, with essays in *Anglo-Saxon Culture and the Modern Imagination*, *Arthurian Literature XXVIII*, and *The Journal of Children's Literature Studies*, and the forthcoming collection *Disney's Middle Ages*. She received her DPhil from the University of Oxford in 2011.

Kate Harvey is a researcher at Trinity College Dublin, where she teaches both early modern literature and children's literature in the School of English. She was awarded a PhD from Trinity College in 2012 for a thesis on adaptations of Shakespeare for children, and continues to research and publish on children's literature, Shakespeare, and visual adaptation, as well as regularly reviewing children's books for *Children's Books Ireland*.

Peter Hunt was the first specialist in Children's Literature to be appointed full Professor of English in a British University. He has written or edited 26 books and has written over 130 articles on the subject. Recent on-line projects include a *Checklist of Books on the History and Criticism of Children's Literature* (Newcastle University, 2012), and the Children's Literature section of the *Oxford Bibliographies Online* (2012). In 1995 the International Society for the Fantastic in the Arts presented him with their Distinguished Scholarship Award, and in 2003 he was awarded the Brothers Grimm Award for services to children's literature, from the International Institute for Children's Literature, Osaka.

Zoë Jaques is a postdoctoral research fellow at Anglia Ruskin University and a part-time lecturer at the University of Cambridge. Her central research interests include children's fiction, posthuman theory, ecocriticism, and gender. She is co-author of *Lewis Carroll's* Alice's Adventures in Wonderland *and* Through the Looking-Glass: A Publishing History (Ashgate: forthcoming). Her second book, *Children's Literature and the Posthuman* (Routledge), is in preparation.

Louise Joy is Fellow and Director of Studies in English at Homerton College, Cambridge. She has published on a range of eighteenth-, nineteenth- and twentieth-century literary topics. Her articles have appeared in journals including *Studies in Romanticism*, *History of European Ideas*, and *European Romantic Review*. She has co-edited a collection of essays entitled *Poetry and Childhood* (Trentham Books, 2010).

Keith O'Sullivan is Lecturer in English at the Church of Ireland College of Education, Dublin. He recently co-edited *Irish Children's Literature: New Perspectives on Contemporary Writing* (Routledge, 2011) and is currently co-editing a volume on children's literature and New York City for Routledge. He was the recipient of the inaugural David Almond Fellowship for Research in Children's Literature, awarded by Newcastle University and Seven Stories in 2012.

Shelley Saguaro is Head of the School of Humanities at the University of Gloucestershire. Recent publications include *Garden*

Plots: The Politics and Poetics of Gardens (Ashgate, 2006), 'Telling Trees: *Eucalyptus*, "Anon", and the Growth of Co-evolutionary Histories' in *Mosaic: a Journal for the Interdisciplinary Study of Literature* (2009), and a chapter on Toni Morrison's *Paradise* in *Literature as History* (Continuum, 2010). She is currently working on Virginia Woolf's late unpublished manuscript 'Anon', and *Between the Acts*.

C. W. Sullivan III is Emeritus Distinguished Professor of Arts and Sciences, retired from East Carolina University, and a Full Member of the Welsh Academy. He is the author of *Welsh Celtic Myth in Modern Fantasy* (Greenwood Press, 1989) and editor of *The Mabinogi: A Book of Essays* (Garland Press, 1996), eight other books, and the on-line journal *Celtic Cultural Studies*. He is a past president of the International Association for the Fantastic in the Arts, and his articles on mythology, folklore, fantasy, and science fiction have appeared in a variety of anthologies and journals. His most recent book, *Heinlein's Juveniles: A Cultural Dictionary*, was published in 2011 by McFarland.

Deborah Cogan Thacker is Subject Group Leader in Humanities at the University of Gloucestershire. She is co-author (with Jean Webb) of *Introducing Children's Literature: From Romanticism to Postmodernism* (Routledge, 2002), and articles and chapters on theoretical approaches to children's literature and the representation of child language in literature. Two of her articles, originally published in *The Lion and the Unicorn*, have been reprinted in *Children's Literature: Critical Concepts in Literary and Cultural Studies*, ed. Peter Hunt (Routledge, 2006). Her essay on 'Fairy Tale and Anti-Fairy Tale: Roald Dahl and the Telling Power of Stories' appears in *Roald Dahl: a New Casebook* (Palgrave Macmillan, 2012).

Introduction

Peter Hunt

Fantasy is literature for teenagers.

(Brian Aldiss)[1]

The Hobbit and *The Lord of the Rings* are probably the most widely read and most imitated works of fantasy ever written; they have affected directly or indirectly a great deal of fantasy produced for adults and for children across the world. Their importance has been increased by the electronic communications revolution, which has blurred the distinctions between print and other forms of text. As Steve Jackson observed, they have had 'a huge influence over all the role-playing games, from Dungeons and Dragons to Warhammer and ... Fighting Fantasy'[2] – and on into vast multiplayer role-playing games such as *World of Warcraft* (Blizzard Entertainment, 2004–). Similarly, readers have become writers to an extent unimaginable when Tolkien's books were published, and 'sub-Tolkien' writing has become a staple of creative writing courses. As Farah Mendlesohn and Edward James note:

> The current popularity of *The Lord of the Rings* has been fuelled by the fantasy genre's recursive plundering of its own material, by 'mentorship' (people handing the book on to their children and to other people's children), the long historical memory of fandom and of course by the impact of Peter Jackson's three spectacular movies.[3]

And, fundamentally, 'most subsequent writers of fantasy are either imitating [Tolkien] or else desperately trying to escape his influence'.[4]

There has been a good deal of discussion as to whether the 'Tolkien effect' has been entirely beneficial: the amateur imitators of Tolkien, in cyberspace or in creative writing classes, may miss many of the subtler characteristics of his books, and replace them with crude tropes and simplistic attitudes to society and gender. Terry Pratchett began his remarkable career as a fantasist in reaction to this kind of writing: 'Originally I just wanted to write a sort of antidote to some of the worst kind of post-Tolkien fantasy, what I call the "Belike, he will wax wroth" school of writing.'[5] Tolkien's cult status, especially in the 1970s, provoked

1

a fierce academic reaction, frequently bound up with, or confused with, issues surrounding the status of fantasy – such as that pointed out by Brian Aldiss in the epigraph to this Introduction. It is only recently that the critical flexibility necessary to deal with the explosion of interest in popular culture and multi-media culture has emerged.

For decades, Tolkien's books, worldwide bestsellers (to their author's somewhat mixed reaction), have been at the centre of debates about quality and popularity: they are at the intersection of discussions about children's books, children's literature, fantasy and 'literature'. Is Tolkien's brand of fantasy essentially trivial and essentially *childish*, and are his books, therefore (and damningly), fit only for immature minds? As Brian Rosebury succinctly put it:

> For Tolkien's hostile critics, patting *The Hobbit* on the head has become something of a tradition: the critic indicates a benevolent receptiveness towards 'fantasy' (when confined to the marginal world of children's books) before proceeding to ridicule the ambitious scale and implied adult readership of *The Lord of the Rings*.[6]

This volume of essays, however, reflects a critical attitude that accepts the intrinsic value of Tolkien's fictions, regardless of genre or intended (or actual) audience, while accepting that genre and audience have an inevitable influence on both texts and interpretations; it seeks to emphasise the positive outcomes of what has often been a negative debate. The essays link Tolkien's major fantasies to their linguistic and cultural roots, to the politics and literature of their times, and consider their relevance to contemporary discussions of fantasy, gender, cultural theory, and film.

But what exactly *are* these books – or this book, for as Edmund Fuller suggests:

> The four-part structure of the work is analogous to Wagner's Ring cycle of operas. A shorter, relatively childlike wonder tale (*Das Rheingold* and *The Hobbit* respectively) in each case introduces a massive trilogy.[7]

And is Fuller placing the books in their correct company? The early reviewers were not certain: of *The Fellowship of the Ring*, H. l'A. Fawcett wrote in the *Manchester Guardian* on 20 August 1954: 'Mr Tolkien is one of those born storytellers who makes his readers ... wide-eyed children.' And presciently, W. J. Lambert wrote in the *Sunday Times* on 8 August 1954: 'Whimsical drivel with a message? No: it sweeps along with a narrative and pictorial force which lifts it above that level. A book for bright children? Well, yes and no.'[8]

Adults' books/children's books

The simplest position, perhaps ironically in view of the negative attitude of a generation of critics to biographical evidence, is that *The Hobbit* not only reflects structural and linguistic characteristics of contemporary children's books, but that it was written, at least initially, for specific children. Christopher Tolkien said in 1937: 'Daddy wrote it ages ago, and read it to John, Michael and me in our Winter "Reads" after tea in the evening,'[9] and in February 1933 Jack (C. S.) Lewis wrote to a friend:

> Since term began I have had a delightful time reading a children's story that Tolkien has just written ... he also grew up on W. Morris and George MacDonald. Reading his fairy tale has been uncanny – it is so exactly what we would both have longed to write (or read) in 1916: so that one feels he is not making it up but merely describing the same world into which all three of us have the entry ... Whether it is really *good* is of course another question: still more, whether it will succeed with modern children.[10]

Tolkien's somewhat ambiguous attitude to the 'childness' of *The Hobbit* is explored in the essays by Keith O'Sullivan (Chapter 1) and Louise Joy (Chapter 5), in this volume; in summary, he seems on the one hand to have regretted those stylistic features which he derived from the 'appropriateness tool-box' of the contemporary children's book, while trying to maintain the connection between fantasy, adulthood, childhood and a kind of intellectual innocence or openness.

As Humphrey Carpenter observes:

> in *The Hobbit* the leaf-mould of Tolkien's mind nurtured a rich growth with which only a few other books in children's literature can compare. For it *is* a children's story. Despite the fact that it had been drawn into his mythology, Tolkien did not allow it to become overwhelmingly serious or even adult in tone, but stuck to his original intention of amusing his own and perhaps other people's children. Indeed he did this too consciously and deliberately at times in the first draft, which contains a large number of 'asides' to juvenile readers ... He later removed many of these, but some remain in the published text – to his regret, for he came to dislike them, and even to believe that any deliberate talking down to children is a great mistake in a story. 'Never mind about the young!' he once wrote. 'I am not interested in the "child" as such, modern or otherwise, and certainly have no intention of meeting him/her half way, or a quarter of the way. It is a mistaken thing to do anyway, either useless (when applied to the stupid) or pernicious (when inflicted on the gifted).' But when he wrote *The Hobbit*

he was still suffering from what he later called 'the contemporary delusions about "fairy-stories" and children' – delusions that not long afterwards he made a conscious decision to renounce.[11]

The Lord of the Rings, on the other hand, was from the outset designed for adults, or at least to inhabit a fictional world designed without children in mind. In October 1938, Tolkien wrote to Stanley Unwin that it was 'forgetting "children" and becoming more terrifying than *The Hobbit* ... It may prove quite unsuitable,' and he wrestled with the problem of appropriateness:

> [*The Lord of the Rings*] was *not* written 'for children', or for any kind of person in particular, but for itself. (If any parts or elements in it appear 'childish', it is because I am childish, and like that kind of thing myself *now*.) I believe children do read it or listen to it eagerly, even quite young ones, and I am very pleased to hear it, though they must fail to under-stand most of it, and it is in any case stuffed with words that they are unlikely to understand – if by that one means 'recognise as something already known'. I hope it increases their vocabularies.[12]

Tolkien seems to have been ambivalent about the status of his characters – Arthur Ransome, who knew exactly the status of *his* characters, 'wrote to Tolkien, describing himself as "a humble Hobbit fancier" and complaining about Gandalf's use of the term "excitable little man" as a description of Bilbo'.[13]

Tolkien's quandaries, as we shall see, have been repeated by many critics – notably, what is the difference between a child reader and a child-like reader? Tolkien might have been amused to find that both books appear in *The Ultimate Book Guide. Over 600 Great Books for 8–12s* – *The Lord of the Rings* being described as 'the Big Daddy of all sword and sourcery fantasy'; one of the child contributors, James Male (aged 11), noted: 'It took me all of the summer holidays to read ... It was the first book I ever read on the beach.'[14] Karen Haber's *Meditations on Middle-earth* cites several examples of authors who had read it from as early as eight years old: Ursula K. Le Guin read it to her children, appreciating the 'rhythmic pattern in *The Lord of the Rings*'; Terry Pratchett first read the trilogy beginning on 'New Year's Eve, 1961' when he was 13.[15] The critic Janet Menzies read it 'about age 10' and concluded: 'At that age the world of sensation and of landscape is very important. It is on those levels that I still think that *The Lord of the Rings* makes its primary impact'.[16]

For many years, conventional wisdom on children's texts would have been that the fact that a book is read by children does not make it a children's book: now, it is the readership that defines the category of 'crossover' books. Fundamentally, *The Lord of the Rings* has crossed from adult to (also) child readership, rather more successfully – ironically – than *The Hobbit* has between child and adult readers. This process has, of course, been partly impelled by marketing: when the film of *The Lion, the Witch and the Wardrobe* was released, the books were re-packaged, uncomfortably, as adult fantasy; other books have made a more natural transition, notably Ursula K. Le Guin's *Earthsea* books, and Philip Pullman's *His Dark Materials*.

One explanation of the status of each book is the 'story shapes' that Tolkien uses. A characteristic of the book for children is, it is commonly assumed, that its plot is 'circular': the protagonist leaves 'home' and security, has adventures, and returns to home and security – often to exactly the same place: classic examples are Lewis Carroll's *Alice's Adventures in Wonderland* (1865), Beatrix Potter's *The Tale of Peter Rabbit* (1902) and Arthur Ransome's *Swallows and Amazons* (1930). The novel of adolescence, or *bildungsroman*, tends to be rather more open-ended: characters start from home, often return towards it, but do not necessarily end there (although there is commonly a sense of some kind of resolution), as in Mark Twain's *The Adventures of Huckleberry Finn* (1884), Noel Streatfeild's *The Circus is Coming* (1938) and Arthur Ransome's *Secret Water* (1939). The characters in an 'adult' novel may have no home to come from or to go to, and their stories may not necessarily be resolved (interestingly, the final book of Ransome's 'Swallows and Amazons' sequence, *Great Northern?* (1947), has this mature shape, beginning and ending away from any home, on board a yacht in the Minches).

By this taxonomy, *The Hobbit, or There and Back Again* is a model for the children's book. Bilbo begins and ends the book in his comfortable home, having circled out into Wilderland and returned a little wiser and richer. His story in *The Lord of the Rings*, however, is far more adult: he begins, a psychologically displaced character in a home that is no longer secure, travels to a temporary home at Rivendell, and finally leaves Middle-earth altogether. The fact that his is not the only story, or the only story-shape in the books, has contributed to the confusion – for all three story-shapes subsist side-by-side. The children's story-shape is 'carried' by Sam, Merry and Pippin: Sam, especially, is as deeply rooted in the idyllic rural Shire as any character, and after his adventures he comes home to the Shire:

> And he went on, and there was yellow light, and fire within; and the evening meal was ready, and he was expected. And Rose drew him in, and set him in his chair, and put little Elanor upon his lap.
> He drew a deep breath. 'Well, I'm back,' he said.[17]

Like Merry and Pippin, who ride back to their homes in Bywater, he has grown, and although as a (temporary) Ring-bearer he will, it is implied, finally pass through the Grey Havens, Sam represents a return to normality and security.

In contrast, Frodo's story (which is, of course, enacted in parallel to Sam's) is a classic *bildungsroman*. He starts from home, is stabbed (literally) by experience, on Weathertop, and although he comes back to the Shire for a time, can never really return home. The circle is not completed, as he joins the Elves and Bilbo to leave Middle-earth. And it is the Elves and the Men, doomed to die, who represent the adult shape of the novel; they were there (as it were) before the novel begins; they pass through it towards decline and departure. The three story-shapes can be read as complementary, but their resonances are so different that it is hardly surprising that the status of *The Lord of the Rings* has seemed hybrid and ambivalent.

Another common confusion lies in the fact that protagonists of children's books are commonly children, and the hobbits are not (exactly) children. Like the central characters of Kenneth Grahame's *The Wind in the Willows* (1908) – another book of ambiguous status – they are adults, but adults who remain largely innocent of the danger-ous and evil ways of the world. They have some ambivalent 'child*like*' characteristics, and so, for the child-audience of *The Hobbit*, and for the kind of adult reader implied for *The Lord of the Rings*, the hobbits can be empathised with. As William H. Green noted, this is an interesting trick:

> So, by omission and contrast, Tolkien achieves indirectly what Goethe must use the machinery of a witch's potion to achieve in *Faust*: he creates a male-menopausal protagonist endowed with the energy and appeal of youth, a children's-book hero.[18]

Critics have consequently attempted to parallel the innate strength of character of the hobbits with the supposed strengths of children in general: they are simultaneously small and vulnerable (and treat Gandalf as a father figure), and yet are (to those with a romantic turn of mind) tenacious, ingenious, and independent.

It is important to distinguish between 'child*like*' and 'child*ish*'; Edmund Fuller, quoting one of the more famous attacks on Tolkien, by Philip Toynbee (in the *Observer*, 1961), that the books were '… dull, ill-written, whimsical and childish', comments:

> Here he has elected the unfavourable suffix, where I would say 'child-*like*.' The kingdom of wonder, like that of Heaven, is one scarcely to be

entered except ye be as a little child. I am afraid that the critic here is too anxious to preserve his adult standing because the work lies within the reach of children and contains elements altogether mistakenly thought by some to be reserved exclusively for them.[19]

Critical confusions

One of the difficulties inherent in discussing Tolkien's books, and bringing fantasy and children's books together, is that we are, despite remarkable changes in critical thinking over the past fifty years, dealing with modes of writing that are not fully 'respectable'. In the 1980s, around the time that the British satirical magazine *Private Eye* commented that *The Lord of the Rings* appeals only to those 'with the mental age of a child – computer programmers, hippies and most Americans',[20] one of the most distinguished of Tolkien's commentators, Tom Shippey, noted that one of the problems that critics had with the books lay in the fact that normal critical tools are not appropriate: 'Tolkien may be a peripheral writer for the theory of fiction. However, it seems time to pay more attention to the peripheries, and less to the well-trodden centre.'[21] Since then, it is frequently asserted, the critical landscape has shifted; fantasy has become part of the mainstream, and the study of children's literature is now a respectable academic discipline.

But despite that, the inclusion of *The Lord of the Rings* in a critical series devoted to children's literature might serve to confirm some worst suspicions – that Tolkien is fit only for children and that children and their books are by definition inferior. It may be over a decade since the idea that a Harry Potter book might take the Whitbread Award aroused derision, but an academic conference on Harry Potter at St Andrews University in May 2012 drew the comment from John Mullan, professor of English at University College London, that 'It's all the fault of cultural studies: anything that is consumed with any appearance of appetite by people becomes an object of academic study ... [Academics] should be reading Milton and Tristram Shandy: that's what they're paid to do.'[22] Which is merely to say that in writing about these books in relation to a less-experienced reading audience, or in relation to a particular mode of literature, it is as well not to take any literary-critical assumptions for granted.

The need for this can be demonstrated by the difficulties that even the supporters of Tolkien get themselves into – even to the extent of covertly or subconsciously resenting the stigma of children's literature being applied to the books. Critics of Tolkien who come from mainstream literary–critical backgrounds encounter problems that are routine for children's literature scholars, with apparent bafflement. What exactly, they ask, *is* the 'child-reader'? (What the generalised adult reader could possibly be like is not addressed.) Thus Paul Kocher, in one of the most admired of early critical works on Tolkien, gropes around for a definition of children: the hobbits, he suggests, are 'a combination, on the one hand, of human children living in a society where the desires of children are ideally institutionalised because there are no grown-ups and, on the other hand, some of the qualities traditionally ascribed to the "little people" of folklore.' The world that children desire constitutes 'endless food, parties, games, and no work; nobody gets sick or dies … and tobacco does not have to be smoked in secret behind the barn … Perhaps even the living in comfortable holes in the ground appeals to the child's love of hiding in small enclosed spaces.'[23] Perhaps, but this is describing the world of *The Wind in the Willows* – the world of regressive adults with rather elemental needs – a world described, with a happy unawareness of irony, by Tolkien's friend C. S. Lewis in his essay 'On Three Ways of Writing for Children'. The lavish tea served early in *The Lion, the Witch and the Wardrobe*, Lewis notes, produced a comment from a friend:

> A man, who has children of his own, said, 'Ah, I see how you got to that. If you want to please grown-up readers you give them sex, so you thought to yourself, "That won't do for children, what shall I give them instead? I know! The little blighters like plenty of good eating."' In reality, however, I myself like eating and drinking. I put in what I would have liked to read when I was a child and what I still like reading now that I am in my fifties.

The assured assumption that there is a correspondence between the tastes of the 53-year-old bachelor and 'the child' bears little examination, although Lewis makes a cognate point in his short essay 'On Juvenile Tastes' (*The Church Times*, 1958), on different sorts of 'writers for children': 'the wrong sort believe that children are a "distinct race" … They dish up not what they like themselves but what that race is supposed to like.'[24]

It is unfortunate that the same kinds of simplistic generalisations made about children can be co-ordinated with simplistic generalisations about (certain kinds of) fantasy literature: the simple predominates over the complex; violence is substituted for negotiation, action for thought, romance for complex relationships. *The Lord of the Rings* may be 'for' adults, but only for certain adults reading in certain ways: in these fantasies, sex is elided – Orcs may plunder, but they are produced asexually and do not rape.

Again, even sympathetic critics indulge in a kind of special pleading; for example, Roger Sale:

> For most of its length *The Hobbit* is the sort of book – *The Wind in the Willows* and the Pooh books are other examples – that appeals to a particular sort of reader, be he [sic] child or adult, whose sense of wit is near his sense of fun and whose willingness to pretend is akin to his ability to remember.[25]

Paul Kocher attempts to work out the age of the implied child-reader from the text: 'young enough not to resent the genial fatherliness of the I–You technique, the encapsulated expositions, sound effects and the rest, yet be old enough to be able to cope with the fairly stiff vocabulary ...'[26] The acceptance of the child audience as an almost infinitely-varied group of individuals who may or may not react to what is implied to be in the text, which is now fundamental to children's literature criticism, is not on the critical radar.

Even Brian Rosebury, citing the moral issues raised by the conflict between Thorin and Bard, concludes that 'although *The Hobbit* is predominantly juvenile fiction, it is not all of a piece. Much of the confusion about it arises from the fact that it contains episodes more suited to the adult mind than the child's.' Similarly, commenting on the narrator's observation in *The Hobbit* that 'If more of us valued food and cheer and song above hoarded gold, it would be a merrier world' (which C. W. Sullivan III sees, in Chapter 4 in this book, as pivotal), Rosebury notes that '*The Hobbit* even in its serious moments retains the self-conscious tone of a children's book ... The anti-acquisitive moral is spelt out more carefully and repeatedly than an adult reader, or possibly any reader, needs.'[27] That may be so, but Rosebury seems to be attempting to make a qualitative distinction – as if the statements by Elrond or Gandalf on similar subjects (*passim*) are any less emphatic.

And, ultimately, for those trying to avoid the stigma of 'children's book', there is always the argument that *The Hobbit* only *looks* like a children's book: it is, as William H. Green suggests, a 'juvenile masterpiece that hides, like a Trojan horse, an adult story'.[28] These issues are explored at length by Keith O'Sullivan in '*The Hobbit*, the Tale, Children's Literature, and the Critics' (Chapter 1 in this volume).

Tolkien and the critical idiom

We have come a long way since the dismissive and (to a twenty-first-century eye) insulting reviews that greeted *The Lord of the Rings*, and 50-year-old attitudes to fantasy which now may verge on the bewildering. Ursula K. Le Guin, for example, wrote in 1974: 'Ten years ago I went to the children's room of the library of such-and-such a city and asked for *The Hobbit*: and the librarian told me "Oh, we keep that only in the adult collection; we don't feel that escapism is good for children.'"[29]

Escapism of this kind was, of course, considered to be bad for adults, too: it did not fit with the accepted canon of literature, or with what Tom Shippey called 'the toolkit of the professional critic'. In privileging the psychologically inward-looking (in the post-Romantic manner), rather than the outward-looking (in the eighteenth-century manner) the 'toolkit' was deeply linked to issues of class and power. As Shippey observed, it

> does not work at all on whole *genres* of fiction (especially fantasy and science fiction, but including also the bulk of 'entertainment' fiction, i.e. what people most commonly read). Furthermore it has a strong tendency to falsify much of what it *does* attempt to explain by assimilating it, often unconsciously, to familiar models.[30]

Tolkien himself took a pragmatic attitude to the problem of negative criticism; as he wrote, famously, in the 1968 'Foreword' to *The Lord of the Rings*: 'Some who have read the book, or at any rate have reviewed it, have found it boring, absurd, or contemptible; and I have no cause to complain, since I have similar opinions of their works, or of the kinds of writing that they evidently prefer.'[31] C. S. Lewis concurred, focusing on the hidden power-premise of the critical attitude:

> Of course a given reader may be ... interested in nothing else ... except detailed studies of complex human personalities. If so he has a good reason for not reading those kinds of work which neither demand nor admit it. He has no reason for condemning them, and indeed no qualification for speaking of them at all. We must not allow the novel of manners to give laws to all literature ... The proper study of man as artist is everything which gives a foothold to the imagination and the passions.[32]

Tolkien's fantasies play by different rules from modern novels – rules which are rooted in language and narrative systems that may not be (have been) critically fashionable, but which remain effective. As Maria Cecire points out in her essay in this book, 'Sources and Successors' (Chapter 2), students reading English at Oxford University, under the syllabus constructed by Tolkien and Lewis, 'were expected to read key medieval literature in English, including *Beowulf, Sir Gawain and the Green Knight*, and works by Chaucer, and to do so with an understanding of the relationship between each narrative and the linguistic moment in which it was written'. Similarly, as C. W. Sullivan III suggests, some elements of Tolkien's work, particularly the modes of storytelling and performance based on specific ancient models, are not amenable to 'conventional' modern critical thinking.

Similarly, the use and importance of characterisation is different: C. S. Lewis again: 'Every good writer knows that the more unusual the scenes and events of his story are, the slighter, the more ordinary, the more typical his persons should be. Hence Gulliver is a commonplace little man, and Alice a commonplace little girl. If they had been more remarkable, they would have wrecked their books.'[33]

But perhaps the most distinctive – and for conventional criticism of the 1960s, troublesome – feature of Tolkien's books was his *worldbuilding*, discussed at length in Catherine Butler's essay in this book (Chapter 7). As Rosebury points out: 'If *The Lord of the Rings* stands at a tangent to the novel as a genre it is … because of a highly specific feature for which precedents are hardly to be found in the novel tradition: the complex, and to an extent systematic, elaboration of an imaginary world.'[34] Butler comments: 'worldbuilding is an absorbing writerly challenge, rather than the precondition of a readerly pleasure. However, it is a challenge that many of Tolkien's readers have also undertaken, at least vicariously. As the abundance of Middle-earth guides, glossaries, dictionaries, atlases and encyclopedias attests, Tolkien's stamina and attention to detail in creating Middle-earth have been rivalled only by those of his readers in learning about it.' It has also been a staple of children's books, from the Lake District of Arthur Ransome to the Island of Sodor in the 'Thomas the Tank Engine' sequence, and the parallel world of the 'Harry Potter' novels, the creation of a complex ludic space in which imaginations can play.

Tolkien constructed a world at once realistic and symbolic, as is demonstrated in his use of forests (see Shelley Saguaro and Deborah Cogan Thacker, 'Tolkien and Trees', Chapter 9), and drew extensively on his study of language and literature; as Jane Suzanne Carroll notes in 'A Topoanalytical Reading of Landscapes in *The Lord of the Rings* and *The Hobbit*' (Chapter 8), the world of Middle-earth is 'not real landscapes, in terms of geology or geography, but the cultural ideas of landscape which have been created over time: just as many of the words in his invented languages ultimately have their origins in medieval languages, many of his landscapes have their roots in medieval texts'.

And, of course, Tolkien drew upon an idyllic view of rural England, epitomised by Kipling's *Puck of Pook's Hill* (1906) and Grahame's *The Wind in the Willows* (1908), chiming with the ambiguously rural and retreatist bent of children's books of the 1920s and 1930s (see Hazel Sheeky Bird, 'The Pastoral Impulse and the Turn to the Future in *The Hobbit* and Interwar Children's Fiction' – Chapter 3). For example, what Tolkien admitted to be 'probably an unconscious source-book ... for the Hobbits',[35] E. A. Wyke-Smith's *The Marvellous Land of Snergs* (1927), which includes episodes of killing the last dragon, travelling through a wood of twisted trees, and underground caverns full of mushrooms, was firmly in this tradition:

> The Snergs are a race of people only slightly taller than the average table but broad in the shoulders and of great strength. Probably they are some offshoot of the pixies who once inhabited the hills and forests of England ... They love company, build houses that go in all directions ... [They] are long-lived people; roughly speaking they live as long as oaks ... They are great on feasts, which they have in the open air at long tables joined end on and following the turns of the street ... Gorbo was a well-known, utterly irresponsible Snerg ... He was of average size for a Snerg and fairly young – possibly two hundred and fifty – and though good-natured to excess he had little intelligence of the useful kind.[36]

In making these links, Tolkien also tapped into a longer and deeper tradition. As Fred Inglis suggests: 'his monumental work constitutes the residual statement of that well-known formulation of Victorian Arthurians and ruralists whose great legacy was inscribed in many forms of the Gothic, from architecture to poetry'. Analysing the texts, one 'must invoke ... some such metaphor as a vast reservoir or field of feeling perpetually in play in British culture, earthed for a moment in such prose and given its terminal or junction point'.[37]

Tolkien and the future

Tolkien's influence on fantasy genres in book-publishing has been well documented. However, with the exponential development of the internet, and the breakdown of the academic literary canon, there has been an explosion of fantasy writing that is not in book form, and/or not mediated through traditional editorial control. This development probably has had more influence on modern popular culture than almost anything else.

On the internet, fantasy rooted in *The Hobbit* and *The Lord of the Rings* appears in blogs, self-published fiction, 'fan fiction', slash fiction and so on. Similarly, creative writing courses and degrees number in the hundreds of thousands, and the help that is offered to writers very often shows its pedigree. Take an on-line guide to helpful websites: *How to Create Fantasy Worlds*, by Paul Nattress.

> Writers who wish to write fantasy fiction will need to set their story in a world different to ours. The most famous fantasy world is Tolkien's Middle Earth. It has its own kingdoms, races, languages and cultures. It has strange beasts, magic and heroes. Tolkein created a rich and wonderful world that was believable. Now, it's your turn.

He goes on to recommend making and using a map, but cautions against copying Tolkien too closely: 'You need elves, dwarves and orcs don't you? Well, no, actually. They've all been done before and I would argue that no one could do them better than Tolkien.' Writers should take their inspiration from folklore and myth, but for those who are less inspired, 'fantasy name generators are ten-a-penny on the web' and 'language creation kits' are readily available.[38]

It can be argued that Tolkien's influence on creative writing classes has been limited by the structure of such classes, which commonly do not cater for writing on Tolkien's epic scale, and that his influence is more likely to have come down through film than through books[39] (see Kate Harvey, 'From Illustration to Film: Visual Narratives and Target Audiences' – Chapter 10). As Mike Foster notes: an assignment to add a chapter to one of Tolkien's books produced results that 'often were merely twee, gory, or simply dull. Asking students to write *about* Tolkien was fair and justifiable; asking them to write *like* him was not. Moreover, mimesis is hardly scholarship; it is literary karaoke.'[40]

It seems unquestionable that Tolkien will continue to have an extraordinary influence on the development of fantasy texts in all their forms, and the essays in this book examine the roots of his appeal, to both adults and children. While experience suggests that the essays are most likely to be read in pursuit of specific materials, rather than as a whole, any reader who dips into several of them will find that they are interlocked. Important quotations recur in different essays, and trigger widely different responses and analyses: Tolkien's language can link us to childhood and folklore (Chapter 5), or to the generally unacknowledged subtleties of the way in which he deals with gender (Chapter 6). Tolkien is a complex writer, pivotal for the discussion of fantasy literature, children's literature, and contemporary popular culture, and these essays demonstrate that his rich materials can generate a rich response.

Notes

1. Quoted in Jon Winoker, *Writers on Writing* (London: Headline, 1987): 39.
2. Daniel Hahn and Leone Flynn with Susan Reuben, *The Ultimate Book Guide: Over 600 Great Books for 8–12s* (London: A. & C. Black, 2002): 112.
3. Farah Mendlesohn and Edward James, *A Short History of Fantasy* (London: Middlesex University Press, 2009): 46–7.
4. Edward James, 'Tolkien, Lewis and the Explosion of Genre Fantasy', in Edward James and Farah Mendlesohn (eds), *The Cambridge Companion to Fantasy Literature* (Cambridge: Cambridge University Press, 2012): 62–78, at 62.
5. Terry Pratchett and Stephen Briggs, *The Discworld Companion* (London: Vista, 1997): 472.
6. Brian Rosebury, *Tolkien: A Cultural Phenomenon* (Basingstoke: Palgrave Macmillan, 2003): 113–14.
7. Edmund Fuller, '"The Lord of the Hobbits": J. R. R. Tolkien', in Neil D. Isaacs and Rose A. Zimbardo (eds), *Tolkien and the Critics: Essays on J. R. R. Tolkien's* The Lord of the Rings (Notre Dame, IN: University of Notre Dame Press, 1968): 17–39 at 18.
8. J. R. R. Tolkien, *The Letters of J. R. R. Tolkien*, ed. Humphrey Carpenter with Christopher Tolkien (London: HarperCollins, 1981): 444.
9. Humphrey Carpenter, *J. R. R. Tolkien: A Biography* (London: Allen & Unwin/Grafton, 1992): 181.
10. Humphrey Carpenter, *The Inklings, C. S. Lewis, J. R. R. Tolkien, Charles Williams, and their Friends* (London: George Allen & Unwin, 1978): 57.
11. Carpenter, *Biography*: 182–3.
12. *Letters*: 310.
13. Carpenter, *The Inklings*: 435.
14. Hahn and Flynn: 148.
15. Karen Haber (ed.), *Meditations on Middle-earth* (London: Earthlight, 2003): 101, 77.
16. Janet Menzies, 'Middle-earth and the Adolescent', in Robert Giddings (ed.), *J. R. R. Tolkien: This Far Land* (London: Vision Press, 1983): 56–72, at 57.
17. J. R. R. Tolkien, *The Lord of the Rings*, 2nd edn (1966; London: HarperCollins, 1993): 1069.
18. William H. Green, *The Hobbit: A Journey into Maturity* (New York: Twayne, [Masterworks], 1995): 9.

19. Fuller: 37.
20. Quoted in Patrick Curry, *Defending Middle-Earth, Tolkien: Myth and Modernity* (London: HarperCollins, 1997): 140.
21. Tom Shippey, *The Road to Middle-Earth* (London: George Allen & Unwin, 1982): 215.
22. http://m.guardian.co.uk/books/2012/may/18/harry-potter-order-60-scholars?cat=books&type=article (accessed 29 July 2012).
23. Paul Kocher, *Master of Middle-Earth: The Achievement of J. R. R. Tolkien* (Harmondsworth: Penguin, 1974): 104.
24. C. S. Lewis, *Of Other Worlds* (London: Geoffrey Bles, 1966): 22, 41.
25. Roger Sale, 'Tolkien and Frodo Baggins', in Isaacs and Zimbardo (eds): 247–88, at 249.
26. Kocher: 25.
27. Rosebury: 25, 112–13.
28. Green: 9.
29. Ursula K. Le Guin, *The Language of the Night: Essays on Fantasy and Science Fiction*, 2nd edn (New York: HarperCollins, 1992): 34.
30. Shippey: 215.
31. *The Lord of the Rings*: 8.
32. Lewis: 65.
33. Ibid.: 64–5.
34. Rosebury: 25.
35. *Letters*: 215.
36. E. A. Wyke-Smith, *The Marvellous Land of Snergs* (London: Ernest Benn, 1927): 7, 9, 10, 35.
37. Fred Inglis, 'Gentility and Powerlessness: Tolkien and the New Class', in Giddings: 23–41, at 27–8, 33.
38. www.oneofus.co.uk/index.php/how_to/how_to_create_fantasy_worlds (accessed 29 July 2012).
39. See Kristin Thompson, *The Frodo Franchise: The Lord of the Rings and Modern Hollywood* (Berkeley: University of California Press, 2007).
40. Mike Foster, 'Teaching Tolkien', in Wayne G. Hammond and Christina Scull (eds), *The Lord of the Rings 1954–2004. Scholarship in Honor of Richard E. Blackwelder* (Milwaukee, WI: Marquette University Press, 2006): 257–67, at 261.

1

The Hobbit, the Tale, Children's Literature, and the Critics

Keith O'Sullivan

While *The Hobbit* is a text for children, and *The Lord of the Rings* adult fiction, the literary–historical relationship between the two is complicated. With the publication of the first volume of *The Lord of the Rings* in 1954 the status of *The Hobbit* as children's literature was problematised: although initially conceived by J. R. R. Tolkien in isolation from its successor, and published as literature for children, it could now be seen as a precursor to a more complex and ambitious narrative – a perception that was only reinforced with the posthumous publication, in 1977, of the third major work of the Tale, *The Silmarillion*.[1] In fact, from the very beginning, *The Hobbit* has occupied a precarious liminal space between fictions thought appropriate either for children or for adults.

Tolkien and the recontextualisation of *The Hobbit*

The extent to which Tolkien played a significant role in this recontextualisation of *The Hobbit* is evident in the emendations he made to the Foreword for the second edition of *The Lord of the Rings* in 1966. The original Foreword was a significant peritext in its own right, in that it situated Tolkien's fictional Middle-earth within the historical continuum of the real world; in doing so, though, it also confused 'real personal matters with the "machinery" of the Tale'[2] by implying that Tolkien's children and friends, to whom the book is dedicated, were distant descendants of hobbits. When the opportunity arose, with the publication of the second edition, to 'cancel' this Foreword, Tolkien did not hesitate in replacing it with the now-standard one. Vladimir Brljak not only argues that 'the story of the maturing of [… Tolkien's] vision is the story of the gradual abandonment and transformation'

16

of the ideas in the initial Foreword but also suggests that the revised Foreword presented Tolkien with the occasion 'to right other regrets, such as the one about having written the children's book that was *The Hobbit*';[3] in correspondence with W. H. Auden, Tolkien stated that it was both 'published hurriedly without due consideration' and 'unhappily meant' as a children's story.[4]

Although it still included *The Hobbit* in the projected Tale that Tolkien envisaged would include *The Silmarillion*, the emended Foreword and the additional peritextual elements – the Prologue, including Notes on the Shire Records – retroactively reconceptualised the contextual framework of *The Hobbit* by ascribing its style to other, fictional authors, thereby positioning Tolkien as editor and translator. While Tom Shippey expresses dissatisfaction with Tolkien's pursuit of this pseudo-translation conceit, because he claims it 'led him … into yet further inconsistencies, or rather disingenuousness', Brljak counters by arguing that 'to exercise our "willing suspension of disbelief", or whatever we choose to call it, and read in accordance with the pseudo-translation device … is to succumb to art, rather than to fraud'.[5] In this Foreword, readers are told that 'many copies were made, especially of the first volume [of the *Red Book of Westmarch* – also known as *Red Book of Periannath*, *The Downfall of the Lord of the Rings* or *Thain's Book*] for the use of the descendants of the children of Master Samwise'.[6] According to Brljak, 'Bilbo's memoirs became a favourite with children and in the process underwent some modification making them more palatable to this audience; the modern editor [in this case Tolkien] is merely translating what has come down to him.'[7]

The almost pleadingly apologetic tone of the 'Note on the Shire Records' suggests Tolkien's awareness of, and disappointment in, the numerous narratorial intrusions that often lead readers to categorise *The Hobbit* solely within the confines of children's literature.[8] However, what the reworked Foreword also shows is that, while he actively attempted to have *The Hobbit* reconceptualised within a continuum that was to include the more adult-orientated *The Lord of the Rings* and *The Silmarillion*, Tolkien did not challenge the fact that children are the implied readers of the text. Aside from the biographical evidence that suggests that he created *The Hobbit* to amuse his children, its legitimacy as a children's text is manifest in a number of its defining characteristics: its simple narrative structure, which focuses on the maturation of a child-like protagonist; the elision of sexual content; the prominence accorded to word play throughout; the suppression of explicit language, especially with regard to depictions of violence; and the didactic nature of the omniscient narrator.[9]

The Hobbit as bildungsroman

That a story concerning a fifty-year-old protagonist living a sedate life can be described as a *bildungsroman* may seem illogical, but, on a number of levels, according to Matthew Grenby, that is exactly what *The Hobbit* is.[10] John Stephens and Jaume Poveda argue that one of the most significant characteristics of the text is that it encourages children to identify with hobbits as ersatz children, especially in terms of their height, personalities and habits; but this identification also prompts child readers to connect with Bilbo's movement from innocence to experience and from egocentricity to social awareness. In particular, Poveda claims that

> hobbit houses ... speak very well to the child's inclination to hide in small places. Just like children, hobbits are fond of riddles, puns and lexical creativity that sometimes transgress grammatical norms. They are also curious to hear old tales and stories. Their habits of eating six times a day, of going barefoot, etc. bring them closer to childlike behaviour.[11]

From Jungian Dorothy Matthews's psychoanalytic perspective, Bilbo's physical journey is a metaphor for the internal processes of identity construction; his adventures, symbolically detailed rites of passage; and his quest, a search for maturity and wholeness.[12] However, his journey towards self-knowledge and worldly knowledge does not involve sexual awakening or experiences, presumably because such content would be at variance with the very traditional adult–child power-dynamic embedded in the dialectic between Tolkien and the text's implied child readership. In fact, according to Poveda, 'the word *sex*' or 'its derivatives' do not appear at all in the fiction of Middle-earth.[13] Nevertheless, Bilbo is shown to *grow up* over the course of *The Hobbit*. On his return to the Shire at the end of his adventures, Gandalf affirms this maturation when he turns to him and says, 'You are not the hobbit you were' – although both his conformity to Shire custom after his return, and his acceptance of limitation, suggest that, despite his adventures, he still remains, in some ways, 'quite a little fellow in the wide world'.[14] While Bilbo's conformity may also be a product of what Timothy Cook describes as Tolkien's predilection for systems where 'individuals gain identity and obtain security within the organic society established according to tradition and natural qualification', what is most significant about Bilbo, as Jean MacIntyre acknowledges, is that, for all his great deeds, he is not cast by Tolkien as the hero of the narrative, a figure of epic stature outside of social and cultural norms.[15] In humanising his heroic deeds, Tolkien enables him not just to represent common humanity but also to empower younger readers, who may yet have to reconfigure their relationships to authority on their own terms.

Language and the implied child reader

With regard to language and an implied readership, C. W. Sullivan III provides numerous examples of different kinds of word play in the text, including the onomatopoeic 'ding-dong-a-ling-dang' of Bilbo's doorbell; the neologising in Bilbo's use of words such as 'confusticate' and 'bebother'; the nonsense in the songs of the elves; the riddling between Bilbo and Gollum; and the use of both traditional proverbs, such as 'Third time pays all', and invented proverbs, such as 'Never laugh at live dragons'.[16] While it is not difficult to recognise the possible attractiveness of this kind of linguistic playfulness to a child readership, what may be less appealing, especially to a more sophisticated young adult or, indeed, an adult one, are the noticeable, and not infrequent, intrusions of the narrator. Many of the narratorial impositions, whose function it is to provide information or offer opinion, are not only directly addressed to the reader in the first-person singular but also imbued with a sense of didacticism:

> If you want to know what *cram* is, I can only say that I don't know the recipe; but it is biscuitish, keeps good indefinitely, is supposed to be sustaining, and is certainly not entertaining, being in fact very uninteresting except as a chewing exercise.[17]

Nonetheless, it is neither mode of address nor tone that most clearly indicates the text's implied readership; rather, it is the manner in which child readers are guided through a sign-posted narrative. When the dwarf Thorin Oakenshield, captured by Wood-elves and lying captive in their Elvenking's dungeon, focalises his and the readers' concerns regarding the welfare of Bilbo and his companions, lost and starving in the forest, the narrator checks the readers' imaginative engagement with the text by asserting that 'that belongs to the next chapter'.[18] Moreover, the end of Chapter IX, 'Barrels Out of Bond', which features more of the same omniscient pronouncements, extends narratorial influence to include directing readers to what ought to be significant, in both their dialogue with the text and their construction of meaning. After Bilbo, who was also captured by Wood-elves, soon after Thorin, escapes the Elvenking's palace, the narrator declares, 'there is no need to tell you much of his adventures that night, for now we are drawing near the end of the eastward journey and coming to the last and greatest adventure, so we must *hurry up* [my italics]'.[19]

Despite the fact that he claimed he had 'no intention of meeting him/her half way, or a quarter of the way'[20] when writing *The Hobbit*, this expurgating of what is thought to be of lesser significance to child readers is not the only example of Tolkien directing or guiding readers through the text. That *The Hobbit* and *The Lord of the Rings* share a concern for the brutalities of war is unsurprising given Tolkien's experiences serving with the Lancashire Fusiliers at the Somme during World War I.[21] Where they differ, however, is in their depictions of such brutalities. While *The Lord of the Rings* perspicuously articulates the savageries of combat in all its horror, *The Hobbit* implies, euphemises, elides:

> It was a terrible battle. The most dreadful of all Bilbo's experiences, and the one which at the time he hated most – which is to say it was the one he was most proud of, and most fond of recalling long afterwards, though he was quite unimportant in it.[22]

In fact, according to Patchen Mortimer, even 'the most direct reference to horror, in the goblin warrens, is a supposition – a description not of what was but what might have been':[23] 'It is not unlikely that they invented some of the machines that have since troubled the world, especially the ingenious devices for killing large numbers of people at once, for wheels and engines and explosions have always delighted them.'[24]

While *The Hobbit* displays many of the characteristics often associated with writing for children, they are the very same ones that Karín Lesnik-Oberstein and Jacqueline Rose focus on to argue that children's literature is frequently regressive, arrested and antipathetic to literary invention in terms of both form and content.[25] Rose's claim that, because of the subject position of the child as reader, there is often 'no disturbance at the level of language, no challenge to [... adult] sexuality, no threat to [... adults] as critics, and no question of [... adults'] relation to the child'[26] seems, in many ways, more than applicable to *The Hobbit*. In fact, it is the partisan nature of the adult–child power-dynamic behind the construct of children's literature that has led scholars such as Peter Hunt, Zohar Shavit, John Stephens and Robyn McCallum, and Jack Zipes to argue that writing for children, more generally, is often involved in processes of ideological acculturation where adult values are transferred onto children.[27]

In the light of the perceived negative connotations of its defining characteristics, it is unsurprising that for some scholars there is limited literary merit to Tolkien's text.[28] For Randel Helms, *The Hobbit* deserves 'little serious, purely literary criticism' in and of itself, because 'it stands at the threshold of one of the most immense and satisfying imaginative creations of our time, *The Lord of the Rings*'.[29] Robert Giddings and Elizabeth Holland also pay it scant scholarly attention, apart from implying that its significance lies, almost exclusively, in the fact that it made Stanley Unwin insist upon a sequel.[30] Even scholars who praise particular elements of the work often censure it in its totality: for instance, Katharyn Crabb, who treats it as an accomplished quest-story, still contends that, as a whole, *The Hobbit* lacks 'complexity in conception, in design and execution', because it is written for a 'naïve' readership of children.[31]

The adult writer of children's fiction

While its structure is simple, its narration didactic and its language playful, these characteristics are neither an unqualified summation of the literariness of *The Hobbit* or, indeed, the preserve of children's literature – for examples of structural simplicity in adult literature, readers need look no further than Ian McEwan's *On Chesil Beach* (2007), didacticism, John Bunyan's *The Pilgrim's Progress* (1678), and, linguistic playfulness, the opening chapter of James Joyce's *A Portrait of the Artist as a Young Man* (1916).[32] In fact, *The Hobbit* becomes more philosophically challenging as the plot unfolds, as its protagonist is increasingly required to maturely consider such complex concepts as *entitlement*, *proprietorship* and *obligation*, particularly in relation to his interest in the dragon Smaug's treasure. Furthermore, despite Tolkien's later rejection of the 'silliness' of the narratorial intrusions in *The Hobbit*, Sullivan argues that their legitimacy as a technique lies in an older literary tradition.[33] Like Jane Chance, who finds narratorial similarities between *The Hobbit* and Chaucer's *The Canterbury Tales*, Sullivan draws comparisons between the invasive and didactic narrator of Tolkien's text and the moralising and judgemental narrators of two other famous medieval poems: the fourteenth-century Celtic *Sir Gawain and the Green Knight* and the eighth- to eleventh-century Scandinavian *Beowulf*.[34] Rather than seeing his narrative technique as deficient, both Sullivan and Chance set Tolkien within an established literary tradition, which they suggest his learning enabled him to draw on.

It is in relation to the language of *The Hobbit*, however, that Tolkien is failed most by scholars. Almost without exception, academic criticism is focused on the arrested features of the text; if it is not, appraisal is limited to Tolkien's linguistic artistry in *The Lord of the Rings* or *The Silmarillion*, as is evident in the scholarship of Michael Drout and Verlyn Flieger.[35] While there are certainly things to excoriate with regard to Tolkien's use of language in *The Hobbit*, there is also much to admire, such as the alliteratively poetic, metrically hypnotic and imaginatively evocative introduction readers receive to the creature Gollum:

> Deep down here by the dark water lived old Gollum, a small slimy creature. I don't know where he came from, nor who or what he was. He was Gollum – as dark as darkness, except for two big round pale eyes in his thin face. He had a little boat, and he rowed about quite quietly on the lake; for lake it was, wide and deep and deadly cold.[36]

Tolkien's skill at employing language that remains free of specialised discourse though lexicographically rich is evident in nearly every chapter, emphasising his willingness to foreground language as the medium of meaning – scholars like Elizabeth Solopova have recognised the relevance of Tolkien as a philologist and examined the linguistic background of his fiction.[37] In *The Hobbit*, the description of the fall of Smaug is subtly inflected with both Tolkien's erudition as a philologist and a sense of literary antecedent, particularly in the epic leaning of its rhetorical and incantatory tone, its echoes of alliterative verse patterns, the Miltonic resonances created by the syntactical placing of the adverb 'full' and the verb 'fell', as well as the hauntingly familiar sounds of the Anglo-Saxon plural noun 'gledes' and verb 'smote':

> The great bow twanged. The black arrow sped straight from the string, straight for the hollow by the left breast where the foreleg was flung wide. In it smote and vanished, barb, shaft and feather, so fierce was its flight. With a shriek that deafened men, felled trees and split stone, Smaug shot spouting into the air, turned over and crashed down from on high in ruin. Full on the town he fell. His last throes splintered it to sparks and gledes. The lake roared in. A vast steam leapt up, white in the sudden dark under the moon. There was a hiss, a gushing whirl, and then silence.[38]

The prominence of story and the reality of fantasy

The fact that *The Hobbit* continues to be sometimes dismissed as unworthy of *serious* scholarly attention is also inextricably linked to

the prominence it accords to *story*; as C. S. Lewis put it: 'Those forms
of literature in which Story exists merely as a means to something
else – for example, the novel of manners ... – have had full justice
done to them; but those forms in which everything else is there
for the sake of the story have been given little serious attention.'[39]
Similarly, Philip Pullman suggests that

> There are some themes, some subjects, too large for adult fiction; they
> can only be dealt with adequately in a children's book. The reason for
> that is that in adult literary fiction [... story is] there on sufferance.
> Other things are felt to be more important: technique, style, literary
> knowingness ... Those ... who truly enjoy story, and plot, and character,
> and who would like to find books in which the events matter and which
> at the same time are works of literary art where the writers have used all
> the resources of their craft, could hardly do better than to look among
> the children's books.[40]

There is the risk, however, of perceiving in the comments of Lewis
and Pullman both an artificial distinction between story and theme,
plot, structure, narration, language, philosophy and ideology, and an
insinuation that contemporary adult literature is incapable of addressing fundamental questions concerning the nature and significance of
human existence – in much modernist literature, for instance, technique, style and literary knowingness are *the story itself*.[41] Nevertheless,
both Lewis and Pullman are passionate in their conviction that the
power of story lies in its capacity to entertain and represent.

Like all good literature, *The Hobbit* offers imaginative experiences through which readers may either escape the humdrum of
everyday life, no matter how fleetingly, or connect in a more potentially profound way, to themselves, to others and to life. While it is
a fantasy narrative, set in a magical pseudo-historical time, offering
liberation from the constraints of the known world, *The Hobbit* posits
metaphysical and moral questions, such as those concerning human
vices like covetousness and maleficence – as is evidenced in Thorin
Oakenshield's pursuit of the Arkenstone, a brilliant, white gem. John
Stephens's contention that the association of *seriousness* with realism in
literature has resulted in the concurrent consigning of fantasy to *non-
serious* or popular literature for audiences, such as children, considered
incapable of complex aesthetic responses is, in fact, probably the crux
of the dearth of scholarly attention afforded *The Hobbit*.[42] However,
implicit in Tolkien's decision to employ the metaphoric or allegorical
discourse mode of fantasy to tell his story is his understanding that,
although fantasy is sometimes commonly misunderstood as being

significantly detached from reality, it exists, as Jules Zanger has argued, in a symbiotic relationship with reality, depending on it for its existence but at the same time reflecting on it, challenging it and illuminating it.[43] In this sense, The Hobbit functions as a text of nostalgia by lovingly idealising the (English) rural landscape as living heritage, something which is developed further in the anti-industrial stance of The Lord of the Rings, where the modernity of Mordor and Isengard contrasts unfavourably with the bucolic simplicity, even authenticity, of Rivendell, Lothlórien, Rohan, Gondor and Fangorn. According to Jason Boffetti, although Tolkien claimed, in his introduction to the Ballantine edition of The Lord of the Rings, that he disliked allegory in all its manifestations, his vexation was, more specifically, with 'pedantic use[s] of allegory' that make 'moral message[s] the primary purpose of writing': Tolkien believed that literature should empower readers to create meaning free from overt authorial moralising.[44]

Intertextuality and crossover fiction

There are two other obvious reasons why fantasy lends itself so well to Tolkien's style of writing: the fact that it is an extremely intertextual genre, and its crossover appeal. Aside from the influences on The Hobbit already mentioned, Tolkien also drew on, amongst other things, children's literature, such as Edward Wyke-Smith's The Marvellous Land of Snergs (1927); fairy tales for its treatment of strangeness and familiarity, adventure and return; Icelander Snorri Sturluson's thirteenth-century mythic collection The Prose Edda for the names of characters; The Völsungasaga, a thirteenth-century Icelandic legendary saga, for his depiction of Smaug; and Arthurian legend for Gandalf's role as wizard and guide for Bilbo.[45] However, it is also true that since 1977 The Hobbit has resounded with the mythopoeic grandeur of The Silmarillion[46] – the amplification of itself as a tale. To read Helm's reconsidered opinion of The Hobbit as The Silmarillion 'writ small', alongside Anne Petty's assertion that 'the most profound and ominous elements' of The Lord of the Rings are 'quarried from' The Hobbit, is to recognise the degree to which the Tale is, for many scholars, an intertextual whole.[47]

Comprised as it is of writings for both children and adults, Tolkien's Tale naturally encourages crossover readings of its individual works, but so, too, does its generic classification as fantasy. Numerous scholars identify fantasy as the crossover genre: Sandra Beckett asserts that 'in the minds of many, crossover literature is synonymous with fantasy'; Melvin Burgess, that 'fantasy shelves are the only part of [... a] bookshop which is browsed freely by kids, teenagers, adults'; Farah Mendlesohn, that readers of fantasy are 'notoriously uninterested in the adult–child divide'; and Ursula K. Le Guin, that fantasy is 'the great age-equalizer'.[48] From the beginning, readers recognised *The Hobbit's* potential to attract an adult readership: an anonymous reviewer, thought to be C. S. Lewis, writing in *The Times Literary Supplement*, suggested that, 'This is a children's book only in the sense that the first of many readings can be undertaken in the nursery'; while Anne Eaton, in *The New York Times*, asserted, 'Boys and girls from 8 years on have already given [... *The Hobbit*] an enthusiastic welcome, but this is a book with no age limits. All those, young or old, who love a fine adventurous tale, beautifully told, will take [... it] to their hearts.'[49] Although he would not have expressed it in such terms, Tolkien, himself, was aware of the crossover appeal of both *The Hobbit* and *The Lord of the Rings*: with regard to the former, he claimed that he was 'not interested in the "child" as such' when writing the text; in relation to the latter, he argued that it was 'not a book written for children at all', despite the fact that many would, quite naturally, 'be interested in it, or parts of it, as they [...] are in the histories and legends of other times (especially in those not specially written for them)'.[50]

The anxiety of influence

The presence of *The Hobbit* in twentieth- and twenty-first-century culture testifies to its wide-ranging popularity and influence. As Shippey claims, 'no modern writer of epic fantasy has managed to escape the mark of Tolkien, no matter how hard many of them have tried'.[51] This 'anxiety of influence'[52] is evident in the writings of Pullman more so than most. That commonalities exist between *His Dark Materials* (1995–2000) and Tolkien's Tale is demonstrable: their fantasy narratives are shaped by quests (Bilbo seeks treasure; Lyra Belacqua, her friend Roger Parslow; and Will Parry, his father); they feature talismanic objects (the ring of Tolkien's Tale and the compass, knife and spyglass of *His Dark Materials*); they are set, in part or whole, in other worlds (Middle-earth and parallel universes); and, they culminate in epic battles between good and evil. However, aware that his use of fantasy to promote his secular humanist worldview would invite comparisons between *His Dark Materials* and the Tale, Pullman made a series of public pronouncements in order to clearly differentiate his work from that of Tolkien and Lewis, but particularly *The Chronicles of Narnia*:[53]

Tolkien ... was like Lewis: a sort of thoroughgoing Platonist, in that they saw this world, this physical universe, as a fallen state created, no doubt, by God but marked and weakened and spoiled by sin ... Well, I passionately disagree with this. The physical world is our home: this is where we live; we're not creatures from somewhere else or in exile. This is our home, and we have to make our homes here and understand that we are physical too: we are material creatures; we are born and we will die.[54]

According to Burton Hatlen, leaving aside the similarities that can be attributed to the generic conventions of fantasy, Pullman's declaration is consistent with the fact that his writing is, when compared with Tolkien's, unpinned by a very different philosophical approach to the contemporary world, hierarchical power structures and the nature of good and evil – while Hatlen bases his argument on *His Dark Materials* and *The Lord of the Rings*, it is also applicable to *The Hobbit*.[55] Where *The Hobbit* is imbued with a nostalgia for medievalism, a proclivity for hierarchical feudal systems and – despite Tolkien's Augustinian theological leanings – a predisposition to moral absolutes, *His Dark Materials* embraces contemporary scientific multiverse theory, advocates the establishment of egalitarian societies and rejects the Christian hope in the Kingdom of Heaven in favour of a secular-humanist republic. Pullman's success in challenging the established nature of Christian authority and cultural idealisations of childhood innocence in Western society, however, has been questioned by scholars like Karen Moruzi, who argue that *His Dark Materials* fails philosophically. She feels that Pullman's use of fantasy (and multiverse) undercuts his insistence on the primacy of the 'here-and-now' *real* world; that, despite its general advocacy of egalitarianism in human relations, Pullman's narrative not only reflects but also creates the reality of the socialisation of children; and that, for all its emphasis on the need for personal and societal transformation, its republic of heaven is not altogether dissimilar, in term of the values it promotes, from the Christian Kingdom of Heaven.[56]

Every fantasist since Tolkien has had to engage with his reputation and legacy, even if only in terms of the inevitability of comparison. Nevertheless, although tropes, events and characterisation in contemporary works – such as J. K. Rowling's *Harry Potter* series (1997–2007) and Susan Cooper's *The Dark Is Rising* sequence (1965–1977) – often suggest a literary ancestry with an origin in Tolkien's Tale, many commonalities are, as Charles Butler contends, as much the corollary of the works' shared generic conventions as any direct imitation.[57] According to Sullivan, 'because it is a form that draws so heavily on the past for virtually all of its context, context, and style, there can be little literary innovation in the genre';[58] as a consequence, similarities are almost inevitable.

What the case of Pullman emphasises is that Tolkien's Tale is as central to twenty-first-century writers of children's fantasy as it was to mid-twentieth-century ones like Lewis. According to Emer O'Sullivan, *The Hobbit* is one of the few works of children's literature that has been accepted into mainstream literature[59] – as well as literary and popular culture studies. As scholars from Paul Kocher to John Rateliff suggest, to categorise it simply as a prelude to *The Lord of the Rings* rather than children's literature in its own right is to lose sight of much of Tolkien's achievement as a writer:[60] it is a failure not just to satisfactorily acknowledge his influence on writers for children, and of fantasy, but also to adequately recognise the implied readership, and crossover potential, of this most seminal of seminal works.

Notes

1. For a magisterial two-volume study of Tolkien's unpublished drafts, revisions and abandoned text of *The Hobbit*, see John D. Rateliff, *The History of the Hobbit* (London: HarperCollins, 2007).
2. J. R. R. Tolkien, *The Peoples of Middle-Earth*, ed. Christopher Tolkien (Boston, MA: Houghton Mifflin, 1996): 26.
3. Vladimir Brljak, 'The Books of Lost Tales: Tolkien as Metafictionist', *Tolkien Studies*, 7 (2010): 1–34, at 18.
4. J. R. R. Tolkien, *The Letters of J. R. R. Tolkien*, ed. Humphrey Carpenter (London: HarperCollins, 1981): 297–8.
5. Tom Shippey, *The Road to Middle-Earth* (1982; reprinted Boston, MA: Houghton Mifflin, 2003): 117; Brljak: 31.
6. J. R. R. Tolkien, *The Lord of the Rings*, 50th edn (1954–5; reprinted Boston, MA: Houghton Mifflin, 2004): 14.
7. Brljak: 18.
8. The term 'children's literature' in this essay connotes both children's literature and Young Adult (YA) literature; for a discussion of the similarities and distinctions between such terms, see Perry Nodelman, *The Hidden Adult: Defining Children's Literature* (Baltimore, MD: Johns Hopkins University Press, 2008): 1–7.
9. For biographical information regarding Tolkien and his children, see Humphrey Carpenter, *The Inklings: C. S. Lewis, J. R. R. Tolkien, Charles Williams* (London: George Allen & Unwin, 1977). For a general discussion on the rhetoric of children's fiction classics, see Lois Kuznets, 'Tolkien and the Rhetoric of Childhood', in N. D. Isaacs et al. (eds), *Tolkien: New Critical Perspectives* (Lexington, KY: University Press of Kentucky, 1981): 150–62.

10. Matthew Grenby, *Children's Literature* (Edinburgh: Edinburgh University Press, 2008): 98.

11. John Stephens, 'Linguistics and Stylistics', in Peter Hunt (ed.), *International Companion Encyclopedia of Children's Literature*, 2nd edn (1996; London and New York: Routledge, 2004): 56–67, at 64; Jaume Albero Poveda, 'Narrative Models in Tolkien's Stories of Middle-Earth', *Journal of English Studies*, 4 (2003–4): 7–22, at 10. For a more general discussion of hobbits, see Marjorie Burns, 'Tracking the Elusive Hobbit: In Its Pre-Shire Den', *Tolkien Studies*, 4 (2007): 200–11.

12. Dorothy Matthews, 'The Psychological Journey of Bilbo Baggins', in Jared Lobdell (ed.), *A Tolkien Compass* (Chicago, IL: Open Court, 1975): 29–42.

13. Poveda: 10.

14. J. R. R. Tolkien, *The Hobbit* (1937; Boston, MA: Houghton Mifflin Harcourt, 2001): 326, 330.

15. Timothy E. Cook, 'Democracy and Community in American Children's Literature', in Ernest J. Yanarealla and Lee Sigelman (eds), *Political Mythology and Popular Fiction* (New York: Greenwood Press, 1988): 39–60, at 55; Jean MacIntyre, '"Time Shall Run Back": Tolkien's *The Hobbit*', *Children's Literature Association Quarterly*, 13(1) (1988): 12–17, at 15.

16. C. W. Sullivan III, 'J. R. R. Tolkien's *The Hobbit*: The Magic of Words', in Perry Nodelman (ed.), *Touchstones: Reflections on the Best in Children's Literature*, vol. 1 (Lanham, MD: Children's Literature Association and Scarecrow Press, 1985): 253–60; Tolkien, *The Hobbit*: 12, 14, 54–5, 82–6, 254, 246.

17. Ibid.: 264.

18. Ibid.: 184.

19. Ibid.: 203.

20. Tolkien, *The Letters of J. R. R. Tolkien*: 200.

21. For more on Tolkien's military experience, see John Garth, *Tolkien and the Great War* (London: HarperCollins, 2003).

22. Tolkien, *The Hobbit*: 305.

23. Patchen Mortimer, 'Tolkien and Modernism', *Tolkien Studies*, 2 (2005): 113–129, at 121.

24. Tolkien, *The Hobbit*: 69–70.

25. Karín Lesnik-Oberstein, *Children's Literature: Criticism and the Fictional Child* (Oxford: Clarendon Press, 1994); Jacqueline Rose, *The Case of Peter Pan, or The Impossibility of Children's Fiction*, 2nd edn (1984; London: Macmillan Press, 1994).

26. Rose, *The Case of Peter Pan*: 20. For a counterargument to Rose's contentions, see Kimberly Reynolds, *Radical Children's Literature: Future Visions and Aesthetic Transformations in Juvenile Fiction* (Basingstoke: Palgrave Macmillan, 2007).

27. Peter Hunt, *An Introduction to Children's Literature* (Oxford: Oxford University Press, 1994); Zohar Shavit, *Poetics of Children's Literature* (1986;

Athens, GA: University of Georgia Press, 2009); John Stephens and Robyn McCallum, *Retelling Stories, Framing Culture: Traditional Story and Metanarratives in Children's Literature* (New York and London: Routledge, 1998); Jack Zipes, *Fairy Tales and the Art of Subversion: The Classical Genre for Children and the Process of Civilization*, 2nd edn (1983; New York and London: Routledge (Routledge Classics), 2012).

28. For details of late twentieth-century scholarship on *The Hobbit*, see MacIntyre: 12.

29. Randel Helms, *Tolkien's World* (Boston, MA: Houghton Mifflin, 1974): 52.

30. Robert Giddings and Elizabeth Holland, *J. R. R. Tolkien: The Shores of Middle-Earth* (London: Junction Books, 1981): 7–9.

31. Katharyn F. Crabb, *J. R. R. Tolkien* (New York: Unger, 1981): 28.

32. Ian McEwan, *On Chesil Beach* (London: Jonathan Cape, 2007).

33. Tolkien, *The Letters of J. R. R. Tolkien*: 297; Sullivan, 'J. R. R. Tolkien's *The Hobbit*: The Magic of Words': 253–60.

34. Jane Chance, *Tolkien's Art: A Mythology for England* (Lexington, KY: University Press of Kentucky, 2001): 71; for Tolkien's erudition concerning *Beowulf*, see J. R. R. Tolkien, *Beowulf: The Monsters and the Critics* (1936; reprinted London: Oxford University Press, 1958).

35. Michael Drout, 'Tolkien's Prose Style and its Literary and Rhetorical Effects', *Tolkien Studies*, 1(1) (2004): 137–63; Verlyn Flieger, *Splintered Light: Logos and Language in Tolkien's World*, 2nd edn (1983; reprinted Kent, OH: Kent State University Press, 2002).

36. Tolkien, *The Hobbit*: 79–80.

37. Elizabeth Solopova, *Languages, Myths and History: An Introduction to the Linguistic and Literary Background of J. R. R. Tolkien's Fiction* (New York: North Landing Books, 2009).

38. Tolkien, *The Hobbit*: 270.

39. C. S. Lewis, *On Stories: And Other Essays on Literature* (1966/1982; Boston, MA: Houghton Mifflin, 2002): 3.

40. Philip Pullman, 'Carnegie Medal Acceptance Speech' (1996), at www.randomhouse.com/features/pullman/author/carnegie (accessed 29 July 2012).

41. See Keith O'Sullivan, 'Democratising Literature: *His Dark Materials* as Crossover Fiction', *Journal of Children's Literature Studies*, 7(1) (2010): 74–86.

42. John Stephens, *Language and Ideology in Children's Literature* (London: Longman, 1992): 241–2.

43. Jules Zanger, 'Heroic Fantasy and Social Reality; Ex Nihilo Nihil Fit', in Roger C. Schlobin (ed.), *The Aesthetics of Fantasy Literature and Art* (Notre Dame, IN: Notre Dame University Press, 1982): 226–36.

44. Jason Boffetti, 'Catholic Scholar, Catholic Sub-Creator', in Paul E. Kerry (ed.), *The Ring and the Cross: Christianity and the Writings of J. R. R. Tolkien* (Lanham, MD: Rowman & Littlefield, and Fairleigh Dickinson University Press, 2010): 193–204, at 200.

45. Edward Wyke-Smith, *The Marvellous Land of Snergs* (Mineola, NY: Dover, 2006); for the importance of fairy tales to Tolkien, see J. R. R. Tolkien, 'On Fairy-Stories', in *Tree and Leaf* (1964; London: HarperCollins, 2001); Snorri Sturluson, *The Prose Edda: Tales from Norse Mythology*, trans. Jean Young (Berkeley, CA: University of California Press, 2002); *The Volsunga Saga*, trans. Eirikr Magnusson and William Morris (1907; reprinted Whitefish, MT: Kessinger Publishing, 2010); for Arthurian legend, see N. J. Higham, *King Arthur: Myth-Making and History* (New York and London: Routledge, 2002).

46. J. R. R. Tolkien, *The Silmarillion*, 2nd edn, ed. Christopher Tolkien (Boston, MA: Houghton Mifflin, 2004).

47. Randel Helms, *Tolkien and the Silmarils* (Boston, MA: Houghton, 1981): 80; Anne C. Petty, *One Ring to Bind Them All: Tolkien's Mythology*, 2nd edn (1979; Tuscaloosa: University of Alabama Press, 2002): 17.

48. Sandra L. Beckett, *Crossover Fiction: Global and Historical Perspectives* (New York and London: Routledge, 2009): 35; Melvin Burgess, quoted in Jasper Rees, 'We're All Reading Children's Books', *Daily Telegraph*, 17 November 2003, at www.telegraph.co.uk/culture/books/3606678/ Were-all-reading-childrens-books.html (accessed 29 July 2012); Farah Mendlesohn, *Diana Wynne Jones: Children's Literature and the Fantastic Tradition* (New York and London: Routledge, 2005): xiii; Ursula K. Le Guin, 'Dreams Must Explain Themselves', in Susan Wood (ed.), *The Language of the Night: Essays on Fantasy and Science Fiction* (New York: Ultramarine, 1980): 47–56, at 55.

49. Anon., 'J. R. R. Tolkien's *The Hobbit*', *The Times Literary Supplement*, 2 October 1937: 714; Anne T. Eaton, 'A Delightfully Imaginative Journey', *The New York Times*, 13 March 1938: 12.

50. Tolkien, *The Letters of J. R. R. Tolkien*: 200; Tolkien, *The Lord of the Rings*: 1.

51. Tom Shippey, *J. R. R. Tolkien: Author of the Century* (London: HarperCollins, 2000): 41.

52. For a more general discussion of the theory of the anxiety of influence, especially in relation to Romantic poets, see Harold Bloom, *The Anxiety of Influence: A Theory of Poetry* (Oxford: Oxford University Press, 1973).

53. For Pullman's censure of Tolkien and Lewis, see Burton Hatlen, 'Pullman's *His Dark Materials*, a Challenge to the Fantasies of J. R. R. Tolkien and C. S. Lewis, with an Epilogue on Pullman's Neo-Romantic Reading of *Paradise Lost*', in Millicent Lenz and Carole Scott (eds), *His Dark Materials Illuminated: Critical Essays on Philip Pullman's Trilogy* (Detroit, MI: Wayne State University Press, 2005): 75–94.

54. Philip Pullman, 'Faith and Fantasy', Radio National Encounter Interview, 24 March 2002, at www.abc.net.au/radionational/programs/encounter/ faith-and-fantasy/3513418 (accessed 29 July 2012).

55. Hatlen: 79.

56. Karen Moruzi, 'Missed Opportunities: The Subordination of Children in Philip Pullman's *His Dark Materials*', *Children's Literature in Education*, 36(1) (2005): 55–68.

57. Charles Butler, 'After the Inklings', in Sarah Wells (ed.), *Ever On: Proceedings of the Tolkien 2005 Conference: 50 Years of The Lord of the Rings* (Coventry: Tolkien Society, 2008): 238–42.
58. C. W. Sullivan III, 'High Fantasy', in Peter Hunt (ed.), *International Companion Encyclopedia of Children's Literature*, 2nd edn (1996; London and New York: Routledge, 2004): 309.
59. Emer O'Sullivan, *Comparative Children's Literature* (New York and London: Routledge, 2005): 20.
60. Paul Kocher, *Master of Middle-earth: The Achievement of J. R. R. Tolkien in Fiction* (1972; London: Penguin, 1974): 22–3; Rateliff: xi.

2

Sources and Successors

Maria Sachiko Cecire

> One writes such a story not out of the leaves or trees still to be
> observed, nor by means of botany and soil-science; but it grows like
> a seed in the dark out of the leaf-mould of the mind: out of all that
> has been seen or thought or read, that has long ago been forgotten,
> descending into the deeps.[1]

In this statement Tolkien reveals his indebtedness as an author to a
wide range of sources: 'all that has been seen or thought or read' over
the course of his life, mixed and merged in his mind like the fertile
soil of a forest floor. Tolkien maintained a lifelong interest in northern
European languages and mythology, medieval literature, fairy stories,
and the genres that became known during his lifetime as science
fiction and fantasy. His career as a philologist (literally translated, a
'lover of language') and medievalist reflects the same fascinations, and
the origins of many aspects of the Middle-earth tales can be traced
to borrowings from medieval languages and literature. However,
Tolkien's acknowledgement of texts and experiences that have 'long
ago been forgotten' also implies the importance of 'low' culture
encounters such as popular culture and childhood reading. In discussing Tolkien's sources and successors – those who influenced him and
those whom he, in turn, influenced – this essay will circle around the
question of how formal and informal encounters with language and
literature contributed to Tolkien's fiction and to the fantasy literature
after *The Hobbit* and *The Lord of the Rings*. (In giving an account of
Tolkien's linguistic and literary influences, this essay must regrettably
overlook many of even his most important personal experiences,
including family and romantic relationships, his lifelong Roman
Catholicism, and his service during the First World War.) Tolkien's
writing as a popular author and his work as an academic were, ultimately, two parts of the same myth-making project for England and
the English-speaking world.

Sources for a new English mythology

In a 1950 letter, after *The Hobbit* had been published but before *The Lord of the Rings*, Tolkien expressed his wish

> to make a body of more or less connected legend, ranging from the large and cosmogonic, to the level of romantic fairy-story ... which I could dedicate simply to: to England; to my country. It should possess the tone and quality that I desired, somewhat cool and clear, be redolent of our 'air' (the clime and soil of the North West, meaning Britain and the hither parts of Europe: not Italy or the Aegean, still less the East), and, while possessing (if I could achieve it) the fair elusive beauty that some call Celtic ..., it should be 'high,' purged of the gross, and fit for the more adult mind of a land long now steeped in poetry.[2]

Although Tolkien called this desire 'absurd' at the time, his Middle-earth writings have been hailed as modern-day myths that have succeeded in fulfilling this aim. As Tom Shippey puts it, Tolkien 'largely created the expectations and established the conventions of a new and flourishing genre', while leaving what he had hoped for such myth to open up: 'scope for other minds and hands' to create further narratives.[3] Brian Attebery defines the fantasy genre as a 'fuzzy set', distinguishable 'not by boundaries but by a centre', with *The Lord of the Rings* as that centre.[4] He argues that 'Tolkien's form of fantasy, for readers in English, is our mental template' for all fantasy.[5]

Attebery's reference to the English language community echoes Tolkien's belief that language and mythology are 'integrally related'.[6] Tolkien saw them as mutually informing one another's development, and expressed regret that the patchwork nature of English history, formed by wave after wave of invasions, meant that the country had no single indigenous mythology. Its legends were, like its language, derived from borrowings from other traditions. He writes of being 'grieved by the poverty of my own beloved country: it had no stories of its own (bound up with its tongue and soil), not of the quality that I sought, and found (as an ingredient) in legends of other lands'.[7] Tolkien lists the mythologies of 'Greek, and Celtic, and Romance, Germanic, Scandinavian, and Finnish (which greatly affected me)', but laments that there is 'nothing English, save impoverished chap-book stuff'. For Tolkien, '[l]anguage is the prime differentiator of peoples', and so he calls Arthurian legends, which are native to the land, 'imperfectly naturalised' because they are 'associated with the soil of Britain but not with English'.[8] Tolkien's lifelong fascination with the creation, transmission, and survival of languages and mythologies resonates in both his fiction and his academic work.

Tolkien was born in 1892, towards the end of a century that provided ample precedent for this dual focus. The nineteenth century had seen an explosion in the collection, chronicling, and at times wholesale invention of national folklores, often undertaken alongside philological research. This nationalistic activity was especially pronounced in northern Europe; the work of Jacob and Wilhelm Grimm is perhaps the best known example today. The Brothers Grimm were philologists and scholars of folklore who sought to capture the spirit of Germany through its 'children's and household tales'. In the preface to the 1819 edition of their *Kinder- und Hausmärchen* (first published 1812) they recount the circumstances that inspired their work: 'we observed that little remained of so many things that had flourished in times of yore and that even their memory was soon to fade away, if it were not for folk songs, some books and legends, and the innocent household tales'.[9] Although many of the stories that they collected were originally of French and Italian origin and edited to appeal to their contemporary reading audience, the Brothers Grimm saw their work as part of a nation-building and identity-building project.

Tolkien knew the Grimms' fairy tales, and the sense of antiquity in such folklore appealed to him. He writes that 'The Juniper Tree' 'has remained with me since childhood; and yet always the chief flavour of that tale lingering in the memory was not beauty or horror, but distance and a great abyss of time, not measurable even by *twe tusend Johr*'.[10] Tolkien quotes from the German here, and in so doing highlights the relationship between the tale, its age, and the cultural significance of the language in which it is told. As Seth Lerer notes, Tolkien 'clearly knows that the phrase 'twe tusend Johr' is not standard High German for "two thousand years" (in which it would be "zwei tausend Jahre")', but a dialect that hints at the special history and cultural identity associated with this tale.[11]

Other northern European countries experienced similar surges of interest in their national mythologies and linguistic histories in the nineteenth century. In Finland Elias Lönnrot compiled a national epic from Finnish folk poetry, giving it a connected narrative arc and publishing it as the *Old Kalevala* in 1835–6 and then as *Kalevala* in 1849. Lönnrot's work soon became 'synonymous around the world with Finnish folklore', and remains the most famous work of Finnish literature outside the country.[12] Tolkien read it as a young man and recalls that he 'was immensely attracted by something in the air of the Kalevala'. During his first year as an undergraduate he became so involved in writing fiction inspired by the work that it had a 'nearly disastrous' effect on his exams that year.[13]

England had also been active in the nineteenth-century search for origins, with popular culture offering both real and imagined examples of early English identity. This began in the preceding century, when Thomas Percy's *Reliques of Ancient English Poetry* (1765) 'made the 1760s the decade in which medieval antiquarianism became widely fashionable and then popular' and brought the stories and 'rude style' of early English ballads and romances into wider circulation.[14] The years 1816 and 1817 saw the publication of two new editions of Thomas Malory's fifteenth century *Morte D'Arthur*, which recounts the stories of King Arthur and his court. The chivalric medievalisms of the *Morte* influenced such prominent artists of the time as Alfred, Lord Tennyson, William Morris, and the Pre-Raphaelites, who borrowed from its narratives, imagery, archaic language, and style for their own new works. There were also surges of interest in England's Anglo-Saxon, Norman, and Old Norse forebears. For example, a 'Cult of Alfred' celebrated the famous Anglo-Saxon king; Sir Walter Scott's novel *Ivanhoe* (1819) depicts the plight of the Saxon-descended English under oppressive Norman overlords; and according to Andrew Wawn, the Victorians not only invented the idea of the Vikings but also coined and popularised the name that we now use for them.[15]

Many of the fairy tales and myths that were collected or created during this period were published in versions for children, concomitant with the rise of the children's publishing industry in the nineteenth century and the Romantic idea that children ought to be exposed to 'those types of literature – fairy tales, folk myths, ballads, romances – that would best stimulate their innate imaginative powers'.[16] After the First World War, when literary attention had turned away from the medievalisms and fantastical adventures that characterised so much writing of the previous century, such tales lived on primarily as children's literature. Tolkien suggests that his first Middle-earth novel, *The Hobbit* (1937), was written as children's literature in part because of such pressures. 'If you're a youngish man and you don't want to be made fun of, you say you're writing for children,' he writes.[17] He also acknowledges that since he had young children at the time he was writing the novel, he 'was accustomed to making up (ephemeral) stories for them' and that he 'had been brought up to believe that there was a real and special connexion between children and fairy-stories'.[18] He writes in 1955 that *The Hobbit* was 'unhappily really meant, as far as I was conscious, as a "children's story," and as I had not learned sense then, and my children were not quite old

enough to correct me, it has some of the sillinesses of manner caught
unthinkingly from the stuff I had served to me'.[19] He claims to have
'freed [him]self from the contemporary delusions about "fairy-stories"
and children' after publishing *The Hobbit*, however, and expressed
'lasting regret' for having tried to cater to children in it.[20]

In the Andrew Lang lecture 'On Fairy-Stories', which he gave in
1939 (it was published in 1947), Tolkien calls the association between
children and fairy-stories an 'accident of our domestic history', and
resists the dismissal of fairy stories as infantile or not sufficiently 'literary'. He asserts that they 'have in the modern lettered world been
relegated to the "nursery," as shabby or old-fashioned furniture is
relegated to the playroom, primarily because the adults do not want it,
and do not mind if it is misused'.[21] This statement reveals the extent
to which Tolkien valued texts that were commonly seen as children's
literature in his day, but did not necessarily appreciate them *as* children's literature.[22] 'Fairy-stories banished in this way [relegated to the
"nursery"], cut off from a full adult art, would in the end be ruined;
indeed in so far as they have been so banished, they have been ruined,'
he wrote.[23] He decided to shift his style to a more 'adult' tone for *The
Lord of the Rings*, and believed that this change was 'entirely beneficial'
to the trilogy, which he says 'was *not* "written for children," or for any
kind of person in particular, but for itself'.[24]

Tolkien writes that 'a liking for fairy-stories was not a dominant
characteristic of [his] early taste'. He 'liked many other things as well,
or better: such as history, astronomy, botany, grammar, and etymol-
ogy', and his 'real taste for fairy stories' only developed as he reached
adulthood, 'wakened by philology on the threshold of manhood,
and quickened to full life by war'.[25] Nonetheless, by the time of
his boyhood there was a wealth of medieval material and works of
medievalism (reinterpretations of the Middle Ages) available for a
child to read in print. The ones that he read joined other texts and
experiences in the 'leaf-mould' of his mind from which Middle-earth
would later spring. He encountered the popular children's literature
of his day, but found that while Lewis Carroll's *Alice* books (*Alice's
Adventures in Wonderland*, 1865, and *Through the Looking-Glass*, 1871),
for instance, 'amused' him he 'had no desire to have either dreams
or adventures' like Alice. *Treasure Island* (1883), with its pirates and
high seas escapades, 'left [him] cool'. He found that tales about 'Red
Indians were better' than these others because of their 'bows and
arrows ... strange languages, and glimpses of an archaic mode of life,
and, above all, forests'.[26] However, he found 'the land of Merlin and
Arthur' even better than the North American 'Red Indian' stories,

and 'the nameless North of Sigurd and the Völsungs, and the prince of all dragons' the 'best of all'.[27]

Tolkien read 'The Tale of Sigurd' in Andrew Lang's *Red Fairy Book* (1890), one of Lang's twelve 'colour' books of collected fairy tales. 'The Tale of Sigurd' recounts a section from the Old Norse *Völsungasaga*, in which the hero Sigurd destroys the dragon Fáfnir for his hoard, acquires a magical ring, awakens and then forgets the warrior maiden Brynhild by means of magic, and dies in the resulting tragedy of their thwarted love. A preface to the tale informs its reader: 'This is a very old story: the Danes who used to fight with the English in King Alfred's time knew this story.'[28] Tolkien recalls the longing that the setting of this magical, ancient tale inspired. 'Such lands were pre-eminently desirable,' he writes; 'the world that contained even the imagination of Fáfnir was richer and more beautiful, at whatever cost of peril'.[29] As a youth Tolkien also read the works of such Victorian authors as William Morris and George MacDonald, who employed medievalisms in their novels about magical otherworlds and heroic quests. As an undergraduate, Tolkien reported modelling one of his own short stories 'on the lines of Morris's romances, with chunks of poetry in between'. And after publishing *The Hobbit*, he declared that it was largely 'derived from (previously digested) epic, mythology, and fairy-story – not, however, Victorian in authorship, as a rule to which George MacDonald is the chief exception'.[30] By this he seems to refer to MacDonald's 'Curdie' books, including the children's novel *The Princess and the Goblin* (1872), from which he borrowed elements of the 'goblin tradition' for *The Hobbit*.[31]

Tolkien also named H. Rider Haggard's adventure novel *She* (1887) as an influence, saying 'I suppose as a boy *She* interested me as much as anything – like the Greek shard of Amyntas, which was the kind of machine by which everything got moving.'[32] In *She* an ancient Greek inscription on a pottery shard sends the English protagonists on a quest to the African interior, where they discover a supernatural queen reigning over the ruins of a lost civilisation. It is telling that Tolkien recalls the shard, which, together with its Latin and English translations, provides access to a hidden past. Notes and signatures on the concave side of the shard reveal how past generations interacted with this object, and the heroes' analysis of the texts from their Cambridge rooms models how linguistic scholarship and mythic adventure might go hand in hand. Tolkien developed a passion for languages at a young age. He recalls making up imaginary languages as a child and claims to have never stopped, stating: 'I have been at it since I could write.'[33] He stumbled upon *A Primer of the Gothic Language* when he was in secondary school, and calls Gothic the first language to 'take [him] by storm, to move [his] heart'.[34] By this point he had already begun learning French, German, and Spanish at home, Greek and Latin in school, and Old and Middle English and Old Norse on his own with the encouragement of a teacher from his school.

Using language primers he first worked his way through the epic poem *Beowulf*, reading in Old English of the hero's youthful triumph over the ogre Grendel and his death in battle against a dragon as an aging king. The young Tolkien moved on to the Middle English romance *Sir Gawain and the Green Knight*, which describes in a distinctive North-West Midland dialect how King Arthur's nephew Gawain enters into a beheading game with a supernatural knight at Christmastime, and what happens when Gawain seeks out the Green Knight to brave the return blow a year later. Tolkien also read *Pearl*, a religious dream-vision with a complex interlocking poetic structure, which exists in the same unique manuscript as *Sir Gawain and the Green Knight* and is believed to be by the same anonymous author. Tolkien next tried his hand at Old Norse, 'reading line by line in the original words the story of Sigurd and the dragon Fáfnir that had fascinated him … when he was a small boy'.[35] These early languages and mythologies of Northern Europe excited him the most, and although he initially went to Exeter College, Oxford, to study Classics, he switched to the relatively new School of English Language and Literature after his first year so as to concentrate on the Germanic languages that he preferred.

It was at this time that he began to develop his ideas about the relationship between legend and language. The two 'began to flow together when I was an undergraduate', he writes, 'to the despair of my tutors and the near-wreckage of my career'.[36] In spite of his disappointing performance in his first-year Classics exams, Tolkien did very well in the English School, earning a first-class degree. By the time war broke out he had solidified his ideas about language and mythology and begun to create new legends to go with his new languages:

> It was just as the 1914 War burst on me that I made the discovery that 'legends' depend on the language to which they belong; but a living language depends equally on the 'legends' which it conveys by tradition … So though being a philologist by nature and trade (yet one always primarily interested in the aesthetic rather than functional aspects of language) I began with language, I found myself inventing 'legends' of the same 'taste.'[37]

Throughout the war and in the years following, Tolkien developed the languages and legends that would give rise to Middle-earth. (He served in the First World War and makes reference to both World Wars' influence on certain aspects of *The Lord of the Rings*, but repeatedly asserted that '[t]here is *no* "allegory", moral, political, or contemporary in the work at all'.[38])

The Oxford English curriculum: leaving a cultural legacy

Tolkien's belief in the interrelated nature of languages and literature not only guided his fiction, but also influenced his career as an academic. After the war and a period at the University of Leeds, Tolkien moved back to the University of Oxford as the Rawlinson and Bosworth Professor of Anglo-Saxon Literature, in 1926. Once there, he began to overhaul the undergraduate curriculum, which would bring together literary and language study, and familiarise all Oxford English students with a range of medieval English texts in their original Old and Middle English. He saw this work as not only important for academic understanding but also, as he called it, a 'patriotic' study of England's literary and linguistic roots.[39] He also developed a friendship with fellow medievalist C. S. Lewis and, in the 1930s, began meeting with the writing group the Inklings. This group was composed of the 'undetermined and unelected circle of friends who gathered around C. S. L.', who 'read aloud compositions of various kinds (and lengths!)' on a regular basis.[40] Tolkien developed *The Hobbit* and *The Lord of the Rings* in this intellectual environment, in the company of colleagues who shared his interests and with the opportunity to meditate on the early texts that he taught in the Oxford English School.

In May 1930 Tolkien published an article called 'The Oxford English School' in the *Oxford Magazine*. This piece articulates his concerns about the stark division between the study of language and of literature in English degree programmes, and at Oxford in particular. Tolkien argues that the 'banishment' of such specialisation in either 'language' or 'literature' 'is probably the first need of reform in the Oxford School'.[41] He suggests changes to the existing curriculum that would require all students – philologically minded and more literature-focused alike – to gain familiarity with English 'as a whole, language and literature hand in hand from the earliest monuments to the latest'.[42] He advocates the study of Old and Middle English literature *as* literature, alongside instruction in these languages, rejecting the idea that such early works are only useful as linguistic exemplars and historical documents. In his essay '*Beowulf*: The Monsters and the Critics' he refers to 'quarrying researchers', who in their mining of the

Old English poem for linguistic evidence overlook its literary merits. He even suggests that '[t]he illusion of historical truth and perspective, that has made *Beowulf* such an attractive quarry, is largely a product of art'.[43] His prescriptions for a revised Oxford curriculum seek to help undergraduates avoid such mistakes, and expose them to the richness of medieval English literature as part of their cultural heritage.

By 1931 Tolkien had succeeded – with the help of Lewis – in introducing the majority of his desired reforms. The new curriculum offered three potential tracks for Oxford English students: Lewis described Course I as 'frankly medieval', requiring the study of Old and Middle English philology, texts, and literature, as well as two additional medieval European languages.[44] It did not require any papers in literature or language after the time of Chaucer. The popular Course III was more modern and emphasised literature, but even this required Old and Middle English language study, a paper on Chaucer and his contemporaries, and three papers in English literature from 1400 to 1830, as well as a paper on modern English philology to accompany the post-medieval texts. Course II was a combination of papers from Courses I and III, extending into the early modern period with a paper on Shakespeare and the option to study Milton and Spenser.[45] All students were expected to read key medieval literature in English, including *Beowulf*, *Sir Gawain and the Green Knight*, and works by Chaucer, and to do so with an understanding of the relationship between each narrative and the linguistic moment in which it was written.

The medieval literature that students read for their degree modelled early literary forms, narratives, and styles, all sanctioned by England's oldest and most prestigious university as authentic 'English' literature. Many of these texts retell existing tales, or claim to do so, and include the supernatural intervention of magic, miracles, and monsters. Writing about the monsters of *Beowulf*, Tolkien suggests that while '[c]orrect and sober taste may refuse that there can be an interest for *us* – the proud *we* that includes all intelligent living people – in ogres and dragons', the poem 'is actually about these unfashionable creatures'.[46] The Oxford English curriculum defied such 'correct and sober taste' in its focus on medieval literature, and demanded that students be able to read these texts in their original languages. Students were not only expected to be able to translate and expound upon the literary characteristics of passages in Old and Middle English, they were also invited to respond to such broad and mythologically significant prompts as '[w]rite on "Faerie" in Middle English poetry' in their exams.[47] John Guillory argues in *Cultural Capital* that literary canons designate valuable cultural knowledge, disseminated through universities and schools. The canon can never give a full picture of cultural identity or capture the 'spirit' of a nation, but must produce 'an imaginary cultural unity never actually coincident with the culture of the nation-state.'[48] Nevertheless, familiarity with the literary canon confers upon students the advantage of cultural capital: that is, a kind of 'symbolic or *cultural*' capital that can be produced, exchanged, distributed, and consumed.[49] Canons vary between languages, cultures, and institutions, and Oxford's medieval-focused, text-based (rather than theory-based) curriculum constructed an image of English identity built on the stories and languages of the nation's distant past.

In this sense the Oxford English School echoed the myth-making academic work of nineteenth-century philologists and folklorists. At the same time, Tolkien was publishing new myths 'for England' in the form of his Middle-earth fiction, for which he borrowed from a broad range of medieval sources and traditions.[50] These projects were, as we have seen, related for Tolkien. Verlyn Flieger notes that Tolkien's 'typical wish upon reading a medieval work' was the wish to 'write a modern work in the same tradition', and refers to a BBC radio interview in which he claimed that he 'hardly got through any fairy-stories without wanting to write one'.[51] As Lewis once said to Tolkien, 'Tollers, there is too little of what we really like in stories. I'm afraid we shall have to try and write some ourselves.'[52] Thus at the same time as the two medievalists taught, wrote criticism, and maintained the English curriculum within the 'high' intellectual space of the university, they also produced 'low', popular-culture texts that reflected their interests.

These texts set the tone for subsequent fantasy in the twentieth and into the start of the twenty-first centuries. Farah Mendlesohn suggests in *Rhetorics of Fantasy* that 'classic quest fantasy ... was set into its "final" form by J.R.R. Tolkien'.[53] Although there had been other quest fantasies before, the decades following the publication of *The Lord of the Rings* and Lewis's *The Lion, the Witch and the Wardrobe* (1950) saw an explosion of fantasy works that sought to emulate, build upon, and re-imagine their visions of magical Anglicised other-worlds and heroic adventure. *The Lord of the Rings* became especially popular in the 1960s, making it the major reference point for subsequent fantasy. While many authors began to write fantasy for adults, *The Hobbit* and Lewis's Narnia books, which were all published as children's literature, kept the door open for a flood of medievalised fantasy aimed at young readers. The cultural belief in 'a real and special connexion between children and fairy-stories' that influenced Tolkien to write *The Hobbit* for children also almost certainly contributed to this popular subgenre.[54]

The legacy of Tolkien and the Oxford curriculum

Given the architects of its curriculum, it is perhaps unsurprising that Oxford's English School produced a number of important children's fantasy authors. Many of these read English from the 1950s onward, including such graduates as Diana Wynne Jones (The *Chrestomanci* series, 1977–2006, *Howl's Moving Castle*, 1986, and *The Dark Lord of Derkholm*, 1998, among others); Susan Cooper (*The Dark Is Rising* quintet, 1965–77); Philip Pullman (*His Dark Materials* trilogy, 1995–2000); and Kevin Crossley-Holland (The *Arthur* trilogy and *Gatty's Tale*, 2000–6). Their contributions to the burgeoning genre of fantasy literature in the twentieth and early twenty-first centuries are often rooted in their studies of early texts, making frequent reference to medieval literature and history as well as to the powerful role of tutors and educational institutions in the development of young heroes. These authors create a link between the Oxford literary canon and popular fantasy literature, transmitting elements of the cultural capital that they acquired through their undergraduate training to a youth readership.

Diana Wynne Jones recalls how Middle English literature 'inspired' her during her education at Oxford: 'suddenly being confronted with the way writers from the Middle Ages handled narratives. They were all so *different*, that was the amazing thing, and all so *good* at it.'[55] She cites Chaucer, Langland, *Sir Gawain and the Green Knight*, and the Middle English fairy romance *Sir Orfeo* (based on the myth of Orpheus and Eurydice; Tolkien made a translation that was published posthumously) as important influences, all of which she read as part of Course III for the 1956 Honour School examinations.[56] Susan Cooper, who also graduated in 1956, draws from a broad range of sources for her Arthurian-inflected *The Dark Is Rising* quintet. She notes that by the time she began to start writing her fantasy series she 'had read almost as much as was then in print, apart from very scholarly studies, about Arthurian legend, partly because I went to Oxford University and the English School at Oxford is very strong on earlier literature'.[57] Although she did not return to medieval literature in preparation for her writing, knowledge of these diverse works seems to have informed her understanding of Britain's relationship to its legendary past.

Kevin Crossley-Holland, whose trilogy also reflects Arthurian material, was especially moved by Anglo-Saxon poetry and language as a student. He attended Oxford between 1959 and 1962, and remembers a period during his undergraduate career (after failing his first-year Old English examinations!) when 'the temper and music of Anglo-Saxon poetry got into my thick head, my nervous system and my bloodstream'.[58] Tolkien asserts a similar emotional connection to Old English poetry by way of its language: *Beowulf*, he asserts,

> is written in a language that after many centuries has still essential kinship with our own, it was made in this land, and moves in our northern world beneath our northern sky, and for those who are native to that tongue and land, it must ever call with a profound appeal – until the dragon comes.[59]

Crossley-Holland states that these words – from the last line of Tolkien's essay '*Beowulf*: The Monsters and the Critics' – 'struck like a gong inside me when I first read them, as a student, and they still do'.[60]

Philip Pullman, meanwhile, received a third-class degree for his Oxford examinations, which he sat in 1986. He writes that he did not 'learn to read' the Oxford idea of English 'very well' – in particular, 'he loathed the Old English element of his course and says he would have got a fourth-class degree if such things had not been abolished'.[61] Pullman's antipathy matches his rebellious approach to children's fantasy: *His Dark Materials* eschews the medievalised setting of most 'high' fantasy and rejects the hierarchies inherent in feudal systems, as well as those that underpin organised religion, adult–child relations, and gender imbalances. However, Pullman does refer to his Oxford education, with the first novel of the trilogy beginning inside an Oxford college and each of the subsequent novels returning to the city as a place of power, politics, and knowledge.

Like the literature and language that they studied at Oxford, these authors' writings are vehicles of cultural knowledge, and, as with all children's literature, may be seen as educative texts. As Peter Hunt suggests, 'it is arguably impossible for a children's book (especially one being read by a child) not to be educational or influential in some way; it cannot help but reflect an ideology and, by extension, didacticism'.[62] Much English-language fantasy after Tolkien (and much in other languages) has been influenced by *The Hobbit* and *The Lord of the Rings*, but the children's fantasy authors educated under Tolkien's English curriculum in many ways continue the project that Tolkien began during his lifetime. Their fiction models other ways of building upon the same texts and languages that inspired Tolkien, and continues to disseminate some of the same literary elements that fascinated him. As children's fantasy authors they take on Tolkien's dual role of educator and storyteller, passing privileged knowledge of ancient literature to future generations, translated into popular narratives for general audiences.

Tolkien writes that after publishing *The Lord of the Rings* his 'philological colleagues [were] shocked at [his] fall into "Trivial literature"'.[63] But, as he argues in '*Beowulf: The Monsters and the Critics*', 'the significance of a myth is not easily to be pinned on paper by analytical reasoning'.[64] The new myth cycle that Tolkien created for Middle-earth has had deep resonance for England and – as befits his philosophy about how language engenders community – for the English-speaking world. Both children's and 'adult' fantasy re-imagines and expands Tolkien's idea of English mythological identity, stretching beyond British 'soil' to take root and grow in English-language communities around the globe. As fantasy works continue to emulate (and try to break away from) his legacy across media and cultures, they breathe new life into the sources that moved Tolkien and return elements of the medieval literatures and languages that he studied into popular circulation.

Notes

1. In Humphrey Carpenter, *J. R. R. Tolkien: A Biography* (London: HarperCollins, 2002): 171.
2. J. R. R. Tolkien, *The Letters of J. R. R. Tolkien*, ed. Humphrey Carpenter and Christopher Tolkien (Boston and New York: Houghton Mifflin, 2000), no. 131: 144–5.
3. Tom Shippey, *J. R. R. Tolkien: Author of the Century* (Boston: Houghton Mifflin, 2002): xvi; and Tolkien, *Letters*, no. 131: 145.
4. Brian Attebery, *Strategies of Fantasy* (Bloomington, IN: Indiana University Press, 1992): 12.
5. Ibid.: 14.
6. Tolkien, *Letters*, no. 131: 144.
7. Ibid.
8. J. R. R. Tolkien, 'English and Welsh', in *The Monsters and the Critics and Other Essays*, ed. Christopher Tolkien (London: HarperCollins, 2006): 166; and Tolkien, *Letters*, no. 131: 144.
9. Jacob and Wilhelm Grimm, 'Preface to the *Kinder- und Hausmärchen gesammelt durch die Brüder Grimm* (1819)', trans. Hans Ulrich Gumbrecht and Jeffrey T. Schnapp, in *Medievalism and the Modernist Temper*, ed. R. Howard Bloch and Stephen G. Nichols (Baltimore, MD: Johns Hopkins University Press, 1996): 481.

10. Tolkien, 'On Fairy-Stories', in *The Monsters and the Critics and Other Essays*, ed. Christopher Tolkien (London: HarperCollins, 2006): 128.
11. Seth Lerer, *Children's Literature: A Reader's History, from Aesop to Harry Potter* (Chicago: University of Chicago Press, 2008): 225.
12. M. A. Branch, 'Introduction', in *Kalevala: The Land of the Heroes*, trans. W. F. Kirby (London and Dover, NH: Athlone Press, 1985): xi.
13. Tolkien, *Letters*, no. 163: 214.
14. Michael Alexander, *Medievalism: The Middle Ages in Modern England* (New Haven, CT: Yale University Press, 2007): 16 and 20.
15. Philip Edward Philips, 'King Alfred the Great and the Victorian Translations of his Anglo-Saxon *Boethius*', in *Global Perspectives on Medieval English Literature, Language, and Culture*, ed. Noel Harold Kaylor, Jr and Richard Scott Nokes (Kalamazoo, MI: Medieval Institute Publications, 2007): 155–73; and Andrew Wawn, *The Vikings and the Victorians: Inventing the Old North in Nineteenth-Century Britain* (Cambridge and Rochester, NY: D. S. Brewer, 2000): 3–4.
16. James McGavran, *Romanticism and Children's Literature in Nineteenth-century England* (Athens, GA: University of Georgia Press, 1991): 4–5.
17. Philip Norman, 'The Hobbit Man', *The Sunday Times Magazine*, 15 Jan. 1967: 36.
18. Tolkien, *Letters*, no. 215: 298.
19. Ibid., no. 163: 215.
20. Norman, 'The Hobbit Man': 36.
21. Tolkien, 'On Fairy-Stories': 130.
22. C. S. Lewis uses this metaphor in the essays in *Of Other Worlds: Essays and Stories*, ed. Walter Hooper (San Diego, CA: Harcourt, 2002): 'On Three Ways of Writing for Children': 26, 'Sometimes Fairy Stories May Say Best What's to be Said': 37, and 'On Juvenile Tastes': 40.
23. Tolkien, 'On Fairy-Stories': 131.
24. Tolkien, *Letters*, no. 234: 310. Emphasis Tolkien's.
25. Tolkien, 'On Fairy-Stories': 135.
26. Ibid.: 134.
27. Ibid.: 134–5.
28. Andrew Lang (ed.), 'The Tale of Sigurd', in *The Red Fairy Book*, illustrated by H. J. Ford and Lancelot Speed (London and New York: Longmans, Green, 1890): 357.
29. Tolkien, 'On Fairy-Stories': 135.
30. Tolkien, *Letters*, no. 1: 7, and no. 25: 31.
31. Ibid., no. 144: 178, and no. 151: 185.
32. In Jared Lobdell, *England and Always: Tolkien's World of the Rings* (Grand Rapids, MI: W. B. Eerdmans, 1981): 7. Originally from a 1967 interview by Henry Resnick, published in the science fiction fanzine *Niekas*.
33. Tolkien, *Letters*, no. 131: 143.
34. Tolkien, 'English and Welsh': 191–2.
35. Carpenter, *J. R. R. Tolkien: A Biography*: 55.
36. Tolkien, *Letters*, no. 257: 345.

37. Ibid., no. 180: 231.
38. Ibid., no. 181: 232. Emphasis Tolkien's.
39. J. R. R. Tolkien, 'The Oxford English School', *The Oxford Magazine*, 29 May 1930: 778–80, at 780.
40. Tolkien, *Letters*, no. 298: 388.
41. Tolkien, 'The Oxford English School': 778.
42. Ibid.: 780.
43. J. R. R. Tolkien, '*Beowulf*: The Monsters and the Critics', in *The Monsters and the Critics and Other Essays*, ed. Christopher Tolkien (London: HarperCollins, 2006): 6–7.
44. C. S. Lewis, 'The Idea of an "English School"', *Rehabilitations and Other Essays* (London: Oxford University Press, 1939): 61.
45. All examination requirements from the *University of Oxford Examination Statutes, together with the Regulations of the Boards for the Academic Year 1932–1933* (Oxford: Oxford University Press, 1932): 143–9.
46. Tolkien, '*Beowulf*: The Monsters and the Critics': 16.
47. *Oxford University Examination Papers: Trinity Term 1956. Second Public Examination: Honour School of English Language and Literature* (Oxford: Clarendon Press, 1956), Section B, Paper 3(b), Question 5.
48. John Guillory, *Cultural Capital: The Problem of Literary Canon Formation* (Chicago: University of Chicago Press, 1993): 38.
49. Ibid.: viii. Guillory takes this term from Pierre Bourdieu, who elaborates on this concept in his works *Distinction* (1984), *The Forms of Capital* (1986), and *The State Nobility* (1996).
50. For detailed analysis of the medieval borrowings in Tolkien, see Tom Shippey, *The Road to Middle-Earth* (Boston: Houghton Mifflin, 1983). For another approach, which opens up medieval literature through Tolkien's writing, see Stuart Lee and Elizabeth Solopova, *The Keys of Middle-earth: Discovering Medieval Literature through the Fiction of J. R. R. Tolkien* (Basingstoke and New York: Palgrave Macmillan, 2005).
51. Verlyn Flieger, *Interrupted Music: The Making of Tolkien's Mythology* (Kent, OH: Kent State University Press, 2005): 7.
52. Tolkien, *Letters*, no. 294: 378.
53. Farah Mendlesohn, *Rhetorics of Fantasy* (Middletown, CT: Wesleyan University Press, 2008): 30.
54. Tolkien, *Letters*, no. 215: 298.
55. Diana Wynne Jones, 'Inventing the Middle Ages'. Talk presented at Nottingham University, 1997, www.leemac.freeserve.co.uk/medieval. htm (accessed 26 July 2010). Emphasis Jones's.
56. *Oxford Examination Statutes* (1955): 179–85.
57. Raymond H. Thompson, 'Interview with Susan Cooper', Cambridge, MA, www.lib.rochester.edu/camelot/intrvws/cooper.htm (accessed 2 July 1989).
58. Kevin Crossley-Holland, 'Translation', www.kevincrossley-holland.com/ translation.html (accessed 26 July 2010).
59. Tolkien, 'The Monsters and the Critics': 33–4.

60. Crossley-Holland, 'Translation'.
61. Alan Franks, 'Philip Pullman Faces his Daemons', *The Times Online*, 17 March 2009, http://entertainment.timesonline.co.uk/tol/arts_and_ entertainment/stage/theatre/article5919020.ece (accessed 26 July 2010). Pullman links to this interview through his personal website, www. philip-pullman.com/.
62. Peter Hunt, *An Introduction to Children's Literature* (Oxford: Oxford University Press, 1994): 3.
63. Tolkien, *Letters*, no. 182: 238.
64. Tolkien, '*Beowulf*: The Monsters and the Critics': 15.

3

The Pastoral Impulse and the Turn to the Future in *The Hobbit* and Interwar Children's Fiction

Hazel Sheeky Bird

To describe Tolkien's *The Hobbit* as an escapist novel has become something of a cliché, and a problematic one at that. Frequently associated with retreatism and nostalgia, and often conflated with pastoralism, escapism is viewed as the defining characteristic of children's fantasy fiction and is also associated with British interwar children's literature in general.[1] As Marcus Crouch argued, although life in 1920s Britain was 'fundamentally changed' it is, nevertheless, 'difficult to see much of this reflected in the children's literature of the decade'.[2] Certainly it is true that anyone seeking to map social and political preoccupations in interwar children's literature is faced with a difficult task.[3] Quite possibly this difficulty arises from what Peter Hunt describes as the indirect effects of events such as the First World War, which 'set the tone' for children's literature of the 1920s and 1930s.[4] Overall, while the interwar years have sometimes been viewed as a period of cultural crisis in Britain – shaped by cultural jeremiads decrying a civilisation on the brink of collapse – children's literature is frequently positioned as a means of escaping the modern world into a pastoral idyll.[5] This essay argues that while *The Hobbit* is undoubtedly a novel that draws upon ideas of escape and pastoralism – ideas that, it has been argued, had great cultural resonance in interwar Britain in general – it does so in a vital and dynamic way.[6] Rather than escape being viewed as a means of denying the effects of modernity, in *The Hobbit* escape offers a means of facing the future with renewed optimism and strength through affirming principles of friendship, mutual understanding and cooperation. It was these principles that had contributed to the founding of the League of Nations in 1919 – but which by 1937, the year *The Hobbit* was published, must have seemed to many at the time to be in short supply. Tolkien's recourse to the pastoral mode in *The Hobbit*, as was true for many other children's novels, was not a means of negating the threats and challenges of the present but of seeking ways to face them individually and collectively.

Nostalgia and escape from modernity?

It is safe to say that in children's literature criticism it is axiomatic to discuss *The Hobbit* as an escapist text, alongside the related but ultimately different impulses of retreatism and nostalgia – all of which often carry implied negative undertones. In their introduction to *Alternative Worlds in Fantasy Fiction*, Peter Hunt and Millicent Lenz observe that for all of *The Hobbit*'s influence on the fantasy genre 'it is easy to see [in it] the same nostalgic, "escapist" characteristics' as shown in Kenneth Grahame and A. A. Milne.[7] Given their observation that fantasy literature oscillates between being viewed as 'an area of advanced literary experimentation' or a regressive form 'associated with self-indulgent catharsis on the part of writers', Hunt and Lenz seem to be expressing a subtle, and possibly unintended, criticism in their use of the terms 'nostalgic' and 'escapist', with regard to *The Hobbit*.[8] Far from singling Tolkien out for criticism though, they contend that the whole tone of fantasy after the First World War was 'retreatist'. Similarly, Colin Manlove refers to 'the strong current of pastoralism in the 1930s ... which was hostile to technology' and claims that 'the primary impulse of post-Great War children's fantasy [was] inward-looking and retreatist ... escapist or consolatory'.[9] In all instances there is an implication that interwar fantasy sought to retreat nostalgically from the modern world towards an earlier pre-industrial landscape.

It is important that we recognise the great extent to which Tolkien's hostility to technology has been cited as a sign of his ultimate rejection of modernity. However, as Patrick Curry puts it, although 'it is ... true that Tolkien was deeply hostile to "modernity"' and that his books are 'certainly nostalgic', it is 'an emotionally empowering nostalgia, not a crippling one'.[10] Moreover, there is 'no reason whatsoever to automatically associate modernity with progressive politics' and by the same token we need not assume that nostalgia necessarily equates to a desire to deny the present and to return, at least imaginatively, to the past.[11]

As with the idea of nostalgia, the subject of pastoralism in children's literature criticism has often confined itself to either employing the term in an implied pejorative sense or adopting a reductive attitude toward the mode. Criticism of Tolkien's pastoralism is usually viewed through the lens of the Georgians who, according to Terry Gifford, 'established in English culture a discourse of escape into rural reassurance that continues today'.[12] However, if we approach both the pastoral and escape in *The Hobbit* from the position that 'the pastoral construct always reveals the preoccupations and tensions of its time', then we see both as performing dynamic functions that reflect the need to draw together and pool strength rather than to run away and hide.[13]

The Treasure of the Isle of the Mist and *The Marvellous Land of Snergs*

Looking briefly at two other examples of British interwar children's fantasy demonstrates the ability of such novels to use escape and nostalgia in different ways. The first, W. W. Tarn's *The Treasure of the Isle of Mist* (first published in 1938 but actually written in 1913–14), uses the idea of escape as a means of ameliorating the effects of the modern world on the individual. The second, E. A. Wyke Smith's *The Marvellous Land of Snergs* (1927), shares far more connections with *The Hobbit*, not least of which is its use of retreat into a pastoral fantasy world as a means of depicting the growth of cooperation and mutual understanding between different people brought about through the agency of children.

The Treasure of the Isle of Mist, described by Manlove as being 'about belonging', is set on an otherworldly version of Skye.[14] When Fiona, in search of the treasure, selflessly saves her neighbour, the Urchin, and his unscrupulous Uncle Jeconiah from the Little People of the Isle, the moral is clear: for Manlove, the treasure is 'rejected for the more contemplative side of "being" and enjoying what is, rather than trying to get more out of the world'.[15] This rejection of individual greed, and the obvious criticism of the grasping Jeconiah, firmly associated with the world of the city, business and commerce, offers readers a gentle critique of selfish individualism. Perhaps more significant is the reward that Fiona receives, which is effectively a means of spiritual escape from the modern world. As the King of the Little People explains:

> You can walk now through the crowded city and never know it, for the wind from the heather will be about you where you go; you can stand in the tumult of men and never hear them, for round you will be the silence of your own sea. That is the treasure of the Isle of the Mist.[16]

This episode places the novel in early twentieth-century discourses on the mass and the individual: it is close to the idea of the 'herd' used to depict either large groups of (often but not always) working-class people or to denote the enjoyment of mass recreation (as in W. Trotter's *Instincts of the Herd in Peace and War, 1872–1939* (1916)).[17] As Fiona's father tells her, man began his evolution as a horde and 'to the horde he still seeks, forming huge crowds during his working days, and on his holidays merely transferring the same crowds in their totality to some other place'. In a sentence that might have been found in F. R. Leavis's *Culture and the Environment* (1934) he continues: 'nothing is more striking to the reflective mind than the abdication of civilisation in the face of meaningless noise'.[18] Tarn's novel is about far more than belonging: it is also about willing separation and the desire to retreat into a quiet, pastoral world as a palliative to the noise and sheer thoughtlessness of mass modern living.

The Marvellous Land of Snergs, on the other hand, demonstrates the ability of children's fantasy novels to address concerns of the age whilst being set in a romantic imaginary world.[19] While notionally set on an island somewhere on Earth, the novel draws upon many features of the chivalric romance novel. The main premise of the book is that two children, Joe and Sylvia, run away from the Society for the Removal of Superfluous Children (S.R.S.C), which has rescued them from a life of neglect and brought them to the island. Besides the Society, the island is also populated by the Snergs, who are 'a race of people only slightly taller than the average table' and 'probably … some offshoot of the pixies who once inhabited the hills and forests of England'. A great river divides the land and acts as a barrier 'keeping the Snergs secure from a horror-haunted land, a land of distressful legends of dragons … and a ruthless king who tyrannized over his people'. Knights, both comic and serious, giants, witches and people who have been turned to stone as punishment for greed, populate the land. When Joe and Sylvia meet the King it is clear that 'there were no signs of ruthlessness' about him; furthermore, the King believes the Snergs to be a 'fierce and cruel race' who live in 'that terror-haunted land beyond the deep river'. Mutual understanding grows between the two people, culminating in their rescue of Joe and Sylvia from the clutches of an unreformed ogre called Golithos.[20]

The moral of the novel, to which Wyke-Smith refers and that he simultaneously downplays, is encapsulated in the unintended outcome of Joe and Sylvia's behaviour, namely, 'the establishment of friendly relations between two countries, and [the] remov[al of] doubts that existed for centuries'.[21] Manlove describes the novel as suggesting 'the kind of cooperation among peoples enshrined in the recent League of Nations'.[22] The obvious cultural misunderstandings shared here between different races and nations, all of which are overcome, demonstrate the contextual relevance of this chivalric and romantic world. Furthermore, the novel places children at the very heart of this new mutually respectful relationship, perhaps suggesting that their innate lack of prejudice can lead the way toward international harmony. What is most significant, however, is that the way forward – toward mutual understanding rather than suspicion – is through this pastoral world. The fact that this offers a retreat from the outside world is evident in the closing lines of the novel:

> The children go on happily year after year, slowly increasing in numbers as fresh cases arrive, and they splash about in the sea and play their various games and roam the woods and fleet the time carelessly as they did in the golden world.[23]

Now Tolkien, unlike Wyke-Smith, was careful not to subscribe to topical readings, writing in his 'Foreword' to *The Lord of the Rings*: 'As for any inner meaning or "message", it has in the intention of the author none. It is neither allegorical nor topical.'[24]

The Hobbit, pastoralism and escape

Unlike Wyke-Smith's pastoral fantasy, Tolkien's Middle-earth is problematic because it is recognisably English. The British Library's decision to include Tolkien's painting of the Shire, complete with enclosed fields and thick hedgerows, in their 2012 exhibition *Writing Britain*, certainly suggests that the equation between the Shire and England is both a popular and an enduring one. Tolkien's illustration, perhaps even more so than the scant description of the Shire that is given in *The Hobbit*, reveals what Alex Potts has described as the view of the English farming scene that became the norm in the 1920s.[25] It is not possible in this essay to explore in detail the highly contested and debated significance of the English countryside during the interwar years. Suffice it to say that following the publication of Martin Wiener's *English Culture and the Decline of the Industrial Spirit* (1981) it has become common to argue that the popularity of this mythical English landscape reflects a society that preferred to look back to Britain's pre-industrial past. As such, so the argument goes, its symbolic importance in the interwar years was based on its ability to offer a conservative, nostalgic antidote to modernity. While this paradigm has been challenged by critics such as David Matless, it still frequently pervades criticism of Tolkien's pastoral Shire.[26]

For some critics the Shire presents an essentially feudal vision of England. According to William Ready, the Shire is 'no Never-Never Land, no Big Rock Candy Mountain' but 'a bit of England' that Tolkien wills to the hobbit.[27] At the beginning of *The Hobbit* the Shire is described as 'a wide respectable country inhabited by decent folk, with good roads [and] an inn or two'. Furthermore we are told that the novel is set 'in the quiet of the world, when there was less noise and more green'.[28] But for Ready, it is an England where the lower classes are 'fore-lock tugging yokels' and where the 'class structure is apparent all through Tolkien's description of Hobbit life'.[29] Likewise, Rosemary Jackson has argued that both *The Hobbit* and *The Lord of the Rings* demonstrate Tolkien's desire to create a 'pre-Industrial, indeed a pre-Norman Conquest, feudal order' and so 'recapture and revivify' a 'lost moral and social hierarchy'.[30] *The Hobbit* is often associated with books such as Eleanor Farjeon's *Martin Pippin in the Apple Orchard* (1921) and to a lesser extent T. H. White's *The Sword in the Stone* (1938), both of which are set in what Manlove describes as a 'Morrisian medieval imaginary world'.[31]

There are once again problems here that are partly the result of conflating nostalgia for a pre-industrial landscape with reactionary politics. Certainly, it is a mistake to refer to pastoral Morrisian fantasy worlds without acknowledging the radical basis of Morris's own atechnological world in his influential novel *The Wood Beyond the World* (1894).[32] As Brian Attebury argues, Jackson interprets Tolkien's recourse to this romantic Morrisian world as a sign of artistic failure and criticises Tolkien for evading 'the writer's responsibility to represent his own age'.[33] Jackson fails to acknowledge the radical nature of Morris's romance and nostalgia and the great influence this had on the development of radical middle-class politics from the 1890s through to the 1930s.[34] This is not to suggest that Tolkien's own politics were aligned with this – as Curry observes, it is 'pointless to spill ink establishing whether Tolkien was "reactionary" or "progressive"' – it is, however, clear that a more nuanced and less reactionary reading of Tolkien's escapist fantasy world is required.[35]

Tolkien signals what he believes is the dynamic function of escape and the pastoral in his essay 'On Fairy-Stories' (1947). For example, he writes:

> it is after all possible for a rational man, after reflection (quite uncon-
> nected with fairy-story or romance), to arrive at the condemnation,

implicit at least in the mere silence of 'escapist' literature, of progressive things like factories, or the machine-guns and bombs that appear to be their most natural and inevitable, dare we say 'inexorable', products.[36]

Tolkien's defence of 'archaism' and condemnation of 'progressive things like factories' has clearly fuelled the argument that his perspective was essentially regressive. However, central to Tolkien's argument is the idea that escape is the key to recovery, which he defines as including the 'return and renewal of health' and as a 're-gaining'. The fact that escape had contemporary relevance for Tolkien is evident in the language he uses to complain that he does not 'accept the tone of scorn or pity with which "Escape" was then so often used'. He continues:

> In using Escape in this way the critics have chosen the wrong word, and, what is more, they are confusing, not always by sincere error, the Escape of the Prisoner with the Flight of the Deserter. Just so a Party-spokesman might have labelled departure from the misery of the Führer's or any other Reich and even criticism of it as treachery. In the same way these critics, to make confusion worse, and so to bring into contempt their opponents, stick their label of scorn not only on to Desertion, but on to real Escape, and what are often its companions, Disgust, Anger, Condemnation, and Revolt.[37]

If we briefly examine Bilbo's escape from Gollum during the riddle competition it becomes clear how escape functions in *The Hobbit*. The episode demonstrates Bilbo's regaining of his own personal strength through his insight into Gollum's own pain and suffering. This is clear when Tolkien writes:

> Bilbo almost stopped breathing, and went stiff himself. He was desperate. He must get away, out of this horrible darkness, while he had any strength left. He must fight. He must stab the foul thing, put its eyes out, kill it. It meant to kill him. No, not a fair fight. He was invisible now. Gollum had no sword. Gollum had not actually threatened to kill him, or tried to yet. And he was miserable, alone, lost. A sudden understanding, a pity mixed with horror, welled up in Bilbo's heart: a glimpse of endless unmarked days without light or hope of betterment, hard stone, cold fish, sneaking and whispering. All these thoughts passed in a flash of a second. He trembled. And then quite suddenly in another flash, as if lifted by a new strength and resolve, he leaped.[38]

It is Bilbo's empathy and growth of understanding – his emotional connection with Gollum – that gives him the strength to make his escape both physically and morally. Arguably, Bilbo trembles due to a realisation of just how close he had come to committing a morally reprehensible act – killing Gollum. The strength and resolve that he gains is then also based on his insight into his own character and the realisation that he has the ability to make the right decision at a time of great danger. The flashes that Tolkien describes here are therefore moments of new understanding and insight for Bilbo: moments of a new vision.

This idea of vision is central to Tolkien's own views on the function of fairy-stories. For Tolkien it is specifically the 'regaining of a clear view ... so that the things seen clearly may be freed from the drab blur of triteness or familiarity' that leads to recovery.[39] This notion aligns Tolkien's observations on the function of fairy-stories with those of Roger Sale on the pastoral mode. For Sale the pastoral mode is characterised by the five key elements of 'refuge, reflection, rescue, requiem, and reconstruction'.[40] In her 2008 article 'Putting Away Childish Things: Incidents of Recovery in Tolkien and Haddon', Alana M. Vincent draws attention to two key aspects of recovery that are useful here. Vincent equates recovery with what she terms a 'freshness of vision' and which in terms of narrative is 'characterized by a strong visual emphasis and an almost overabundance of descriptive detail and sensory language'.[41] Recovery is achieved firstly though the recognition of things as separate from ourselves and secondly through the insight that is gained by viewing the familiar in this new way. Or, as Tolkien put it, looking 'at green again and be[ing] startled anew (but not blinded) by blue and yellow and red'.[42] Where Vincent discusses Tolkien's *The Lord of the Rings* in relation to Mark Haddon's 2003 novel *The Curious Incident of the Dog in the Night-Time*, there are other forms of writing more contemporary with Tolkien that are perhaps more relevant.

Camping and tramping fiction

Given their reputation for heralding a new age of realism in interwar children's writing, it may appear strange to bring David Severn's camping and tramping 'Waggoner' novels (1942–6) into a discussion of fantasy fiction. At first sight *The Hobbit* appears to share little in common with a genre described by Victor Watson, as 'a popular kind of British novel in which the narrative was mostly devoted to the excitements of hiking, exploring, boating, map-reading and the practicalities of camping'.[43] In fact, when camping and tramping novels and *The Hobbit* are discussed in terms of their genre, they appear to be oppositional rather than in sympathy with one another. However, just as Graham Greene's *The Power and the Glory* (1940) and *The Lord of the Rings* (1954) may appear to be (as Thomas Wendorf demonstrates) 'odd literary bedfellows', they have 'more complex relations and can effect similar truths'.[44] Both *The Hobbit* and the 'Waggoner' novels demonstrate the ability of interwar children's literature to use escapism and pastoralism in a vital and dynamic way.

Just like children's fantasy of the 1930s, camping and tramping novels have frequently been described as either escapist or nostalgic.[45] Once again this description has served to mask the affirmative way that both ideas function in these narratives. While the Shire of *The Hobbit* is recognisably English but imaginary, camping and tramping novels were set in equally romantic and imaginative countryside – namely the mythical English national countryside which was 'a refuge from the more violent and thrusting tendencies of the modern world' and where 'the dominant note is one of nostalgia, of a sense of fragile unreality, of retreat from ideas of energy to ones of still and delicate beauty'.[46] The 'Waggoner' series provides a particularly useful point of comparison with *The Hobbit* in a number of ways. Severn (who was the son of Tolkien's publisher Stanley Unwin) depicts the caravan holidays of a group of school friends, and, as he wrote in his memoirs, he had (unlike Tolkien) 'an urge to proselytise, to sing the praises of the English countryside, to reach out to children – and there were enormous numbers of them – locked away in the big cities and unable to escape … [On] sunny, blue-sky days I found it a physical agony to be shackled to my desk. I lived for the weekends and my escape into the countryside.'[47]

The theme of escaping from the constraints of modern life is developed through the series, notably in *A Cabin for Crusoe* (1943) and *Hermit in the Hills* (1945); what is key for Severn, and where he differs from Tolkien, is that his rural vision is based on the real environment rather than a fantastic or magical one. However, as Wendorf demonstrates, it is useful to bear in mind the distinction that C. S. Lewis drew between 'realism of content' and 'realism of presentation'. Where 'realism of content' refers to the 'probable or true to life', 'realism of presentation' refers to the 'bringing [of] something close to us' in 'sharply observed or sharply imagined detail'.[48] For Wendorf, while Tolkien's work is clearly improbable and unlike Severn's does not strive for 'realism of content', nevertheless it does sustain 'realism of presentation'. If viewed in this way, the accuracy of content evident in Severn's writing need not position his writing in opposition to Tolkien's.

There are two key ways that Severn's novels are connected with *The Hobbit* and which in turn depict both a sense of renewal through escape and pastoralism, and growth of personal and communal understanding. As with Tolkien, renewal in Severn is closely linked to the idea of a regaining of sight and how this brings to the individual a sense of connectedness. For example, when describing the sunrise in *Hermit in the Hills*, Severn writes:

> The minutes passed like seconds, and the sun, steadily climbing and gaining power and brilliance, darted a first, faint warmth across the sky and touched Diana's cheek. From crimson to fiery red, red to orange, orange to yellow, so the sun had changed colour and strode above the hills and the restless sea of clouds, while the sky turned a deeper blue above her.[49]

There are some differences between Diana's vision – that makes her feel connected to the natural world around her – and the 'clear view' that Tolkien considered key to recovery. Whereas Diana feels that 'all this was hers' and that she was linked 'so closely' to the world that she was 'completely one' with it, Tolkien argued that things that are seen clearly are freed from 'possessiveness' and characterised by separateness. Diana's experience at sunrise makes her realise that 'life up here would be filled with something more than happiness' and that 'compared with the hermit, they might be looking through dusty windows!' This last observation has striking resemblance to Tolkien's own observation that we need 'to clean our windows; so that the things seen clearly may be freed from the drab blur of triteness or familiarity'.[50] Commenting on the work of Richard Jefferies, Potts observes that for Jefferies 'the intense individual experience of natural beauty and light at one level acted as a metaphor of the as-yet-unrealised possibilities of a major transformation of society'.[51] It is exactly this sense of possibility that characterises the pastoralism of both David Severn's 'Waggoner' series and Tolkien's *The Hobbit*.

The 'Waggoner' novels eventually come to offer a radical vision of communalism, not dissimilar to the fellowship that grows in *The Hobbit* between Bilbo and the Dwarves. In the Severn novels this fellowship is effected through the connection that is made between the middle-class campers and trampers and groups of Romany gypsies, and is symbolised through the sharing of campfires, an engagement with gypsy customs and an appreciation of both the romance and hardships of their lives. Thus, Severn's 'escapist' novels carry a similar truth to both *The Hobbit* and *The Marvellous Land of Snergs*, that it is possible for very different people to come to understand and respect each other. Tolkien would, of course, develop this idea further in *The Lord of the Rings*, particularly through the relationship between Gimli and Legolas. In *The Hobbit* it is only Thorin's moral blindness resulting from his desire for Smaug's treasure, and Bilbo's 'theft' of the Arkenstone, that makes him temporarily forget his newfound respect for Bilbo. This is largely based on the role Bilbo plays in bringing about the Dwarves' escape from both the spiders of the forest and the dungeons of the Wood Elves. It takes another moment of escape, this time overtly linked to recovery and consolation, for Thorin to regain and confirm his clear vision.

For Tolkien, joy was an essential element of the consolation inherent in fairy-stories; they were moments of 'sudden and miraculous grace: never to be counted on to recur'. For William Green, *The Hobbit* is filled with such moments, characterised by 'a catch of the breath, a beat of the lifting heart'.[52] While the context is very different from that of Severn's novel, the clearest of these turns to joy comes towards the end of the novel during the Battle of the Five Armies when it seems to all as though the battle is lost. Bilbo reflects that they will all be 'slaughtered or driven down and captured', which is, he thinks, 'enough to make one weep, after all one has gone through'. It is at this darkest point that Bilbo sees the Eagles: 'He gave a great cry; he had seen a sight that made his heart leap, dark shapes small yet majestic against the distant glow.' This marks the turning point in the battle and the defeat of the enemy horde.[53]

The return of the Eagles, and this turn to joy, is significant as it completes the union of the races and marks the beginning of a new period of shared prosperity, and, more importantly, of peace and understanding. Rather than being something that is fought over, the treasure is shared and becomes symbolic of new friendships and alliances. Like *The Treasure of the Isle of Mist*, *The Hobbit* also suggests that greed for material goods leads to destructive competition. It is noteworthy that when Bilbo returns to the Shire he finds that his relatives are busy selling his possessions in a bid to improve their material wealth. However, unlike Fiona in *The Treasure of the Isle of Mist*, Bilbo's reward is not to separate himself from others but to connect to them and to forge respectful friendships that have great significance for the stability of Middle-earth. Bilbo's joy on seeing the Eagles return symbolises far more than the shifting fortunes of battle; it opens the path to reconciliation and recovery through mutual understanding and cooperation.

While it is quite possible to argue that Tolkien's recourse to the pastoral suggests that for him the modern world seemed devoid of a willingness to see through another's eyes, or to sacrifice one's own gain for the good of others, a contrary argument is equally possible. *The Hobbit* can be seen as a novel that time and again tells us that people can be loyal, brave, and pull together for a common good. For Tom Shippey, 'adventure in Middle-earth embodies a modern meaning' but 'it does not exist to propagate it'.[54] Rather than escape and pastoralism being ways of avoiding the realities of modern life, they were instead a powerful means of drawing strength for the future – and by 1937 the need for a gathering of strength and mutual understanding must have been more than apparent to most. If we can for a moment set aside all of the pejorative notions that have come to surround notions of escape, nostalgia and pastoralism, then this modern meaning becomes clear. It is the sense of connection, resulting from moments of escape and consolation, that ultimately makes *The Hobbit* a far more optimistic and forward looking novel than is often recognised.

Notes

1. Lucie Armitt, *Theorising the Fantastic* (London: Edward Arnold, 1996): 1.
2. Marcus Crouch, *Treasure Seekers and Borrowers* (1962; London: The Library Association, 1963): 38.
3. See Kimberley Reynolds, *Modernism, the Left and Progressive Publishing for Children, 1910–1949* (Oxford: Oxford University Press, forthcoming 2015).
4. Peter Hunt, *An Introduction to Children's Literature* (Oxford: Oxford University Press, 1994): 105.
5. Richard Overy, *The Morbid Years: Britain Between the Wars* (London: Allan Lane, 2009), and see Owen Dudley Edwards, *British Children's Fiction of the Second World War* (Edinburgh: Edinburgh University Press, 2007).
6. For representative work on the subject of the cultural significance of pastoralism and the English countryside during the interwar years, see David Lowenthal, 'British National Identity and the English Landscape', *Rural History*, 2 (1991): 205–30, and Judy Giles and Tim Middleton, *Writing Englishness 1900–1950: An Introductory Source Book on National Identity* (London: Routledge, 1995).
7. Peter Hunt and Millicent Lenz, *Alternative Worlds in Fantasy Fiction* (London: Continuum, 2001): 32.
8. Ibid.: 2, 19.
9. Colin Manlove, *From Alice to Harry Potter: Children's Fantasy in England* (Christchurch: Cybereditions, 2003): 58, 62.
10. Patrick Curry, *Defending Middle-Earth: Tolkien, Myth and Modernity* (1997; New York: Houghton Mifflin, 2004): 15
11. Patrick Curry, '"Less Noise and More Green": Tolkien's Ideology for England', in Proceedings of the J. R. R. Tolkien Centenary Conference,

ed. Patricia Reynolds and Glen Goodnight, *Mythlore*, 21(2) (Winter 1996): 126–37, at 128.

12. Terry Gifford, *Pastoral* (London and New York: Routledge, 1999): 71.
13. Ibid.: 82.
14. W. W. Tarn, *The Treasure of the Isle of Mist: A Tale of the Isle of Skye* (1938; London: Oxford University Press, 1959).
15. Manlove: 53, 54.
16. Tarn: 148–9.
17. W. Trotter, *Instincts of the Herd in Peace and War, 1872–1939* (London: T. Fisher Unwin, 1916); see also Q. D. Leavis, *Fiction and the Reading Public* (London: Chatto & Windus, 1932).
18. Tarn: 20.
19. E. A. Wyke-Smith, *The Marvellous Land of Snergs* (1928; Mineola, NY: Dover Publications, 2006).
20. Ibid.: 7, 71, 167, 169.
21. Ibid.: 216.
22. Manlove: 61.
23. Wyke-Smith: 220.
24. Quoted in Chris Hopkins, 'Tolkien and Englishness', Proceedings of the J. R. R. Tolkien Centenary Conference, ed. Patricia Reynolds and Glen Goodnight, *Mythlore*, 21(2) (Winter 1996): 278–80, at 278.
25. Alex Potts, 'Constable Country Between the Wars', in *Patriotism: The Making and Unmaking of British National Identity*, Volume 3: *National Fictions*, ed. Raphael Samuel (London: Routledge, 1989): 160–85.
26. Martin Wiener, *English Culture and the Decline of the Industrial Spirit* (Cambridge: Cambridge University Press, 1981). David Matless, and more recently Ysanne Holt and David Corbett, have examined how calls for preservation position some interwar attitudes to the countryside within discourses of modernity rather than against them. See David Matless, *Landscape and Englishness* (London: Reaktion Books, 1998), and *Geographies of Englishness: Landscape and the National Past 1880–1940*, ed. David Peters Corbett, Ysanne Holt and Fiona Russell (New Haven, CT and London: Yale University Press, 2002).
27. William Ready, *The Tolkien Relation: A Personal Inquiry* (Chicago, IL: Henry Regnery, 1968): 81–2.
28. J. R. R. Tolkien, *The Hobbit or There and Back Again* (1937; London: Allen & Unwin, 1966): 29, 3.
29. Ready: 81–2.
30. Rosemary Jackson, *Fantasy* (London: Methuen, 1981): 91, 1.
31. Manlove: 55.
32. For a more radical interpretation of Morris's nostalgic romantic vision, see Alastair Bonnett, *Left in the Past: Radicalism and the Politics of Nostalgia* (London: Continuum, 2010).
33. Brian Attebery, *Strategies of Fantasy* (Bloomington and Indianapolis: Indiana University Press, 1992): 22.

34. On Morris' influence on British socialism, see Jan Marsh, *Back to the Land: The Pastoral Impulse in Victorian England from 1880 to 1914* (London: Quartet Books, 1982).
35. Curry, '"Less Noise and More Green"': 126.
36. J. R. R. Tolkien, 'On Fairy-Stories', in *Tree and Leaf* (London: Allen & Unwin, 1964): 55, 56, 58, 63.
37. Ibid.: 54.
38. Tolkien, *The Hobbit*: 80.
39. Tolkien, 'On Fairy-Stories': 53.
40. Roger Sale, *English Literature in History, 1780–1830: Pastoral and Politics* (London: Hutchinson, 1983): 17.
41. Alana M. Vincent, 'Putting Away Childish Things: Incidents of Recovery in Tolkien and Haddon', *Mythlore*, 26 (Spring 2008): 101–18, at 106.
42. Tolkien, 'On Fairy-Stories': 53.
43. Victor Watson (ed.), *The Cambridge Guide to Children's Books in English* (Cambridge: Cambridge University Press, 2001): 124.
44. Thomas A. Wendorf, 'Greene, Tolkien, and the Mysterious Relations of Realism and Fantasy', *Renascence*, 55(1) (Fall 2002): 78–101, at 78.
45. Owen Dudley Edwards, *British Children's Fiction of the Second World War* (Edinburgh: Edinburgh University Press, 2007): 44 and 470.
46. Potts: 173.
47. David Severn, *Fifty Years with Father: A Relationship* (London: George Allen & Unwin, 1982): 95 and 98.
48. Wendorf: 78.
49. David Severn, *Hermit in the Hills* (London: John Lane, 1945): 194, 202.
50. Tolkien, 'On Fairy-Stories': 53, 63.
51. Potts: 170.
52. William H. Green, *The Hobbit: A Journey into Maturity* (New York: Twayne, 1995): 11.
53. Tolkien, *The Hobbit*: 261–2.
54. Quoted in Curry, *Defending Middle-Earth*: 8.

4

Tolkien and the Traditional Dragon Tale: An Examination of *The Hobbit*

C. W. Sullivan III

C. S. Lewis once wrote that we have ignored 'story as story' as we pursued, among other approaches, the 'delineation of character' or the 'criticism of social conditions'.[1] Needless to say, literary theory has put story even further into the background. In few instances has this been more evident than in the post-1966 attempts to delve into the 'meaning(s)' of J. R. R. Tolkien's most popular works, *The Hobbit* and *The Lord of the Rings*; fewer such analytical assessments have been attempted with *The Silmarillion* – and for good reason. But Brian Rosebury has argued that modern and post-modern critical approaches to Tolkien's fiction have yielded, at best, mixed results: 'There is something about Tolkien's art which eludes the conventional strategies of contemporary criticism, even when these are deployed with sympathy and patience.'[2] Following Rosebury's argument, I would argue that we should return, building on the lead provided by C. S. Lewis, to the story itself and to Tolkien as a storyteller.

This means looking at Tolkien not just as a storyteller but as a traditional storyteller. By traditional storytellers, I mean the creators of oral narratives, from the anonymous poets who recited or chanted *Beowulf*, *The Iliad*, and *The Odyssey* to the unknown first tellers of the Irish cycles and Welsh *Mabinogi*. As structural analysis has shown, these tales have essentially similar plots from era to era, from culture to culture, but as performance analyses of contemporary tellers and singers have shown, each traditional teller shapes his narrative in an individual way, creating a variation on a formula. In other words, to best understand Tolkien as a traditional storyteller, we should use the critical approaches that have proved profitable when applied to ancient, originally oral, narratives; for it is my argument that Tolkien was a traditional storyteller in that ancient sense, the difference being that he was able to present his 'oral narrative' in a modern medium – print. In addition, and as unlikely as it might seem at first blush, it is important to study *The Hobbit* as one would any traditional performance; that is, to use the performance approach to understand Tolkien's story as a production in context, a production that comes from a specific performer in a specific time and a specific place.

What such an approach will reveal, looking at the children's literature classic *The Hobbit* for specific examples (although the same approach will also work with the more adult-oriented *The Lord of the Rings*), is that Tolkien did, indeed, tell a traditional story, a story with a structure similar to the structures of the ancient narratives, and that, at a certain point in his tale, he both fulfilled and departed from that ancient structure to create a narrative performance of his own, a traditional narrative that is also unique to its teller, its time, and its place.

The dragon-slayer story

We know the basic dragon-slayer story; it begins with a young man of either humble or noble birth, a maiden, a village or countryside menaced by a dragon, and the dragon itself, often an eater of maidens and/or hoarder of gold, whom the young man must slay to save the maiden, village, or countryside, becoming a Hero, as Joseph Campbell, among others, would define the term, in the process. The earliest western version of the story probably comes from Scandinavian mythology.

> [Thor] asked to go fishing with Hymir, and when sent off to get some bait, he took the giant's biggest ox and cut its head off to take with them. ... [w]hen [Thor] threw the ox-head out into the sea, it was indeed the [Midgard Serpent] which took the bait. Thor had to exert all his divine strength, and before long, digging his heels through the boat and pushing hard against the sea bottom, he hauled up the monster, and they stared fiercely into one another's eyes. At this terrible sight, Hymir was panic-stricken, and as Thor raised his hammer, he cut the line. The serpent sank back into the depths of the sea, and Thor in anger knocked the giant overboard and waded back to shore.[3]

Thor and the Midgard Serpent meet again during Ragnarok, the final battle in which almost all creation is destroyed; Thor slays the serpent, but staggers back nine paces 'before he falls down dead, on account of the poison blown on him by the serpent'.[4]

The story of Thor's fishing expedition, unlike such humorous stories as Thor's dressing as a bride to reclaim his hammer, Mjollnir, from the giants, was taken very seriously and corresponds to stories in other mythologies that relate the 'conquest of a World Monster by the

God of the Sky'.[5] Thor's most obvious and immediate descendants are Beowulf and Sigurd the Volsung. Beowulf's ultimate battle is with a dragon; he slays it with the help of a kinsman, Wiglaf, but dies almost immediately of his wounds. Sigurd slays the dragon Fáfnir, but that act will lead, in the convoluted way of Scandinavian sagas, to his own death as well. Since then, and for a variety of cultural reasons, dragon-slayers have been more successful. St George slew his Dragon in Libya, became a patron saint of England, among other places, and was cited by Shakespeare in *Richard III* and, perhaps, *King Lear*; Spenser's Red Crosse Knight, after some struggle, slew the Dragon of Errour in the First Book of *The Faerie Queene*. That both were Christian knights is not irrelevant, Christianity triumphing over what had become a symbol of evil.

A narrative such as the dragon-slayer story that has been in oral and literary circulation for centuries develops a characteristic narrative structure. As folklore scholar Linda Dégh notes:

> The Märchen [magic tale] tells of an ordinary human being's encoun-
> ter with the suprahuman world and his becoming endowed with qual-
> ities that enable him to perform supernatural acts. The Märchen is, in
> fact, an adventure story with a single hero. ... The hero's (or heroine's)
> career starts, as everyone else's, in the dull and miserable world of reality.
> Then, all of a sudden, the supernatural world involves him and challenges
> the mortal who undertakes his long voyage to happiness. He enters the
> magic forest, guided by supernatural helpers, and defeats evil powers
> beyond the boundaries of man's universe. Crossing several borders of
> the Beyond, performing impossible tasks, the hero is slandered, tortured,
> trapped, betrayed. He suffers death by extreme cruelty but is always
> brought to life again. Suffering turns him into a real hero: as often as
> he is devoured, cut up, swallowed, or turned into a beast, so does he
> become stronger and handsomer and more worthy of the prize he seeks.
> His ascent from rags to riches ends with the beautiful heroine's hand ...
> kingdom, and marriage. The final act of the Märchen brings the hero
> back to the human world; he metes out justice, punishes the evil, rewards
> the good.[6]

Dégh's structural outline includes all of the possible elements that might be in a traditional narrative, but most narratives do not include every one, and some narratives create variations. Bilbo's death and rebirth scene in symbolically-appropriate tunnels far beneath the Earth's surface includes a subterranean encounter with Gollum and the finding of a magic ring, while Luke Skywalker's takes place when he is pulled below the 'water' in the garbage disposal of an immense space vehicle.[7] The omission of some elements, the changing of others, and the introduction of original elements function to create what folklorists call 'variations' on the basic 'formula'. The teller of a traditional narrative, then, does not slavishly follow a previous version or try to tell the original version (if such could be known) of a story – whether it be 'Cinderella', 'Tatterhood', or 'The Dragon-slayer' – but tells the story with variations that suit him or her, especially in regard to place and time; nor does writing the traditional story down and publishing it guarantee that there is a permanent form to be accepted by all, as feminist 'retellings' of 'Cinderella' and other folk and fairy tales prove. Even dragon-slayer tales are not immune from such recastings. In Gordon Dickson's *The Dragon and the George* (1976), a human from this world finds himself in the body of a dragon on another world; and in Barbara Hambly's *Dragonsbane* (1985), all of the commonplaces of Medieval Romance are reversed – and the dragon is 'slain' in the middle of the story. (Novels like those of Dickson and Hambly were, of course, published for the adult market, but like Tolkien's *The Lord of the Rings*, they are also widely read by younger readers.) It is within this matrix of oral and written, formula and variation, derivative and innovative that *The Hobbit* must be examined.

Before discussing what *The Hobbit* is, it is important to understand what it is not. In spite of its publication date, 1937, *The Hobbit* is not a modern novel. Modern novelists try to succeed by producing something new and original, something innovative; traditional story-tellers tell the stories that everyone wants to hear over and over again. Gerhard Herm, commenting on a bard's training, in *The Celts*, asserts that the apprentice had to learn 'all of the old stories circulating that the public invariably wished to hear again and again, in the same traditional form'.[8] Modern novelists are trying to move the form into the future and are judged on how well they *create*; traditional storytellers are judged on how well they tell the old stories, how well they *recreate*. The past provides the standards by which all traditional performers and performances are judged: a holiday dinner at home is judged by how well it compares to past holiday dinners ('That was the *best* Christmas dinner ever!'), a fiddler's performance of the blue grass/ country staple 'Orange Blossom Special', is judged according to all the previous performances of that tune the hearers have experienced ('That boy sure can fiddle!'), and a tale about dragon slaying is judged on how well the teller presents a narrative of which we all know the basic structural outline, the basic story. Tolkien was telling a traditional story and told it well.

In the 'Introduction' to the 1974 edition of *The Mabinogion*, editor Gwyn Jones says: 'It helps if we remember how much is still unknown about the art and craft of medieval prose narrative, both oral and written, its authorship and transmission, its concepts of construction, relevance, timing, delivery, its means and ends generally ... The tellers of the native tales knew no foreshadowings of nineteenth-century critical logistics; their hearers had not heard of the 'well-made' novel; and it is in the nature of the wondertale to transcend factual consistency'.[9] In *Beowulf: The Poem and Its Traditions*, John Niles, commenting on the aesthetics of the *Beowulf* poet, argued that such 'poets rely on both memory and certain habitual structures of words and ideas to recreate a [narrative] fluently without having it fixed in a single form'.[10] The comments of Jones and Niles in regard to ancient narratives indirectly support the idea that Tolkien, a student and scholar of ancient and medieval narratives, was writing such a narrative in *The Hobbit*.

Tolkien and the traditional tale

The external evidence of Tolkien's interest in traditional dragon-slayer stories in particular is certainly there. In his biography of Tolkien, Humphrey Carpenter quotes a Tolkien comment about his own youth: 'I desired dragons with a profound desire', and notes that at about age seven, Tolkien 'began to compose his own story about a dragon';[11] Carpenter attributes this interest to Tolkien's having read the story of the hero Sigurd and the dragon Fáfnir in Andrew Lang's *Red Fairy Book*. Tolkien spent prize money he had won on books by William Morris, including *The Volsunga Saga* and *The House of the Wolfings*, the former a translation of the Icelandic saga in which Sigurd and Fáfnir appear, the latter a prose-and-verse romance by Morris himself. Tolkien was 22 at the time.[12] Carpenter asserts that Tolkien found *The House of the Wolfings* 'absorbing' because Morris was trying to 'recreate the excitement he himself [Tolkien] had found in the pages of early English and Icelandic narratives', and Tolkien was impressed with Morris's ability to 'describe with great precision the details of his imagined landscape'.[13] Tolkien's studies in philology, especially under the direction of Joseph Wright, were also leading him further into the study of old northern European (as opposed to 'Classical') languages, and it was Wright who told Tolkien, 'Go in for the Celtic, lad; there's money in it.'[14] The 'money' part turned out to be quite true, although not in the way that Wright had probably envisioned.

Fantasy critics often overlook an early essay of Tolkien's, '*Beowulf: The Monsters and the Critics*', published one year before *The Hobbit* and therefore, I think, germane to Tolkien's thinking about ancient, traditional narratives. In it Tolkien defends the seriousness of the monsters in the poem against the critics who would see them as lapses in artistic taste or as simple allegories. The monsters, he argues, must first be read as monsters – or else the heroic level of the poem makes no sense. Far more attention has been paid to Tolkien's comments in 'On Fairy-Stories'; the seriousness of his attention to traditional folk and fairy tales here is certainly relevant to the seriousness with which he wrote his first novel. And in 'English and Welsh', the 1955 O'Donnell Lecture (delivered the day after the publication of *The Return of the King* but not itself published until 1963 – and also often overlooked by Tolkien scholars), Tolkien apologises for his tardiness in presenting this lecture, saying that there were many tasks to be done first, including 'the long-delayed appearance of a large "work," if it can be called that, which contains, in the way of presentation that I find most natural, much of what I have received from the study of things Celtic'.[15]

In addition to his academic interest in ancient narratives and traditional stories, there is also evidence that Tolkien was interested in the role of the storyteller. As Tom Shippey suggests, 'Like Walter Scott or William Morris before him, [Tolkien] felt the perilous charm of the archaic world of the North recovered from bits and scraps by generations of inquiry. He wanted to tell a story about it simply, one feels, because there were hardly any complete ones left.'[16] Tolkien himself remarked in the preface to *The Fellowship of the Ring* that the 'prime motive [for writing *The Lord of the Rings*] was the desire of a tale-teller to try his hand at a really long story that would hold the attention of the readers, amuse them, delight them, and at times maybe excite them or deeply move them'.[17] I find it significant that Tolkien, who knew deeply the meanings of words, uses the very words 'tale-teller', and not 'writer' or 'author', to refer to himself and the word 'story', and not 'novel', to refer to *The Lord of the Rings*.[18]

For the most part, *The Hobbit* reads and feels like a traditional story; indeed, it was begun as an oral tale told to Tolkien's sons. The story begins on an ordinary morning in the mundane world with the soon-to-be main character calmly smoking a pipe outside his door after breakfast. He is not technically an orphan, but his parents have passed away, and he has no siblings. Along comes a wizard and the next day some dwarves, and Bilbo Baggins is soon off into the magic forest on an adventure, and not just any adventure but the grandest quest of all – to slay a dragon and reclaim a treasure. Bilbo, in the company of his mentor, the wizard Gandalf, and his new dwarf companions, faces a traditional series of increasingly difficult tests, tests in which he is increasingly successful. In Chapter 2, he finds the trolls, because he moves more quietly than the dwarves, but he gets caught; in Chapter 4, he is able to shout a warning that allows Gandalf to escape although he and the dwarves are captured by the goblins; in Chapter 5, he triumphs over Gollum, albeit with a questionable riddle; in Chapter 8, he rescues the dwarves from the spiders; in Chapter 9, he rescues the dwarves from the wood elves' prison; in Chapter 11, he finds the door into the mountain; and in Chapter 12, he saves the dwarves from the dragon's attack. Through those incidents, in which he is increasingly central and increasingly successful, Bilbo progresses from '*a little fellow bobbing on the mat*' (italics in the original) at the beginning of the story[19] to become the acknowledged leader of the expedition by the middle of Chapter 12. At the end of the story, he does come home changed. Gandalf remarks, 'My dear Bilbo! ...You are not the hobbit that you were,'[20] and he must restore order there, in a way, reclaiming his home and possessions from the Sackville-Bagginses.

But Bilbo does not kill the dragon, Smaug, nor do any of the dwarves, despite Thorin's earlier boasting to the contrary. Indeed, the dragon is killed almost off stage. After Smaug has flown out in the night to wreak havoc on Laketown at the end of Chapter 12, Bilbo and the dwarves spend 40 pages exploring the mountain and refortifying it against the expected attack. Finally, in Chapter 14, we hear about the death of Smaug but this is presented almost as a sidebar to the rest of the story. As the residents and mayor of Laketown panic, one figure rallies the soldiers, Bard, a descendant of the Lords of Dale and possessor of a portentous 'black arrow' that has never failed to find its mark. Having been told by an old thrush of the weak spot on the dragon's underside, Bard aims carefully and brings the dragon crashing down – an event of which Bilbo and the dwarves remain ignorant for some time. Moreover, the dragon has been slain with five chapters still to go in the story.

Tolkien's originality

Up to this point, Tolkien has been telling a traditional dragon-slayer story, but now he makes the story his own. Bilbo is challenged by the dragon, certainly, but in an unexpected way. In Chapter 12, when Bilbo heads, all alone, down toward the dragon's lair for the first time, he reaches a point at which he stops.

> Going on from there was the bravest thing he ever did. The tremen-
> dous things that happened afterwards were as nothing compared to it.

He fought the real battle in the tunnel all alone, before he ever saw the vast danger that lay in wait.[21]

This is Bilbo's challenge, a test not of strength and skill, but of courage and will — something very different from the battles entered into by Beowulf and Sigurd the Volsung. The alert reader, the reader experienced in dragon-slayer tales (aren't we all?), must have been wondering for some time who was going to kill the dragon, must have known that Bilbo was not a dragon-slayer, and must have figured out that dwarves who once ran away from a dragon would not be the ones to slay it. Moreover, Bilbo was hired as a burglar, after all, though he has done much more than that. Bilbo makes two more trips down that tunnel by himself. In the second, he does triumph, successfully challenging Smaug in a duel of words but then getting singed by dragon fire for his last bit of audacity; on the third trip, he finds the dragon gone.

The contrast between Bilbo and Bard is more complex than who does or does not kill the dragon. Bard, in spite of his brief appearances in the narrative, is the inheritor of the Beowulf/Sigurd tradition. He slays the dragon with a magic weapon that pierces the unprotected spot on the dragon's underside, and survives the encounter (Sigurd); and his destruction of the dragon results, after the Battle of the Five Armies, in a great deal of treasure to be disbursed among the winners. Bard and Dain, the new leader of the dwarves, give much of their shares away to the profit of their communities and friends (Beowulf). While he plays some part in all of these adventures, Bilbo, while now the leader of the expedition, confronts the dragon more as a Trickster than a Hero. On his first visit to Smaug's lair, he steals a cup and indirectly awakens the dragon's fury (parallel to the actions of the slave in *Beowulf*), and on his second trip, he engages in crafty word play with the dragon, not physical confrontation. At the end of each scene, Bilbo 'flees' up the tunnel.[22] It is true that, by relating comments about the dragon's soft spot to the dwarves where a thrush can hear them and relay them to Bard, and by stealing the Arkenstone, Bilbo moves the action along, but these are enabling actions rather than heroic ones. And after slaying the dragon, Bard proudly announces his lineage to the Laketown people, whereas Bilbo craftily keeps his identity secret when talking with Smaug.

Tolkien handles the split hero, which he may have understood from his study of Icelandic sagas,[23] much differently in *The Lord of the Rings*, dividing the Bilbo and Bard duties between Frodo and Aragorn. Frodo, like Bilbo, is there throughout the novel, but his task is to sneak into Mordor and cast the One Ring into the fires of Mount Doom;

he is not supposed to confront Sauron or battle his armies. Aragorn, first presented as an unknown stranger, with no history or heritage (the Märchen orphan, as it were), in Chapter Nine of *The Fellowship of the Ring*, is slowly discovered throughout *The Lord of the Rings* to be more than a mere woods-roving ranger; he is the rightful heir to the Kingdom of Gondor, carries the reforged sword-that-was-broken, can rouse the cursed and sleeping knights to aid in the penultimate battle, weds the elf maiden, Arwen, challenges Sauron's army at Mordor's gates, and will, in the end, be the High King in Middle-earth. But Tolkien had more 'room' to create with Frodo and, especially, Aragorn in *The Lord of the Rings* than he had had with Bilbo and Bard in *The Hobbit*.

Tolkien and the First World War

Tolkien did not suddenly realise that Bilbo was not a dragon-slayer, find himself stuck for a hero, and end up at the last minute dragging in Bard from the wings to do the job. Tolkien was after a larger and more pertinent foe. It is important to note that none of the dwarves (or anyone else we might have developed a fondness for in the story) dies as a result of the dragon quest. Thor, Beowulf, and Sigurd the Volsung all die, directly or indirectly, from their battles with dragons, while St George, Spenser's Red Crosse Knight, and numerous grade B modern fantasy heroes tame or slay their dragons. But characters we care about do die – in the Battle of the Five Armies. Thorin dies surrounded by a pile of slain enemies, and Fili and Kili die with him, a fitting death as he was their mother's brother. It is war, war caused by greed, that is the real danger in this tale.

In the traditional tale, Dégh's Märchen, for example, the ending is almost always about unalloyed triumph; the hero comes home with the treasure, marries the princess, and becomes king to restore order and rule wisely over the land. By not creating an ending of unalloyed triumph, Tolkien makes the traditional tale his own, relevant to himself and his time, a time when the spectre of the First World War still hung heavy over Europe. Tolkien was in France, although not yet on the front lines, when the first day of the Battle of the Somme resulted in some 20,000 Allied dead, and he lost his two best friends, Rob Gilman and G. B. Smith, and many, many acquaintances in that war.

In *War and the Works of J. R. R. Tolkien*, Janet Brennan Croft uses Tolkien's letters and essays to establish connections between the war and his novels. Croft quotes a letter in which Tolkien wrote that 'The Dead Marshes and the Morannon owe something to Northern

France after the Battle of the Somme,' and then she notes that the 'hopeless bravery he observed in the trenches' may have connected with the northern European theory of courage without hope that Tolkien discusses in 'Beowulf: The Monsters and the Critics', courage that may well lead to defeat.[24] As Bilbo watches what appears to be the beginning of the victory of the goblins over the dwarves and elves, he comments, 'Misery me! I have heard songs of many battles, and I have always understood that defeat may be glorious. It seems very uncomfortable, not to say distressing.'[25] Bilbo, excited by but also sceptical about adventures from the beginning and often wishing he were home again during the course of the events of the story, finds what Tolkien might have considered the Christian fallacy of Ragnarok in particular, the Scandinavian mythos in general, and the glorious death in a losing cause: the sheer waste. (Tolkien's The Children of Hurin, posthumously published under the editorship of Christopher Tolkien, is as bleak a working out of fate as any in the original Icelandic sagas and may well be Tolkien's version and acknowledgement of the bleakness of that particular Scandinavian vision.)[26]

W. A. Senior, in 'Loss Eternal in J. R. R. Tolkien's Middle-earth', asserts that there is 'one concept that ... provides Tolkien with his most pervasive and unifying component of atmosphere and mood: the sustained and grieved sense of loss, of which death is but one form, that floods through the history of Middle-earth'. Discussing not only The Hobbit and The Lord of the Rings, but also The Silmarillion and some of Tolkien's other posthumously-published tales to illustrate the pervasiveness of this sense of loss in all of Tolkien's fiction, Senior concludes that there is 'in volume after volume, tale after tale ... the incalculable devastation and annihilation faced by the denizens of Middle-earth from Feanor to Frodo'.[27] Senior traces that sense of loss to Tolkien's experiences in and immediately after the First World War.

As The Hobbit draws to a close, Tolkien finalises the variation he has made on the traditional dragon–slayer story formula. Bilbo, the protagonist, has not become the hero by slaying the dragon; he has a more important role to fulfil for Tolkien. When Bilbo reaches Thorin's side after the battle has ended, he finds a dying and repentant dwarf who tells him, 'Since I leave now all gold and silver, and go where it is of little worth, I wish to part in friendship from you, and I take back my words and deeds at the Gate,' and his final words to Bilbo are Tolkien's most direct statement of the theme of the novel: 'If more of us valued food and cheer and song above hoarded gold, it would be a merrier world.'[28] At the very end of the novel, years later, when knowledge of his adventure his damaged Bilbo's reputation among the staid hobbits of Hobbiton and his Mithril coat of mail is on loan to a museum, Bilbo and Gandalf are reminiscing about the adventure, and Gandalf does not tell Bilbo that he, Bilbo, was a hero in the tale; rather, he says, 'You are a very fine person, Mr. Baggins, and I am very fond of you; but you are only quite a little fellow in a wide world after all!' to which Bilbo replies, 'Thank goodness!'[29]

Evaluated by the standards of the structure and content of the traditional Hero Tale or Märchen, Bilbo, though successful, is not a Hero. His successes are important and do contribute to the successful outcome of the action, but they do not come as a result of direct confrontation with and victory against an opponent. Even his confrontation with Gollum is tainted by the tricky question, not a riddle at all, that he asks to win the ring, and it is the power of the ring to render him invisible that allows him to trick the guards and escape from the mountain, to attack the spiders that have captured the dwarves, to roam the halls of the wood elves and free the dwarves from captivity there, to approach the dragon, and finally, perhaps, to escape death in the final battle. Bilbo, like other traditional Trickster figures with whom Tolkien was well acquainted, Loki, Odysseus, Reynard the Fox, and others, was not destined to be a Hero.

But evaluating *The Hobbit* from a performance perspective and attempting to assess what Tolkien was doing with the structure and content of the traditional dragon-slayer's tale, how and why he changed the structure and content to make the story his own and make it relevant to himself, his time, and his place, yields a better sense of the work as a whole. That approach discovers the themes of *The Hobbit* to be about greed and war, themes different from those of heroism or heroic death in a lost cause that Tolkien had found in the sagas and in other northern writings, themes directly traceable to his experiences in and reflections on the First World War. The dragon is slain, by the right person, with relative ease; war is a much more complex and costly affair. War, Tolkien is saying, is about loss, and it is much more dangerous than dragons.

Notes

1. C. S. Lewis, 'On Story', in *Of Other Worlds*, ed. Walter Hooper (New York: Harcourt Brace, 1975): 3.
2. Brian Rosebury, *Tolkien: A Critical Assessment* (New York: St Martin's, 1992): 4.

3. H. R. Ellis Davidson, *Gods and Myths of Northern Europe* (New York: Penguin, 1975): 35.
4. Snorri Sturluson, *The Prose Edda*, trans. Jean I. Young (Berkeley: University of California Press, 1966): 88.
5. Davidson: 81, 82.
6. Linda Dégh, 'Folk Narrative', in Richard Dorson (ed.), *Folklore and Folklife* (Chicago, IL: University of Chicago Press, 1972): 53–85, at 63.
7. C. W. Sullivan III, 'J. R. R. Tolkien and the Telling of a Traditional Narrative', *Journal of the Fantastic in the Arts*, 7(1) (1996): 75–82, at 76.
8. Gerhard Herm, *The Celts* (New York: St Martins, 1975): 239.
9. Gwyn Jones and Thomas Jones (ed. and trans.), 'Introduction', *The Mabinogion*, rev. edn (London: Dent, 1974): xxxviii.
10. John Niles, *Beowulf: The Poem and Its Traditions* (Cambridge, MA: Harvard University Press, 1983): 33.
11. Humphrey Carpenter, *J. R. R. Tolkien: A Biography* (Boston, MA: Houghton Mifflin, 1977): 22, 23.
12. Ibid.: 69.
13. Ibid.: 70.
14. Ibid.: 56.
15. Ibid.: 224.
16. Tom Shippey, *The Road to Middle Earth* (Boston, MA: Houghton Mifflin, 1983): 54.
17. J. R. R. Tolkien, *The Fellowship of the Ring*. New Edition (New York: Ballantine, 1989): 11.
18. C. W. Sullivan III, 'J. R. R. Tolkien and the Rediscovery of the North', in Jenö Bárdos (ed.), *Husse Papers 2005: Proceedings of the Seventh Biennial Conference* (Veszprém: University of Veszprém, 2006): 244.
19. J. R. R. Tolkien, *The Hobbit* (1937; rev. edn, New York: Ballantine, 1989): 18.
20. Ibid:. 300.
21. Ibid.: 212–13.
22. Ibid.: 214–15.
23. Theodore M. Andersson, 'The Displacement of the Heroic Ideal in the Family Sagas', in John Tucker (ed.), *Sagas of the Icelanders* (New York: Garland, 1989): 40–70.
24. Janet Brennan Croft, *War and the Works of J. R. R. Tolkien* (Westport, CT: Greenwood, 2004): 17, 19.
25. Tolkien, *The Hobbit*: 284.
26. J. R. R. Tolkien, *The Children of Hurin*, ed. Christopher Tolkien (Boston, MA: Houghton Mifflin, 2009).
27. W. A. Senior, 'Loss Eternal in J. R. R. Tolkien's Middle-earth', in George Clark and Daniel Timmons (ed.), *J. R. R. Tolkien and His Literary Resonances* (Westport, CT: Greenwood, 2000): 173, 174.
28. Tolkien, *The Hobbit*: 288.
29. Ibid.: 303.

5

Tolkien's Language

Louise Joy

Langue and *parole*

If we start from the rudimentary position that *The Hobbit* is a work of children's literature since, at the point of composing and publishing the text, J. R. R. Tolkien understood himself to be writing for young people, then it is tempting to assume that its very language – what Tolkien termed its 'linguistic matter'[1] – must somehow relate to children. After all, what is there to a text, to any text, if not language? What else, if not its linguistic matter, could make *The Hobbit* a children's novel? Of course, there are the illustrations; but as Tolkien's early critic, the ten-year-old Rayner Unwin, averred: 'This book, with the help of maps, does not need any illustrations it is good and should appeal to all children between the ages of 5 and 9'[2] (punctuation his own). Tolkien, however, was vehement in his antipathy to the idea that literature must be morphologically altered to make it fit for children: 'Do not write down to Children or to anybody. Not even in language,'[3] he enjoined in 1959, two decades after the publication of his children's masterpiece. While by this point in time, Tolkien had made his peace with the fact that *The Hobbit* and *The Lord of the Rings* did appeal to children, he was nonetheless insistent that if this was so, it was certainly not on account of anything he had consciously *done* to them: 'I am not specially interested in children,' he wrote, and 'certainly not in writing for them: i.e. in addressing directly and expressly those who cannot understand adult language.'[4] Two years later he elaborated on this: 'Children are not a class or kind, they are a heterogeneous collection of immature persons, varying, as persons do, in their reach, and in their ability to extend it when stimulated. As soon as you limit your vocabulary to what you suppose to be within their reach, you in fact simply cut off the gifted ones from the chance of extending it.'[5] Quite clearly, at least according to the author himself, if the 'linguistic matter' of *The Hobbit* makes any concessions to children, then it is not on account of the words of which it is comprised.

Unsurprisingly, given his idiosyncratic – not to mention professional – fascination with languages and their origins, the words Tolkien uses have for long fascinated critics, whose starting point is often Tolkien's own comment in relation to *The Lord of the Rings* that 'the invention of languages is the foundation. The "stories" were made rather to provide a world for the languages than the reverse.'[6] Studies of Tolkien's language have painstakingly uncovered the intricate systems of words in his fiction, explicating the etymologies of the words he borrowed and analysing the significance of the words he coined.[7] Such studies have exhaustively shown how Tolkien's 'mythology' derives from, is animated by, or is an 'outgrowth of,'[8] his invented languages. Elizabeth Kirk, for example, analyses how Tolkien creates a 'model' for 'the relationship of language to action, to values and to civilization'; and Margaret Hiley interrogates the ways in which Tolkien's language has mythical signifying systems superimposed upon it.[9] But suppose we begin from a different starting point. Suppose we take language not to mean the diction Tolkien uses or the systems within which his words function (*langue*), but instead the forms in or methods by which words are uttered (*parole*).[10] This would shift the emphasis away from Tolkien's vocabulary (about which there is anyway surely little more to be said), and towards the ends to which Tolkien *uses* his vocabulary – his narrative techniques or his speech acts – a dimension of Tolkien's language which has received much less concerted critical attention. If it is not the words that Tolkien uses that make *The Hobbit*'s language suitable for, and moreover appealing to, a child reader, then it must be what he does with them.

Direct speech

Narrative theorists going back to Plato have tended to agree that there are two main ways in which literature uses language: *diegetically* (by telling) and *mimetically* (by showing). In a novel, these two narrative modes are epitomised by, on the one hand, what Gerard Genette calls 'narrative of events' ('a transcription of the (supposed) non-verbal into the verbal'), and on the other, what he terms 'narrative of words' ('the discourse of characters').[11] To put this more crudely, action can either be presented through the words of the narrator or it can be presented through the words of the characters themselves. Naturally, novels for children, like novels more generally, tend to make use of a combination of narrative of events with narrative of words. However, it has often been proposed that 'children's literature characteristically focuses on showing rather than telling'.[12] This means that children's novels tend to create an illusion that the reader is witnessing first-hand events as they unfold, rather than being presented with a version of events that has already been filtered through the eyes of a narrator. Maria Nikolajeva, who distinguishes between 'external representation' ('including description, comments, actions, and speech') and 'internal representation' (which 'allows us to penetrate the characters' minds, to take part in their innermost thoughts and mental states'), observes that there is 'a clear tendency in fiction for younger children toward external characterization, while young adult fiction frequently employs internal means'.[13] On account of this propensity for children's novels to appear to present rather than *re*present the scene at hand, John Stephens has suggested that 'with children's fiction ... more attention needs to be paid to direct speech dialogue ... because it exists in a higher proportion'.[14] Certainly, a quick survey of influential children's texts written contemporaneously to *The Hobbit* indicates that by the mid-1930s direct speech had become a major ingredient of the children's novel. In novels such as Arthur Ransome's *Swallows and Amazons* (1930), John Masefield's *The Box of Delights* (1935) and Alison Uttley's *A Traveller in Time* (1939), a large portion of the narrative is presented via direct speech. Needless to say, children's novels do not have a monopoly on direct speech, in the 1930s or at any other point in literary history; but when one considers the comparatively minor role that direct speech plays in some of the notable examples of adult literature from the same decade, for example in works by Virginia Woolf, William Faulkner and George Orwell, we can see in sharper focus its importance as a factor which might determine, or at least influence, the ages included within a text's likely audience.

The Hobbit almost exclusively uses external rather than internal character representation. This means that invariably Tolkien's reader does 'not know any more about [the characters] than other characters would', a position which, at least for Nikolajeva, befits 'the cognitive level of [the] implied readers' of children's literature.[15] Accordingly, direct speech is a fundamental element of the novel. This is not to say that most of the novel is conducted through dialogue – it is not; most of the novel is comprised of omniscient third-person narrative, often, though not always, focalised through Bilbo Baggins. But it is to observe that dialogue – of which there is plenty – occurs at seminal moments of the novel, not because Tolkien resorts to direct speech as a vehicle for the dramatisation of sensational events, but because at such moments, language *is* the event. At the novel's many dramatic peaks, it is spoken language – talk – which makes things happen. In this way, Tolkien's language reconnects with what the anthropologist Bronislaw Malinowski, in his influential essay 'The Problem of Meaning in Primitive Languages' (1923), termed 'its primitive function and original form'. Such language, Malinowski wrote, is 'a mode of behaviour, an indispensable element of concerted human action'.[16] Interestingly, given that what we are concerned with in this essay is the ways in which Tolkien's language might appeal to the child reader, Malinowski perceived the function of language among primitive peoples (his field work was conducted in Papua New Guinea) to share something vital in common with the function of language among children: 'When the child clamours for a person, it calls and he appears before it. When it wants food or an object … its only means of action is to clamour, and a very efficient means of action this proves to the child.'[17] He concludes that, both among what today we would call 'uncontacted people' and among children, words are therefore not only a means of expression, but 'the word gives power, allows one to exercise an influence over an object or an action'.[18] In *The Hobbit* too, words, especially words as they are presented through direct speech, make things happen. Tolkien's use of direct speech in *The Hobbit*, then, secures the appeal of the novel among children not merely because a child reader might find external character representation less arduous than internal character representation; it also secures the appeal of the novel among children because, if we accept Malinowski's theory, children already recognise the potential for spoken language to change the environment. For a child reader, Tolkien's attribution of power to words does not require any leap of faith. At the same time, though, the use of such language does not make children the only appropriate audience for his fairy-story, as Tolkien was keen to stress: fairy-stories will always appeal to a *de facto* audience comprised of readers of any age who wish, as he put it, to 'open a door on Other Time', to 'stand outside our own time, outside Time itself, maybe' – or to pick up on Malinowski's term, to return to a more 'primitive' existence. The rest of this essay seeks to chart *The Hobbit*'s childish, or 'primitive', use of 'verbal magic'[19] wherein spoken language becomes precious artillery capable of transforming the world in which it is sounded.

Conversation

The Hobbit opens with a scene-setting narrative overview addressed directly to the reader. It is surely this awkward direct address, clumsily reminiscent of children's novels from several decades earlier by authors such as Beatrix Potter, E. Nesbit or J. M. Barrie, which Tolkien later had in mind when he criticised the 'whims[ical]' and even 'facetious' mode in which the novel begins.[20] Certainly, his discomfort with the use of second-person address ('you will see whether he gained anything in the end'[21]) can be judged by the fact that he almost entirely abandons use of this technique after the first four pages, when the narrative moves into direct speech and the novel proper gets under way. But here we encounter something interesting. While, following the logic outlined above, the direct representation of talk might provide a point of entry for the child reader, in fact the novel's first dialogue – between Bilbo Baggins and Gandalf – reveals conversation to be a fundamentally adult (and hence regrettable) preoccupation:

> 'Good morning!' said Bilbo, and he meant it. …
> 'What do you mean?' [Gandalf] said. 'Do you wish me a good morning, or mean that it is a good morning whether I want it or not; or that you feel good this morning; or that it is a morning to be good on?'
> 'All of them at once,' said Bilbo. 'And a very fine morning for a pipe of tobacco out of doors, into the bargain. If you have a pipe about you, sit down and have a fill of mine! There's no hurry, we have all the day before us! …
> 'Very pretty!' said Gandalf. 'But I have no time to blow smoke-rings this morning. I am looking for someone to share in an adventure that I am arranging, and it's very difficult to find anyone.'
> 'I should think so – in these parts! We are plain quiet folk and have no use for adventures. Nasty disturbing uncomfortable things! Make you late for dinner! I can't think what anybody sees in them,' said our Mr Baggins. … 'Good morning!' he said at last. 'We don't want any adventures here, thank you! You might try over The Hill or across The Water.' By this he meant that the conversation was at an end.
> 'What a lot of things you do use *Good morning* for!' said Gandalf. 'Now you mean that you want to get rid of me, and that it won't be good till I move off.'
> 'Not at all, not at all, my dear sir!'[22]

Scholars have often proposed that the hobbit provides a point of identification for the child reader on account of his diminutive stature, and there is perhaps some truth to this; but it is important to note that the hobbit's small talk has a pungent whiff of the old man about it. While Bilbo, navigating his way through the fraught business of shaking off an unwelcome visitor within the bounds of politeness, participates in a decidedly adult comedy of manners, Gandalf emerges as the more energetic, uninhibited, and hence childlike, figure, a figure at home in the child's adventure story. If, as Stephen Miller suggests, we can distinguish between *conversation*, which is 'purposeless', and *talk*, which is 'purposeful',[23] we might see Bilbo as a master of conversation, frustrating Gandalf's desire to talk. But it is not quite the case that Bilbo's conversation is purposeless. He is using language to attempt to 'establish [a bond] of personal union between [two] people brought together' rather than to 'frame and express thoughts'.[24] And his efforts indicate that he has fully digested some of the basic rules of conversation: for example, he takes pains to avoid his interlocutor losing face, by directing him off to The Hill and The Water;[25] he avoids open disagreement, by never directly asking Gandalf to leave;[26] and, crucially, he ensures that there are no embarrassing silences, respectfully responding to all questions and volunteering comments in exchange. Bilbo emerges as a morally upright character, someone who takes seriously the view expressed by John Mahaffy that conversation is a *duty*.[27] But this encounter is not what Milton Wright would characterise as 'resultful', since 'to be successful, a conversation must be interesting to the persons taking part in it. This means to *all* of the persons.'[28] And such interest is contingent, as Daniel Menaker points out, on 'the main part of a conversation, particularly with a new acquaintance, establish[ing] some kind of common ground'.[29]

Far from bringing the two characters together, this conversation has driven them apart, exposing the oppositional positions that they occupy. In part the opposition Tolkien sets up here is an opposition between taking risks and playing it safe – or what the novel goes on to characterise as *Tookishness* versus *Bagginsishness*. At the same time, though, it is an opposition between using words to do things (for example, to convey meaning, like Gandalf) and using words to not do things (for example, to obfuscate one's meaning, like Bilbo Baggins). In addition, it is implicitly an opposition between a modern way of life, rooted in the home, and a pre-modern way of life, let loose in the great outdoors. So we have here a cluster of associations: on the one hand the Baggins, a grumpy, though polite, old man whose civility is epitomised by his capacity to use words to deflect meaning (every word in the phrase 'Not at all, not at all, my dear sir!' is a lie); and on the other, the Took, an upbeat, if uncivilised, childlike figure ('I am looking for someone to share in an adventure') whose primitive nature is epitomised by his desire for words to *mean* something. If dialogue is the narrative hook with which Tolkien ensnares his child reader, it is a hook he uses to expose the ridiculousness of conversation – or, more specifically, the ridiculousness of polite sociability in the modern, adult world. The child reader does not want to hang around blowing smoke rings outside the hobbit hole; the child wants to go on the trip. The function of this conversation, then, is to galvanise the reader's frustration precisely with conversation. What the reader wants from direct speech, Tolkien assumes, is *direct* speech – which is to say, speech that cuts to the chase, or, moreover, speech that *is* the chase.

When Bilbo Baggins undertakes to go on Gandalf's adventure, he evolves (or perhaps regresses) from a figure who uses language in place of action into one who uses language *as* action. He changes from a character whose default utterances are moans about the lack of creature comforts ('I am dreadfully hungry'[30]) to one who can use language to materialise absent food and shelter ('you will take me along quick to a fire, where I can dry'[31]). He acquires the capacity to use language in this way from the example of Gandalf, whose talk luxuriates in the possibility for words to alter the things to which they relate. Gandalf is liberal in his use of imperatives ('Be good, take care of yourselves – and DON'T LEAVE THE PATH!'[32]), fully invoking the privileges accorded to him by virtue of his superior social position. This position also gives him licence to ask the questions, forcing his companions, the dwarves and the hobbit, into the subservient role of supplying answers. But it is in his interaction with their enemies that Gandalf's talk is most manifestly bewitching. He sets the precedent for how to use spoken language to make things happen when the voyagers encounter their first hurdle: the three trolls in the wood. Bilbo and the dwarves have already succumbed to the trolls' greater physical strength, but Gandalf, crucially, is invisible, and hence can – indeed must – rely on the power of the voice alone to get his way. When Gandalf intervenes, the trolls are preoccupied by an undirected conversation of the kind that Gandalf despises:

> 'Blimey, Bert, look what I've copped!' said William.
>   'What is it?' said the others coming up.
>   'Lumme, if I knows! What are yer?' …
>   It was just then that Gandalf came back. But no one saw him. The trolls had just decided to roast the dwarves now and eat them later – that was Bert's idea, and after a lot of argument they had all agreed to it.
>   'No good roasting 'em now, it'd take all night,' said a voice. Bert thought it was William's.
>   … [A]nd so the argument began all over again.[33]

The coarse speech of the trolls reflects an aggressive misuse of language; their colloquialisms ('copped') betray their immunity to the beauty of a well turned phrase, their indifference to aesthetic beauty mirroring their indifference to moral virtue. When Gandalf enters the affray, he demonstrates his understanding that it is not what is said that is significant to these crude conversationalists, but that *something* is said. By weighing in with a remark which opens up an argument that is already finished, he wilfully misconstrues one form of conversational silence for another: effectively he turns a 'lapse' (which occurs when talk has been discontinued) into a 'pause' (which occurs when one speaker hands over to another).[34] In so doing, he propels the interlocutors into conflict, violating the guiding maxim of conversation, which is precisely to avoid discord – and in so doing, saving the day, since the trolls squabble themselves into a death-trap.

Among the many vitalising effects of Gandalf's performative utterances[35] is their effect on Bilbo Baggins, who, in imitation, gradually begins to relinquish his comparatively unambitious desire for language simply to be constative – 'All the same, I should like it all plain and clear'[36]. The hobbit is first called on to conjure words which do more than merely describe, in his encounter with Gollum, where he is required to tread that ever-precarious line between providing witty banter and not causing offence. True to form, Baggins is initially conservative, intuitively adhering to the three golden rules of polite conversation: don't impose; give options; and be friendly.[37] But his interlocutor is a slippery operator, and it is not clear that politeness alone will secure the outcome that Bilbo seeks (being shown the way out). Gollum, it should be remembered, has not of late had much exposure to conversation, and what he seeks from the hobbit is the simple satisfaction of reciprocated talk. Bilbo, therefore, must deliver what Gollum requires, ensuring that the dialogue keeps moving forward through 'simple pairs of initiative and reaction moves'.[38] But at the same time, Bilbo becomes aware that 'holding the floor is a position of power';[39] he therefore cannot afford to fail to come up with something to say. Verbal gymnastics are not, at this early point in the novel, the hobbit's forte, and his conversational ineptitude is redeemed only by the fact that Gollum's is even worse: '[Bilbo's] tongue seemed to stick in his mouth; he wanted to shout out: "Give me more time! Give me time!" But all that came out with a sudden squeal was: "Time! Time!" Bilbo was saved by pure luck. For that of course was the answer.'[40] Through his accidental verbal prowess, the hobbit quickly realises that if he is to get what he needs out of the conversation, then he will have to start to dictate the terms on which it operates:

'What has it got in its pocketses? Tell us that. It must tell first.' …
'Answers were to be guessed not given,' [Bilbo] said.

'But it wasn't a fair questions,' said Gollum. 'Not a riddle, precious, no.'
'Oh well, if it's a matter of ordinary questions,' Bilbo replied, 'Then
I asked one first. What have you lost? Tell me that?'
  'What has it got in its pocketses?' ...
  'What have you lost?' Bilbo persisted.[41]

Disrupting the smooth sequence of initiative and reaction moves, the
hobbit sneaks in a question of a completely different order (particular,
not abstract) which thrusts Gollum from a position in which he holds
the power (knowledge of the way out) to one in which he lacks it
(knowledge of what Bilbo has in mind). By taking the initiative in this
way, Bilbo alters the power dynamics between the two interlocutors,
transforming the encounter from one in which Bilbo is subject to
Gollum's whims to one in which Gollum is subject to his. Essentially,
by substituting one kind of question for another, he has seized the
advantage; by assuming the role of question-master, which enables
him to dictate what kinds of questions can be asked, he relegates
Gollum to a position in which he must provide reactive rather than
initiative conversational moves. By enfeebling Gollum in this way, the
hobbit makes it possible to get what he wants (his liberty) without
surrendering in return what he can't afford to give (the ring).

Speech acts

Although Bilbo does succeed in outwitting Gollum, it is more
through good fortune than design, and he still has some way to go
before he is able to wield words with the finesse displayed by Gandalf.
This is because Gandalf has realised that in order most effectively to
work their magic, words must give pleasure to their audience: we
'must have stories in any conversation in order to carry it forward.
People cannot discuss abstractions for a considerable time without
becoming wearied; they must have narratives, recitals of what people
said or did.'[42] This is most vividly demonstrated by the elaborate and
impeccably timed story he tells Beorn in order to seduce him into
offering the travellers food and shelter. By telling a tale so captivat-
ing and so suspenseful, Gandalf places his listener in a position of
such eagerness for the words to continue that he is prepared to offer
whatever Gandalf desires in return. 'Oh let 'em all come! Hurry up!
Come along, you two, and sit down! ... But now please get on with
the tale,' begs Beorn.[43] In effect, Gandalf uses words as a kind of
currency. In a variation on the childish use of words to clamour for
what is wanted (usually food), in so doing materialising it, Gandalf

offers words in exchange for what he wants (food again), arousing in his interlocutor a hunger to hear more which rivals his companions' hunger to eat: 'If all beggars could tell such a good [tale],' observes Beorn, 'they might find me kinder. You may be making it all up, of course, but you deserve a supper for the story all the same. Let's have something to eat!'[44]

But equally important as the use of language to allure is its use to repel – using language not merely to exert power over the environment, but to *over*power it. The old adage might proclaim that 'sticks and stones will break my bones but words will never hurt me'. But of course, the very fact that a mantra is required to deny the potency of words suggests that the opposite is true: words *do* hurt. The capacity for words to cause injury rests, as Bilbo Baggins resolutely discovers, on the appropriation of power involved in naming. As Malinowski has noted, 'a name has the power over the person or thing which it signifies',[45] and to assume the role of endowing something with a name is to decide upon, and hence control the parameters of, its identity. When the hobbit is confronted by an enormous spiderlike creature in the wood, he fearlessly chants:

> *Old Tomnoddy, all big body,*
> *Old Tomnoddy can't spy on me!*
> *Attercop! Attercop!*
> *Down you drop!*
> *You'll never catch me up your tree!*[46]

By arrogating the right to name the creature, Bilbo subjects it to his rule, since the spider can do nothing to influence Bilbo's choice of words. In addition, by employing inane monikers which domesticate and hence enervate the creature ('Old Tomnoddy', 'Attercop'), he de-escalates the threat, transforming it from something undefined, and hence unassailable, into something knowable and consequently surmountable. The solution, it transpires, is spellbindingly simple – the hurling of verbal abuse.

Bilbo's resort to offensive rhymes is a child's tactic, drawn straight from the repertoire of playground lore. Childish as the trick may be, though, it is devastatingly effective: 'they stopped advancing, and some went off in the direction of the voice. "Attercop" made them so angry that they lost their wits.'[47] Bilbo drives his antagonists into a frenzy by assaulting them with words calculated to wound. This is a speech act in a forcible sense: his words stun the spiders, ambushing them by bending them to his will. In a book concerned with magic, it is tempting to see Bilbo's song as a kind of incantation which enchants those who hear it; but in fact, to use language to 'repuls[e] outer things' is 'an arrangement biologically essential to the human race', one which we find even in 'the early articulated words sent forth by children [to] produce the very effect which these words *mean*'.[48] Tolkien's protagonist has reconnected with his childish, primal instincts and rediscovered his capacity to use words to transfigure, potentially even to annihilate, the world he inhabits.

It is the hobbit's newfound linguistic ingenuity which ultimately proves to be his greatest contribution to the adventure, since it is this that enables them to vanquish the dragon whose crimes they have travelled so far to avenge. In a virtuoso solo performance, when Bilbo Baggins is brought face to face with Smaug, he steps up to the occasion, bringing into play his entire range of newly acquired (or recalled) strategies in a remarkable performance of verbal pyrotechnics:

> 'No thank you, O Smaug the Tremendous! ... I did not come for presents. I only wished to have a look at you and see if you were truly as great as tales say. I did not believe them.'
>
> 'Do you now?' said the dragon somewhat flattered, even though he did not believe a word of it. ... 'Who are you and where do you come from, may I ask?'
>
> 'You may indeed! I come from under the hill, and under the hills and over the hills my paths led. And through the air. I am he that walks unseen.'
>
> 'So I can well believe,' said Smaug, 'but that is hardly your usual name.'
>
> 'I am the clue-finder, the web-cutter, the stinging fly. I was chosen for the lucky number.'[49]

Keenly aware of the need to avoid aggravating the volatile dragon, the hobbit cajoles him with wheedling falsities. Not only is this essential for keeping him on side (a basic skill for a good conversationalist), in addition to biding valuable time while the hobbit calculates his next move, it moreover works performatively to debilitate the dragon. The hobbit's flattery serves to make the dragon forget that he is conversing with a probable enemy, ensnaring him into the fateful trap of exposing his unprotected breast: '"Dazzlingly marvellous! Perfect! Flawless! Staggering!" exclaimed Bilbo aloud, but what he thought inside was: "Old fool! Why there is a large patch in the hollow of his left breast as bare as a snail out of its shell!"'[50] By pandering to the dragon's ego, the hobbit's sycophantic words cause the dragon to reveal his weakness. Crucially, Bilbo Baggins succeeds in doing this because he has first piqued the dragon's interest through his witty repartee. Gandalf has taught the hobbit well; Bilbo recognises that the most effective means of harnessing the outcome he wants is to prove an entertaining interlocutor, hence his recourse to riddles – the form which served him so well with (against) Gollum. By this late point in the novel, though, the hobbit has gained the confidence to compose his own riddles and not merely to rely on other people's. The hobbit's creative flair elicits the grudging admiration of his antagonist, seemingly reversing the power dynamics between them. Thus the tiny hobbit, the burglar, whose only credible tools are his words, steals the dragon's thunder – setting in motion a trajectory of events that will result in the fearful creature's eventual demise and the accomplishment of the task that the adventurers had set out to complete.

If *The Hobbit* dramatises the appeal of Tookishness over Bagginsishness, then it also testifies to the appeal of active language over static language. While the performativity of Tolkien's direct speech nostalgically transports the adult reader back to an imagined collective past in which words do not merely refer to things, they actually *do* things, it also tantalises the newly literate child with the power that is theirs to be had through an imperious command of language.

Notes

1. J. R. R. Tolkien, *Letters of J. R. R. Tolkien*, ed. Humphrey Carpenter with Christopher Tolkien (London: George Allen & Unwin, 1981): 219.
2. Quoted in Wayne G. Hammond and Christina Scull, *The Art of the Hobbit by J. R. R. Tolkien* (London: HarperCollins, 2011): 7.
3. Tolkien, *Letters*: 298.
4. Ibid.: 297.
5. Ibid.: 310.
6. Ibid.: 219.
7. Prominent studies of Tolkien's language include: Verlyn Flieger, *Splintered Light: Logos and Language in Tolkien's World* (Grand Rapids, MI: Eerdmans, 1983); Tom Shippey, *The Road to Middle-Earth* (London: Allen & Unwin, 1982); William Provost, 'Language and Myth in the Fantasy Writings of J. R. R. Tolkien', *Modern Age: A Quarterly Review*, 33(1) (1990): 42–52; Alan McComas, 'Negating and Affirming Spirit through Language: The Integration of Character, Magic, and Story in *The Lord of the Rings*', *Mythlore: A Journal of J. R. R. Tolkien, C. S. Lewis, Charles Williams, and the Genres of Myth and Fantasy Studies*, 19(2) [72]: 4–14; 19(3) [73]: 40–9; Mary Zimmer, 'Creating and Re-Creating Worlds with Words: The Religion and the Magic of Language in *The Lord of the Rings*', *Seven: An Anglo-American Literary Review*, 12 (1995): 65–78; C. W. Sullivan III,

III, 'J. R. R. Tolkien's *The Hobbit*: The Magic of Words', in *Touchstones: Reflections on the Best in Children's Literature*, ed. Perry Nodelman and Jill May (West Lafayette, IN: Children's Literature Association, 1985), 1: 253–61; Michael Livingstone, 'The Myths of the Author: Tolkien and the Medieval Origins of the word *hobbit*,' *Mythlore: A Journal of J. R. R. Tolkien, C. S. Lewis, Charles Williams, and the Genres of Myth and Fantasy Studies*, 30 [117/118]: 129–46.

8. Douglas A. Anderson, *The Annotated Hobbit*, rev. edn (London: HarperCollins, 2003): 4.

9. Elizabeth D. Kirk, '"I Would Rather Have Written in Elvish": Language, Fiction and *The Lord of the Rings*'. *NOVEL: A Forum on Fiction*, 5(1) (1971): 5–18; Margaret Hiley, 'Stolen Language, Cosmic Models: Myth and Mythology in Tolkien', *Modern Fiction Studies*, 50(4) (2004): 838–60.

10. I have in mind here the distinctions laid out by Ferdinand de Saussure in *Course in General Linguistics*, ed. Charles Bally and Albert Sechehaye, trans. Roy Harris (La Salle, IL: Open Court, 1983).

11. Gerard Genette, *Narrative Discourse: An Essay in Method*, trans. Jane E. Lewin (Ithaca, NY: Cornell University Press, 1980): 165, 170.

12. Perry Nodelman, *The Hidden Adult: Defining Children's Literature* (Baltimore, MD: Johns Hopkins University Press, 2008): 214. Nodelman echoes a view which is commonly accepted among critics of children's literature.

13. Maria Nikolajeva, *Aesthetic Approaches to Children's Literature: An Introduction* (Lanham, MD: Scarecrow Press, 2005): 161–3.

14. John Stephens, 'Analysing Texts: Linguistics and Stylistics', in Peter Hunt (ed.), *Understanding Children's Literature* (London: Routledge, 1999): 73–85, at 82.

15. Nikolajeva: 161, 162.

16. Bronislaw Malinowski, 'The Problem of Meaning in Primitive Languages', in *The Meaning of Meaning: A Study of the Influence of Language upon Thought and of the Science of Symbolism* (London: Kegan Paul, Trench, Trübner, 1923): 481.

17. Ibid.: 486.

18. Ibid.: 490.

19. Ibid.

20. Tolkien, *Letters*: 298.

21. J. R. R. Tolkien, *The Hobbit* (1937; London: HarperCollins, 1996): 4.

22. Ibid.: 5–6.

23. Stephen Miller, *Conversation: A History of a Declining Art* (New Haven, CT and London: Yale University Press, 2006): 14.

24. Malinowski: 479.

25. Elizabeth Traugott and Mary Pratt, *Linguistics for Students of Literature* (New York: Harcourt Brace Jovanovich, 1980).

26. Klaus P. Schneider, *Small Talk: Analysing Phatic Discourse* (Marburg: Hitzeroth, 1988).

27. John Pentland Mahaffy, *The Principles of the Art of Conversation* (New York: J. P. Putnam's Sons, 1888).

28. Milton Wright, *The Art of Conversation, and How to Apply Its Technique* (London: Whittlesey House, 1936): 15, 31.
29. Daniel Menaker, *A Good Talk: The Story and Skill of Conversation* (New York: Hachette, 2010): 18.
30. Tolkien, *The Hobbit*: 89.
31. Ibid.: 242.
32. Ibid.: 127.
33. Ibid.: 34–8.
34. Schneider: 49.
35. John L. Austin, *How to Do Things with Words* (Oxford: Clarendon Press, 1962).
36. Tolkien, *The Hobbit*: 21.
37. Robin Lakoff, 'The Logic of Politeness; Or, Minding Your p's and q's', in *Papers from the Ninth Regional Meeting of the Chicago Linguistic Society* (Chicago, IL: University of Chicago Press, 1973): 292–305.
38. Schneider: 34.
39. Ibid.: 48.
40. Ibid.: 73.
41. Ibid.: 76-77.
42. Wright: 187.
43. Tolkien, *The Hobbit*: 112.
44. Ibid.: 114.
45. Malinowski: 478.
46. Tolkien, *The Hobbit*: 145.
47. Ibid.: 149.
48. Malinowski: 487.
49. Tolkien, *The Hobbit*: 200.
50. Ibid.: 203–4.

6

There and Back Again: The Gendered Journey of Tolkien's Hobbits

Zoë Jaques

Authority is male. It's a fact. My fantasy dutifully reported the fact. But is that all a fantasy does – report facts? (Ursula K. Le Guin)[1]

ARE YOU A GUY OR A GIRL?
I've heard the question all my life. The answer is not so simple, since there are no pronouns in the English language as complex as I am, and I do not want to simplify myself in order to neatly fit one or the other ... We have a history filled with militant hero/ines. Yet therein lies the rub! How can I tell you about their battles when the words woman and man, feminine and masculine, are almost the only words that exist in the English language to describe all the vicissitudes of bodies and styles of expression. (Leslie Feinberg)[2]

The Hobbit and *The Lord of the Rings* have always sat a little awkwardly as part of the canon of children's fiction. While *The Hobbit* was probably composed, at least initially, with a child audience in mind, its position on what Randall Helms calls 'the threshold of one of the most immense and satisfying creations of our time, *The Lord of the Rings*',[3] has often led to the former being relegated to the position of a children's story that informs the more noteworthy and adult latter tales. Conversely, critics such as Colin Manlove see *The Lord of the Rings* as itself merely a rewrite of *The Hobbit*, suggesting that the series is purely an 'overblown version' which is more 'simple and one-sided'[4] than its counterpart. J. R. R. Tolkien's own comments on the books have added to the confusion of categorisation, as while he stated that his trilogy 'was not specially addressed to children or to any other class of people' but was instead directed 'to any one who enjoyed a long exciting story',[5] the complexity of the books and the narrative length Tolkien here alludes to demands, not necessarily an older, but certainly a more mature reader than *The Hobbit*. Children's literary critics have therefore been somewhat divided as to which of Tolkien's texts should be in the canon, with one, all, or none variously included.

Yet Tolkien's fiction and children's literature are similar in that both have been heavily criticised for depicting outdated or stereotypical models of gendered behaviour. Children's literature is satiated with prostrate, encumbered or servile damsels supposedly in need of some form of rescue; as Maria Tatar has observed, when folktales were transformed into texts for children, nineteenth-century adapters were 'astute enough to know that ... to turn a heroine into a tragic martyr often required little more than putting a broom in her hand'.[6] The children's fantasy genre too, which relies so heavily upon the hero tale, has frequently marginalised women, with Philip Pullman famously declaring the Narnia series 'ugly and poisonous',[7] an opinion based in part upon Lewis's exclusion of Susan from salvation in *The Last Battle* because of her interest in 'nylons and lipstick and invitations'.[8] Even more recent children's fantasy, such as Rowling's hugely successful 'Harry Potter' series, has been criticised as 'formulaic and sexist'.[9] Similarly, the scarcity of female characters in Tolkien's fiction has led to some critical derision of his work for being 'overtly patriarchal'[10] and 'pushing the women to the margins of stories'.[11] While some critics have concluded that such a depiction is merely in keeping with the period and milieu of composition, resulting in a Middle-earth that is very 'Inkling-like, in that while women exist in the world, they need not be given significant attention',[12] others have argued that such appeals to context fail 'to adequately explain Tolkien's sexism'.[13] Thus, while Tolkien's place in the canon of children's fiction is ill-defined, his work does align with one of the more problematic and itself contested facets of the form.

There are, of course, many works of children's fiction that offer more complicated interpretations of gender than this brief summary might imply, and in recent years critics have been vocal in recovering lost female literary traditions and exploring more modern texts for children which challenge limiting gender ideologies.[14] Tolkien's fiction too, while on the surface offering a fairly constrained gender spectrum, can be read in a more nuanced manner, as Jane Chance has demonstrated in her discussion of the ways in which Tolkien critiques and vilifies 'the isolation of those who are different, whether by race, nationality, culture, class, age, or gender'.[15] This essay will suggest that there is, in fact, a marriage to be found between Tolkien's contribution

to children's fantasy fiction and his stance on the gendered development of his protagonists. The longstanding critical focus on the relative
absence of female characters in his books overlooks the fact that one
does not require characters identified as female to find gender. Gender
is a mode of behaviour, separate from sex, in which cultural norms
associated with sex are enacted, resisted, and reshaped. As such there
can be no text(s) without gender, or with *less* gender. Yet Tolkien goes
beyond the mere representation of gender to offer an interventionist
narrative about what it means for a child to engage with a gendered
world. The central characters of the books – the hobbits – operate as
ciphers for children, and by implication, child readers. It is a lesson
disclosed in *The Two Towers*, when Aragon asks whether Éomer has
found the bodies of Merry and Pippin amongst the slain Orcs:

> 'Did you search the slain? Were there no bodies other than those of orc-
> kind? They would be small, only children in your eyes, unshod but clad
> in grey.'
> 'There were no dwarves nor children,' said Éomer. ...
> 'We do not speak of dwarves or children,' said Gimli. 'Our friends
> were hobbits.'
> 'Hobbits?' said Éomer. 'And what may they be? It is a strange name.'
> 'A strange name for a strange folk,' said Gimli. 'But these were very dear
> to us. It seems that you have heard in Rohan of the words that troubled
> Minas Tirith. They spoke of the Halfling. These hobbits are Halflings.'
> 'Halflings!' laughed the Rider that stood beside Éomer. 'Halflings!
> But they are only a little people in old songs and children's tales of the
> North. Do we walk in legends or on the green earth in daylight?'[16]

While hobbits are a species – one amongst the wealth of different beings
that populate Tolkien's fantasy space – they also can easily be viewed as
children, not only in the eyes of the Riders of Rohan but in those of the
human reader. These 'Halflings', or 'little people', begin their adventures
in an embryonic state that is loosely 'gendered', or at least in as close to
such a state as might be said to exist, yet their journeys through Middle-
earth offer opportunities for gendered development, identity negotiation
and growth that the child might ideally be exposed to (metaphorically at
least). But they are also creatures of fantasy – not only as part of Tolkien's
landscape but as alluded to here in the reference to the old songs and
children's tales – and their dual role as both fantastical beings and metaphors for children offers a unique opportunity for a model of gendered
development which eschews binaries and embraces fluidity.

Judith Butler famously aligns gender with a kind of performativity, suggesting that 'there is no gender that is "expressed" by actions,

gestures, speech, but that the performance of gender was precisely that which produced retroactively the illusion that there was an inner gender core'.[17] The 'performance' Butler identifies is socially compelled through 'a ritualized repetition of conventions';[18] in other words, gender performs a pre-written script, you don't extemporise. Yet Tolkien's fantasy world necessitates exposure to moments where gender questions have to be decided upon in ways that lead to no obvious scripts. Here crises of the body or crises of the nation lead to moments of gender *frisson*, where 'doing gender' is created in response to situations for which there is no pre-defined performance, or at least no entirely satisfactory one. It is here, perhaps, that we might find an answer to the questions posed in the two epigrams that open this essay. Fantasy has the opportunity to do more than 'report facts', offering instead the subversive possibilities of a world divorced from ritualised binaries of gendered behaviour that are both socially constructed and constricted. The constraints identified by Butler in terms of the fixities of gender ideologies that lead to pre-scripted performance need not exist in fantasy, even fantasy that relies on northern European mythlore as its source and which is distinctly conservative in its aims. The spectrum of beings which populate Tolkien's narratives enact a range of gendered behaviours between hyper-masculinity and suffocating maternity, and while the books explore the excitement of such alternative genders, they also foreground dangers inherent both in gender extremes and in a lack of exposure to a range of models of gendered expression. Tolkien places his most important characters – the developing hobbits, and by association, developing children – on a journey whereby they encounter and learn from a range of gendered types, demonstrating that there is no ideal 'inner gender core' to be aspired to but rather a synergy of roles which lead to a fully developed self. The evolved 'hobbit', then, having encountered and learned from a world peppered with all kinds of 'vicissitudes of bodies and styles of expression', might well become a substitute term for the more debilitated and limited words 'woman and man, feminine and masculine'. As such, Tolkien's child reader is able to see representations of the optionality of gender – a freedom which is a product of fantasy, and, potentially, an unintended one.

Defining the species: gendering the nascent Hobbit

Perhaps unsurprisingly it is in the first of Tolkien's volumes – the one more universally considered suitable for a child audience[19] – that we encounter the most embryonic of hobbit forms. Although he is not characterised as a young hobbit himself – being portly, in his fifties and initially found 'standing at his door after breakfast smoking a long wooden pipe[20] – the behavioral traits we encounter in homely Bilbo bespeak a developmentally immature being, if not a physically young one. We are immediately informed of the primacy of his living quarters, which as several critics have commented is 'a dwelling interestingly womb-like'[21] in its warmth, comfort and protection. Bilbo need not venture far beyond the security of this nurturing space, for from it he is able to fulfil his central desires in the form of sustenance and, importantly, relative isolation from the outside world. Although it is explained several times in the opening chapter that hobbits enjoy the company of others, as suggested by the 'lots and lots of pegs for hats and coats'[22] that presuppose the arrival of many welcome visitors, in practice Bilbo is not especially keen on companionship. His initially friendly exchanges with Gandalf quickly dissolve as Bilbo realises that the wizard 'was not quite his sort'[23] and he soon wishes that the troublesome fellow might leave him in peace. The arrival of the numerous dwarves puts further strain upon the reclusive hobbit's hospitality, as he worries that the 'cakes might run short, and then he … might have to go without', becomes increasingly 'hot, and red in the face, and annoyed' over the course of the evening, and finally heads to bed resolved that he 'was not to bother to get up early and cook everybody else's wretched breakfast'.[24] The comforts of a hobbit hole are principally designed for single occupation, and by the end of the first chapter Bilbo's resentment of the peculiarities of 'others' and their potential dependence upon him is paramount.

This representation of Bilbo's homely character marks him out as an unlikely adventurer; he does not have the obvious traits of a hero. Bilbo embodies and yearns for the comforts of the traditionally maternal domestic space of home and hearth – a desire he has to navigate throughout this later adventure, and in which he is not entirely successful. But his position within the comfortingly maternal also hints at more complex potential for this isolated being. In only the fourth paragraph of the book, Tolkien introduces the adventurous nature of Bilbo's mother, Belladonna Took, which, as William Green has pointed out, is a curious inclusion given that the book includes 'no living female characters, human or animal'.[25] Although Tolkien is quick to assert that Belladonna did not have 'any adventures after she became Mrs Bungo Baggins' and moved into what was later to become Bilbo's 'luxurious hobbit hole',[26] the term 'Tookish' is quickly encoded with a sense of adventurous spirit aroused in Bilbo by the arrival of Gandalf and the company of dwarves. Thus the passing of the evening sees Bilbo wrestling with a Tookish desire to 'explore the caves, and wear a sword instead of a walking-stick'[27] and then shrieking in fear and requiring a period of repose 'out of the way on the drawing-room sofa'.[28] Here Tolkien's initial allusion to traits often aligned with stereotypical and outdated models of masculinity or femininity – such as medieval sword wielding or Victorian fits of hysteria – are aligned with an oppositional gender spectrum, so that a clear-cut negotiation of what it means to be male or female is not easily defined. Bilbo might be said at this nascent stage to be in a state of ungendered non-being. Just as a child in the womb might be sexed but not gendered, Bilbo is biologically male but his gender identity has not yet been refined. Yet this state does not offer Bilbo any fluidity of gender expression, for Tolkien's opening chapter firmly establishes him as static, isolated and fairly selfish – a character who, as a result of living in a personal cocoon, is not yet individuated and hasn't formed a composite identity through negotiating his behaviour in relation to that of others. The journey, or maturation process of moving from childhood to adulthood, is an opportunity to be exposed to a range of gendered behaviours that the old-but-young Bilbo has not been offered in the comforts of the Shire, despite his distant background of adventurous maternity and domesticated paternal influence.

The opening of *The Lord of the Rings* is narratologically similar to *The Hobbit*, but Tolkien also expounds upon the nature and identity of hobbits here through metatextual apparatus. In his introduction to Bilbo he quickly dispenses with details of the species, noting that the reader knows 'enough to go on with',[29] while *The Fellowship of the Ring* is prefaced with a note 'Concerning Hobbits' which gives broader details on the species and briefly recalls Bilbo's earlier adventure. The description here again evokes a sense of the child; hobbits are described as 'a little people' who 'dressed in bright colours' and prefer to go about bare-foot than shod. Their faces are 'broad, bright-eyed, red-cheeked, with mouths apt to laughter, and to eating and drinking' and their fondness for 'simple jests at all times', 'six meals a day' and delight 'in parties, and in presents'[30] further reinforces their immaturity. Yet while our introduction to the hobbit hero of this later tale is placed in a similar context, drawing attention to the pleasant but child-like nature of these 'charming, absurd, helpless'[31] beings, as the normally tranquil Shire is this time upset by a 'long-expected' as opposed to 'unexpected' party, Frodo's inauguration is set against a more turbulent history than was the case for Bilbo. Firstly, the previous adventures of Frodo's 'uncle' create unease and excitement in the hobbit populace, and while his birthday party is largely celebrated by its many visitors, there is a sense that some strangeness surrounds Bilbo thanks to his encounters with 'outlandish folk'[32] like dwarves and conjurers. This peculiarity becomes transposed onto Frodo as he too begins 'to carry on Bilbo's reputation for oddity'[33] and is seen 'far from home walking in the hills and woods under the starlight'.[34] But secondly, and perhaps more importantly, this opening also hints at a troubled exterior to the comfortable space of the Shire, predicting a journey born not of the awakening of a dormant desire to adventure, as in Bilbo's more individuated case, but a necessitated call to fellowship for the good of a nation. Tolkien here hints that the pleasant peace and isolation of the hobbits in the Shire, by which they 'heeded less and less the world outside where dark things moved',[35] is not necessarily a natural order nor assumed as a fixed state. Despite his maturation journey in *The Hobbit*, Bilbo remains an isolated being, as Tolkien notes that the 'many reports and complaints of strange persons and creatures prowling about the borders, or over them: the first sign that all was not what it should be' go unheeded by Bilbo himself, who 'yet had any notion of what it portended'.[36] Thus while his journey in *The Hobbit* offers the possibility for adventure and partial development of the self, the journey of Frodo and his hobbit companions relies upon exposure to a wider variety of such 'dark things' and 'strange persons', which variously enact a broader range of gendered behaviours that they must combat, reenact, or learn from as part of the development, not just of themselves but of themselves as part of a wider community.

Encountering the other: hobbits and hyper-gender

Both *The Hobbit* and *The Lord of the Rings* are thus structured as developmental journeys for their central, child-like characters, but the exposure to a variety of different gender models is far more limited in the former than the latter. Bilbo's encounters with crudely masculine trolls, goblins, and even a dragon, are essentially a series of momentary and cyclical trials with folkloric or mythological staples, each of which is only partially developed, and dispatched with relative ease, offering Bilbo limited exposure to models of gendered expression. Here the most successful method of defeating what might appear to be an invincible foe is primarily through acts of silence or invisibility – variously playing with the notion of the ideal child being 'seen and not heard' but also delighting in the childish devilment of oral word-play from a relatively safe distance. Bilbo's appointment to the company of dwarves is based upon Gandalf's inability to find a 'mighty Warrior, even a Hero'[37] to attack the dragon's hoard, settling instead on the more subtle science of burglary. Like the Artful Dodger of *Oliver Twist*, Bilbo has a certain knack for the craft, being light-footed and less inclined to producing the 'dwarfish racket'[38] of his companions. Successful thievery thus becomes Bilbo's primary role as the narrative develops, and he graduates from a failed attempt at pick-pocketing a troll early in the story, through to successfully reliev-ing a drunken elf guard of his keys and finally to snatching away a cup from Smaug's precious hoard. To be successful in his ventures, Bilbo need only maintain the same principles that provided him with security in his hobbit hole; he must remain unseen, keep a safe distance, and rely on wit rather than physicality to keep him safe. Conversely, the hobbits who venture on the journey to destroy the ring encounter many of the same types of beings, but in their more extreme and hyper-gendered versions, and they have to learn to model their behaviour differently. For Frodo and his companions, acts of avoidance, silence or oral trickery are rarely enough to ensure the continuation of the quest.

One of the more important encounters mirrored in both narra-tives is the hobbits' battles with spiders. In *The Hobbit* the event largely replicates the earlier encounter with trolls, but offers Bilbo the opportunity to save his friends without the assistance of Gandalf. Yet while Bilbo here achieves some development as an adventurer, not only through saving his friends but through acts of spider killing which make him feel 'much fiercer and bolder in spite of an empty stomach',[39] the creatures themselves remain largely underdeveloped and merely representative of a 'loathsome' mass. William Green has observed that Bilbo's success here and elsewhere is in avoiding the 'motif of *bagging*' which dominates the narrative: 'Bilbo – born Mr. Baggins of Bag End – achieves heroism because he repeatedly avoids being "bagged" by his foes.'[40] For Green, being bagged is akin to 'absorption into the passive female principle',[41] yet, like the other beasts the company encounter, the spiders are sexed male and there is little to suggest that they differ from the trolls or goblins in represent-ing nascent evil as opposed to specifically gendered beings. Tolkien himself, commenting on spiders in general, stated that they were 'the particular terror of northern imaginations', but also differentiated between the male and female: '[t]he female monster is certainly no deadlier than the male, but she is different. She is a sucking, strangling, trapping creature.'[42] It is the latter being which Frodo and Sam have to battle at the close of *The Two Towers*.

While shaped as a mammoth arachnid, Shelob is more 'an evil thing in spider form',[43] unnatural in both size and body:

> Great horns she had, and behind her short stalk-like neck was her huge swollen body, a vast bloating bag, swaying and sagging between her legs; its great bulk was black, blotched with livid marks, but the belly underneath was pale and luminous and gave forth a stench. Her legs were bent, with great knobbed joints high above her back, and hairs that stuck out like steel spines, and at each leg's end there was a claw.[44]

Although clearly a manifestation of evil, much like the spiders of *The Hobbit*, the singularity of this being and the narrative's repetitive instance upon her identity as female marks Shelob as an important example of a specifically gendered creature; as Margery Hourihan has contended, the creature might well be 'the most striking instance of a devouring female in twentieth-century young adult or children's fiction'.[45] Shelob is the embodiment of monstrous maternity; isolated and evil, her vast smothering form lies swollen in the mountains in a space that cruelly inverts the comforts of the hobbit hole, and in order to progress, Frodo and Sam must escape her vile and murderous appetite by successfully navigating her lair. Addressing maternal origins in Shakespearean drama, Janet Adelman has commented on the dangers of returning to the maternal body, suggesting that the male protagonist must 'break away from the suffocating matrix, each in his own way recovering his manhood by taking a terrible vengeance on the woman in whom it is represented'.[46] Such a reading might well be applied to Sam's attack on Shelob, and certainly critics have read this moment as a masculine rite of passage in which the smaller, weaker male penetrates and escapes the vast female body, thus surviving her malicious intent. Perhaps the most extreme critical reading in this regard is that offered by Brenda Partridge, who sees the moment as ripe with sexual symbolism:

> The description of Sam's battle with Shelob is not only a life and death struggle of man and monster, good against evil, but also represents a violent struggle between man and woman. Shelob's 'soft squelching body' is a metaphor for the female genitals swollen and moist in sexual arousal. … Her impenetrable skin hangs in folds like the layers of the labia … The male organ puny compared with the vast, evil smelling mass of the female is described in euphemistic sexual terms as 'his little impudence'.[47]

Partridge suggests that for Tolkien 'the female linked with sexuality is seen as evil',[48] and certainly with so few female characters in Tolkien's fantasy landscape it is easy to see why such an extreme portrayal of femininity has led to some critical disdain. The fact that Sam's eventual triumph over Shelob is through his wielding of a feminine artefact – the phial gifted to him by the powerful but incorruptible Galadriel – does little to appease a sense of polarisation of women so that 'female virginity and sexuality are opposed, and equated, respectively, with good and evil'.[49] By this reading, Tolkien's monstrous female seems little more developed than a fairy-tale wicked queen, while Galadriel's token is a talisman of the glorified damsel.

Yet this hyper-gendering of Shelob, and the oppositional portrayal of more idealised females such as Galadriel, or the elf-maiden Arwen, have their counters in the representation of extremes of masculinity in Tolkien's fiction too. Shelob herself, while isolated in her mountain lair, is carefully aligned with Sauron, both of whom delight 'in their own devices' and fear 'no assault, nor wrath, nor any end of their wickedness'.[50] As Melanie Rawls has suggested, Shelob can be interpreted as 'what happens when the feminine concern with the individual and with the inner life is taken too far',[51] yet such an extreme can also be located in Sauron, in keeping with her suggestion that for Tolkien both feminine and masculine 'principles' are 'equal yet other'.[52] In this way, Shelob might be read as 'Sauron's visible half – the horrifying, slime-drenched, fleshy feminine counterpart to his spectral masculine'.[53] Successful hobbit- or child-development, then, is not merely achieved by avoiding the monstrous female but rather through learning to negotiate extremes of either gender which polarise and delimit identity formation. In *The Hobbit*, Bilbo's exposure to the more extreme versions of masculinity is limited. Gandalf, for example, is here a more kindly wizard than the Balrog-battler of the later trilogy, although William H. Green has gone so far as to suggest that the characterisation of Gandalf is one of the 'submerged feminine' motifs of the book, arguing that he 'seems to function as Bilbo's fairy godmother, wand and all, and his actual physical form, though nominally masculine, is no less maternal than other fairy-tale proxies for the dead mother'.[54] Furthermore, whilst the dwarves of *The Hobbit* might be gruff and gold-hungry, they are nonetheless rather more bumbling than their subsequent axe-wielding representative Gimli, and the heroics shown by Bard and his followers against the invasion of Smaug take place entirely outside of Bilbo's sight, removing him from the masculine aggression of the battlefield not once but twice (for Bilbo is also excluded from the Battle of Five Armies, having been hit on the head by a stone). Yet the far-reaching consequences of Sauron's quest for dominion in *The Lord of the Rings* encodes these books with a more direct and immediate display of hyper-masculinity, which Frodo cannot avoid but must engage with.

While on the one hand Tolkien here validates instances of violence and displays of masculine aggression in the context of war, this is also tempered and endorsed only in so far as that violence works to protect and subvert more extreme expressions of expansionist politics. Homi K. Bhabha strongly aligns masculine identity with national identity and patriotism, whereby the enactment of gender identity is done on behalf of the father/nation. He notes, in this tendency, a connection between masculinity and extremes of expansionist national identity: "'phallic respect" leads periodically to the resurgence of the fascination with fascism'.[55] The dangerous ideological journeys of the various beings depicted in Tolkien's trilogy expose just this potential danger in gender construction. Doubtless, individuated masculinity is celebrated in acts of violence that protect localised geographical areas, but it is in the coming together of nations, rather like Britain and then America joining the Second World War, that true acts of masculine identity are celebrated. While validating the masculinity of direct violence, the dangers inherent in relying upon self-sufficiency are also exposed. The success of the fellowship, then, is necessitated by the union of different kinds of masculinities – be they that of the Wizards, Elves, Men, Dwarves, or Hobbits – who come together to protect Middle-earth through compassion and companionship. But such idealism is also linked with a form of masculinity that embodies the fantastical possibilities of fairy-tale, as exposed by the lament of the old wife and servant Ioreth, as she weeps over Faramir's wounded body:

> 'Alas! if he should die. Would that there were kings in Gondor, as there were once upon a time, they say! For it is said in old lore: *The hands of a king are the hands of a healer.* And so the rightful king could ever be known.'[56]

Ioreth here makes a direct appeal to the tradition of 'once upon a time', and in keeping with such narrative expectations Faramir goes on to later marry Éowyn, who herself embodies the very principles of kingly behaviour Ioreth identifies: 'I will be a shieldmaiden no longer, nor vie with the great Riders, nor take joy only in the songs of slaying. I will be a healer, and love all things that grow and are not barren.'[57] While some critics have read Éowyn's renouncement of her role as a capable warrior as a disappointing return to traditional female roles,[58] it might also be said to emphasise the importance of both sexes focusing on remedial over-destructive behaviours as part of a quest to return a nation to a state of peace. The importance of healing, of love and of growth is integral to the numerous unions that Tolkien makes central to his longer narrative – be they created through marriage or through the bonds of fellowship – standing in contrast to the more individuated journey which Bilbo experiences in his own quest for maturation.

(D)evolving the gendered self: from isolation to domestication

Tolkien thus positions his hobbits' encounters with a variety of gendered beings alongside the importance of creating bonds between peoples – the multiple marriages towards the close of *The Lord of the Rings* might be said to emphasise Tolkien's interest in evolving his characters from isolated individuals into domesticated communities. Critics have been vocal, and polarised, in their readings of the sexual politics of Tolkien's unions, with some viewing the camaraderie of the male protagonists as indicative of 'submerged homoeroticism' in the text, and others focusing on the heterosexual marriages as a reinforcement of Tolkien's more conservative values.[59] Yet regardless of which position on sexuality he might be said to be taking, Tolkien is validating fellowship and underscoring the importance of avoiding isolation, and it is perhaps this lesson that most potently connects with the child's maturation journey.

Nowhere is this link more apparent than his depiction of Gollum/Sméagol – a being that Tolkien encodes with his moral stance on the derogating effects of operating alone, so that he comes to represent the shadowy and hollow possibilities of isolated masculinity. As a fable of Darwinian devolution, which Gollum's animal-like and adaptive behaviour clearly emulates, his degeneration might well be seen as one of a number of warnings in children's literature about the debilitating effects of selfish and immoral behaviour, such as the lessons taught to Tom about becoming an eft in Kingsley's *The Water-babies* or those encoded in Collodi's tale of Pinocchio's transformation into a donkey. Yet unlike those of Tom or Pinocchio, Gollum's journey does not conclude in redemption, but is rather a slow decline into increased alienation and degeneration, marked by various displays of violence and cruelty. Although starting life as an 'inquisitive and curious-minded hobbit',[60] after killing his friend Déagol in a desire to posses the ring, Sméagol is expelled by his grandmother from the matriarchal influence of her hobbit hole and is driven into the roots of the mountains. Here he inhabits a space that mocks the comforts enjoyed by hobbits in its darkness, coldness and scarcity of food, his only companionship coming in the form of the other half of his divided self. Gollum thus embodies an isolated masculinity of violence, self-sufficiency and degradation not unlike the consumptive femininity of Shelob, and it is perhaps unsurprising that his only real communal action is to become her servant. Gollum's othering, and yet ultimate connection to the central beings a child reader might identify with, serves as a crucial warning against seclusion.

Isolation is thus Tolkien's key to developmental failure. Gollum's life is frequently spared in both narratives thanks to the hints of kinship which Bilbo, Frodo and Sam variously see in the 'forlorn, ruinous, utterly wretched'[61] former hobbit, but he remains an isolated and irredeemable figure until his last act of uncalculating violence to Frodo on the edge of Mount Doom, where, in a perverse inversion of the marriage ceremonies which occur elsewhere in the narrative, Gollum bites off Frodo's ringed finger and then topples into the abyss. Yet it is not only in Gollum that Tolkien offers a warning against degenerative forms of masculine independence, and even non-violent practices are shown to limit the development of both the individual and a race. The ents, for example, endorse an isolating mechanism of gendered behaviour whereby the 'Entwives made gardens to live in' but the 'Ents went on wandering, and ... only came to the gardens now and again.'[62] This rather stereotypical model of separate spheres is flawed in Middle-earth, for its eventual outcome is the potential extinction of the species, a fear potently embodied in Treebeard's explanation of the Ents' most pressing concern: 'There have never been many of us and we have not increased. There have been no Entings – no children, you would say, not for a terrible long count of years. You see, we lost the Entwives.'[63] Community, which in this case requires both male and female union, becomes essential to Tolkien's vision.

The desire or act of being alone – as shown through the conditioning of the Ents, Gollum, Sauron or Shelob – is a degenerative and unnatural condition in Tolkien's world. These individuated, and in some cases hyper-gendered beings seem distinct from the central hobbits of the tale, yet Bilbo and Frodo also disclose an inclination towards isolation and Tolkien offers these child-like beings an opportunity to undergo a journey of maturation and gender development based around communal living. Yet the dual narratives do not offer equal levels of exposure to contrasting gender models, despite the fact that they take place on a similar landscape, and the extent to which either tale models a successful gendered rite of passage for a child reader might be contested. Tolkien's first volume can be read as an incomplete gendered quest, and although Bilbo's trials in this book offer some development, the story ends with him having experienced a relatively one-sided model of gender identity. Frodo, conversely, encounters a far broader range of gendered behaviours in his quest to destroy the ring and he might be said to come to embody traits of each member of the fellowship, developing the valour of men, the endurance of dwarves, the wisdom of wizards and the quiet stoicism of elves. Yet despite his experiences, Frodo's return to the domestic is even more awkward than Bilbo's. Tolkien suggests that there are dangers implicit in the developmental journey and the same wistful longing to leave the comforts of domesticity that haunts the opening of the tale for Bilbo also mars Frodo's return to the Shire. The journey, for Frodo at least, has scarred him too deeply, and it is only Sam who truly evolves in the domestic realm, made 'solid and whole'[64] through developing his community and marriage to Rosie.

Although clearly offering conservative endings, the various gendered journeys of the central protagonists may have differing effects on the child reader. In one, the supposedly more child-friendly *The Hobbit*, gender is fairly monolithic and masculine in shape. In the supposedly more adult-friendly *The Lord of the Rings*, gender finds a fuller range of expression. Such gendering and generic categorisation might say something about adult readers' expectations about what is 'child-appropriate'. But it leads to a false sense that these are books for boys at best, or books for adult men at worst. In fact a teleological focus on what *happens* to the male characters ignores what they *experience*, and what the child reader experiences alongside them. Many critics see in Tolkien a stance that is either actively misogynist or passively ignorant of gender issues, yet it is a distinct interest in gender that drives and shapes character development, particularly of those characters who are coded as children as much as they are hobbits. This process aligns hobbits with childhood development, whereby fantasy permits a fluidity of gender that allows a perhaps unintended, but nonetheless potent, fantasy of informed gendered development. Tolkien's tales thus offer an impressive, one might say fantastical, range of gendered behaviours that all disclose the complexities of forming a gender identity when also trying to 'grow up'.

Notes

1. Ursula K. Le Guin, *Earthsea Revisioned* (Cambridge, MA: Children's Literature New England, 1993): 11.

2. Leslie Feinberg, *Transgender Warriors: Making History from Joan of Arc to Denis Rodman* (Boston, MA: Beacon Press, 1996): ix.

3. Randall Helms, *Tolkien's World* (Boston, MA: Houghton Mifflin, 1974): 80.

4. Colin Manlove, *From Alice to Harry Potter: Children's Fantasy in England* (Christchurch: Cybereditions, 2003): 69.

5. J. R. R. Tolkien, *The Letters of J. R. R. Tolkien*, ed. Humphrey Carpenter with Christopher Tolkien (Cambridge, MA: George Allen & Unwin, 1981): 297.

6. Maria Tatar, *Off with their Heads! Fairy Tales and the Culture of Childhood* (Princeton, NJ: Princeton University Press, 1992): 6–7.

7. Philip Pullman, 'The Dark Side of Narnia', *The Guardian*, 1 October 1998: 6.

8. C. S. Lewis, *The Last Battle* (1956; London: HarperCollins, 1998): 165.

9. Jack Zipes, *Sticks and Stones: The Troublesome Success of Children's Literature from Slovenly Peter to Harry Potter* (London: Routledge, 2001): 171. The topic of gender in the Harry Potter series has been a particularly vexed one: see Ximena Gallardo-C. and C. Jason Smith, 'Cinderfella: J. K. Rowling's Wily Web of Gender', in *Reading Harry Potter: Critical Essays*, ed. Giselle Liza Anatol (Westport, CT: Praeger, 2003): 191–205; Eliza T. Dresang, 'Hermione Granger and the Heritage of Gender', in *The Ivory Tower and Harry Potter: Perspectives on a Literary Phenomenon*, ed. Lana A. Whited (Columbia, MO: University of Missouri Press, 2004): 211–42; Mimi Gladstein, 'Feminism and Equal Opportunity: Hermione and the Women of Hogwarts', in *Harry Potter and Philosophy*, ed. David Baggett and Shawn E. Klein (Chicago, IL: Open Court Publishing, 2004): 49–60; Annette Wannamaker, 'Men in Cloaks and High-heeled Boots, Men Wielding Pink Umbrellas: Witchy Masculinities in the Harry Potter Novels', in *Boys in Children's Literature and Popular Culture: Masculinity, Abjection, and the Fictional Child* (New York: Routledge, 2008): 121–45.

10. Candice Fredrick and Sam McBride, *Women Among the Inklings: Gender, C. S. Lewis, J. R. R. Tolkien, and Charles Williams* (Westport, CT: Greenwood Press, 2001): 109.

11. William H. Green, '"Where's Mama?" The Construction of the Feminine in *The Hobbit*', *The Lion and the Unicorn*, 22(2) (2008): 188–95, at 190.

12. Fredrick and McBride: 108.

13. Melissa McCrory Hatcher, 'Finding Woman's Role in *The Lord of the Rings*', *Mythlore*, 25(97–8) (2007): 43–54, at 43.

14. Lissa Paul uses the helpful phrase 'Reading Otherways' to define this process, *Reading Otherways* (South Woodchester: The Thimble Press, 1998). For more on feminist approaches to children's literature, see, for example: Barbara Lyon Clark and Margaret Higonnet (eds), *Girls, Boys, Books, Toys: Gender in Children's Literature and Culture* (Baltimore, MD: Johns Hopkins University Press, 1999); Kerry Mallan, *Gender Dilemmas in Children's Fiction* (Basingstoke: Palgrave Macmillan, 2009); Claudia Nelson, *Boys will*

be Girls: The Feminist Ethic and British Children's Fiction, 1857–1917 (New Brunswick, NJ: Rutgers University Press, 1991); Kimberley Reynolds, *Girls Only? Gender and Popular Children's Fiction in Britain, 1880–1910* (New York: Harvester Wheatsheaf, 1990); Roberta Seelinger Trites, *Waking Sleeping Beauty: Feminist Voices in Children's Novels* (Iowa City, IA: University of Iowa Press, 1997); Jack Zipes, *Happily Ever After: Fairy Tales, Children and the Culture Industry* (London: Routledge, 1997).

15. Jane Chance, 'Tolkien and the Other', *Tolkien's Modern Middle Ages*, ed. Jane Chance and Alfred Siewers (New York: Palgrave Macmillan, 2005): 172.

16. J. R. R. Tolkien, *The Two Towers* (1954; London: HarperCollins, 1999): 32–3.

17. Judith Butler, 'Melancholy Gender/Refused Identification' in *Constructing Masculinity*, ed. Maurice Berger, Brian Wallis and Simon Watson (New York and London: Routledge, 1995):31.

18. Ibid.: 31.

19. Although the structure, rhetoric and narrative voice of *The Hobbit* implies a young readership, Tolkien himself discounted this specific intention: 'I'm not interested in the "child" as such, modern or otherwise, and certainly have no intention of meeting him / her half way, or a quarter of the way' (*Letters*: 200).

20. J. R. R. Tolkien, *The Hobbit* (1937; London: HarperCollins, 1999): 5.

21. Dorothy Matthews, 'The Psychological Journey of Bilbo Baggins', in *A Tolkien Compass*, 2nd edition, ed. Jared Lobdell (Peru, IL: Open Court Publishing, 2003): 27–40, at 30.

22. Tolkien, *Hobbit*: 3.

23. Ibid.: 6.

24. Ibid.: 9, 11, 26.

25. Green, '"Where's Mama?"': 88.

26. Tolkien, *Hobbit*: 4, 16. Tolkien also includes a wry aside here, commenting that the hobbit hole in question was built 'partly with her [Belladonna's] money' (p. 4).

27. Ibid.: 16.

28. Ibid.: 17.

29. Ibid.: 4. It should be noted that this type of narrative aside is one of the features which have led critics to read *The Hobbit* as more expressly interested in the experience of the child reader. Paul Kocher, for example, has noted that from 'the opening pages hardly a page goes by in which the narrator does not address the child in the first person singular', and suggests that the best route to understanding the book is 'to think of Tolkien, or another adult, in a chair by the fireside telling the story to a semicircle of children sitting on the floor facing him' (Paul Kocher, *Master of Middle Earth: The Achievement of J. R. R. Tolkien* (London: Thames & Hudson, 1972): 19.

30. J. R. R. Tolkien, *The Fellowship of the Ring* (1954; London: HarperCollins, 1994): 2.

31. Ibid.: 64.
32. Ibid.: 31.
33. Ibid.: 55.
34. Ibid.: 56.
35. Ibid.: 7.
36. Ibid.: 14.
37. Ibid.: 21.
38. Tolkien, *Hobbit*: 33.
39. Ibid.: 146.
40. William H. Green, 'The Four-Part Structure of Bilbo's Education', *Children's Literature* 8 (1980): 133–40, at 136.
41. Ibid.
42. Charlotte and Dennis Plimmer, 'The Man who Understands Hobbits', *Daily Telegraph Magazine*, 22 March 1968: 31.
43. Tolkien, *The Two Towers*: 414.
44. Ibid.: 417.
45. Margery Hourihan, *Deconstructing the Hero: Literary Theory and Children's Literature* (London: Routledge, 1997): 190.
46. Janet Adelman, *Suffocating Mothers: Fantasies of Maternal Origin in Shakespeare's plays, Hamlet to the Tempest* (New York: Routledge, 1992): 38.
47. Brenda Partridge, 'No Sex Please – We're Hobbits: The Construction of Female Sexuality in *The Lord of the Rings*', in *J. R. R Tolkien: This Far Land*, ed. Robert Giddings (London: Vision Press, 1983): 179–97, at 190.
48. Ibid.: 191.
49. Hourihan: 191.
50. Tolkien, *The Two Towers*: 416.
51. Melanie Rawls, 'The Feminine Principle in Tolkien', *Mythlore*, 10(4) (1984): 5–13, at 10.
52. Ibid.: 13.
53. Jes Battis, 'Gazing Upon Sauron: Hobbits, Elves, and the Queering of the Postcolonial Optic', *Modern Fiction Studies*, 50(4) (2004): 908–25, at 916.
54. William H. Green, *The Hobbit: A Journey into Maturity* (New York: Twayne Publishers, 1995): 67.
55. Homi K. Bhabha, 'Are you a man or a mouse?' in *Constructing Masculinity*, ed. Maurice Berger, Brian Wallis and Simon Watson (New York and London: Routledge, 1995): 57–67, at 63.
56. J. R. R. Tolkien, *The Return of the King* (1955; London: HarperCollins, 1999): 154.
57. Ibid.: 292.
58. See, for example, J. Neville, 'Women', in *Reading* The Lord of the Rings: *New Writings on Tolkien's Classic*, ed. Robert Eaglestone (London: Continuum, 2005): 101–10.
59. For more on the homosexual and heterosexual aspects of Tolkien's writing, see: Battis (2004); Partridge (1983); Ty Rosenthal, 'Warm Beds are Good: Sex and Libido in Tolkien's Writing', *Mallorn*, 42 (2004): 35–42.

60. Tolkien, *The Fellowship of the Ring*: 69.
61. Tolkien, *The Return of the King*: 263.
62. Tolkien, *The Two Towers*: 87.
63. Ibid.: 86.
64. Tolkien, *The Return of the King*: 372.

7

Tolkien and Worldbuilding

Catherine Butler

What is worldbuilding?

One of Tolkien's distinctive contributions to fantasy writing lies in the example he set as a builder of worlds. Fantasy and science-fiction novelists, game designers, and role-play enthusiasts all acknowledge Tolkien as a master in the art of constructing a universe with its own history and geography, flora and fauna, cultures and languages, magic and physics. Tolkien may be known as the builder of only *one* world – Middle-earth[1] – but it is a world almost six decades in the making, and has a depth and detail to which other writers, whether for adults or children, can only aspire.

The labour of creating Middle-earth, in its various phases, revisions and versions, has become a subject of study in its own right, to which much academic attention has been devoted. It is no part of my present purpose to compete with the work of such scholars as Douglas A. Anderson, John Rateliff, Christina Scull, Wayne G. Hammond, and above all Tolkien's son Christopher, whose editions of his father's unpublished work, starting with *The Silmarillion* in 1977, have done much to enlarge and enhance our understanding of Middle-earth's evolution. Rather, I wish to explore the implications and ramifications of the act of worldbuilding, especially as it was conceived and practised by Tolkien. In particular, this essay will consider the ways in which considerations of audience may have affected the representation of Middle-earth. *The Hobbit* and *The Lord of the Rings* are set in the 'same' world, yet it looks quite different in important respects. How far should these differences be understood as reflecting the 17 years of development between their publication, and how far are they attributable to considerations of genre and of the capacities and interests of their respective audiences?

Worldbuilding and sub-creation

Tolkien's most extensive statement on the art of making worlds comes in his 1939 essay 'On Fairy-Stories', and this seems to the obvious place to begin our investigation. It is here that he introduces the concept of the writer as a 'sub-creator', a position analogous in some ways to that of God as the creator of our own world. For Tolkien, sub-creation arises from the imaginative ability of humans to recombine elements of reality (the 'Primary World') in new ways. When these recombined elements are arranged and expressed through art, they result in a new, Secondary World, which may in turn induce in readers the kind of imaginative absorption Tolkien refers to as Secondary Belief, and it is on the ability to evoke Secondary Belief that the Secondary World's claim to be a successful sub-creation depends.

Given the nature of Tolkien's own fiction, it is important to stress that the creation of a Secondary World in this sense is not in itself to be identified with the making of a world such as Middle-earth. Rather, a Secondary World may be an imaginative space of any kind, as long as that space is sufficiently well rendered to enable Secondary Belief. The world Thackeray conjures in *Vanity Fair*, for example, is as legitimate an example of sub-creation as Middle-earth, despite its more 'realistic' setting. It is only those sub-creations characterised by the qualities of 'strangeness and wonder' that Tolkien labels Fantasy, and even within Fantasy many texts are still rooted in the everyday. For example, the genre Tolkien labels 'Chestertonian fantasy', or *mooreeffoc* ('coffee room' spelt backwards), is concerned rather with defamiliarisation and revealing 'the queerness of things that have become trite' through habituation than with constructing a radically new setting. However, Tolkien prefers the fairy-story, as 'a thing built on or about Fantasy, of which Fantasy is the core', and in which 'simple or fundamental things, untouched by Fantasy ... are made all the more luminous by their setting'.[2]

'On Fairy-Stories' can be read as a revealing account (and justification) of Tolkien's intentions and method in *The Hobbit*, published two years previously, which by this definition is a fairy-story *par excellence*. Here we do indeed find a fantasy setting in which 'simple and fundamental things', such as friendship and the domestic but resilient virtues exemplified by Bilbo Baggins, are made more luminous than they could appear within a realist novel of manners. If we look to the essay for an account of his fantasy world in itself, however, rather than of its rhetorical presentation and effect, we shall be disappointed. 'On Fairy-Stories' deals with settings primarily in terms of their interaction with narratives and readers rather than in isolation. To this extent, despite its talk of sub-creations and Secondary Worlds, the essay sheds only an oblique light on the nature of Middle-earth – a world that Tolkien had, by the time of 'On Fairy-Stories', been building for over twenty years, and that had gradually acquired an existence in many ways independent of the stories that he chose to set there.

Aspects of worldbuilding

Luckily, 'On Fairy-Stories' is not the only place to seek insights into Tolkien's ideas about worldbuilding. By considering his practice in his published (and posthumously-published) works, along with the views he expressed in other essays and letters, it is possible to identify a number of the ingredients he strove for and valued in the making of his fictional world.

Central among these is a requirement for depth and richness of detail. Two letters written by Tolkien in September 1954 illuminate complementary aspects of his desire to create a world that has been 'thought through' to a far greater extent than is required by the plot. The first, written to Hugh Brogan (then an undergraduate, but an enthusiast for *The Hobbit* from his childhood), lays out one advantage of such a world from the point of view of the reader: 'If you want my opinion, a part of the "fascination" [of *The Lord of the Rings*] consists in the vistas of yet more legend and history, to which this work does not contain a full clue.'[3] The sense that there is more to the world of a story than the story itself, that its scenery is not a mere stage prop, can to an extent be faked by the judicious insertion of references to non-existent events and people, but Tolkien's readers knew – or would, he hoped, be able to sense – that the various legends and lays of Middle-earth, and the monuments and ruins littering the landscape through which Bilbo and Frodo walk, had a far fuller existence, if only (at that time) in Tolkien's own mind and his unpublished manuscripts. This is certainly a quality Tolkien valued as a reader. In his 1936 essay '*Beowulf*: the Monsters and the Critics', he praises the *Beowulf*-poet for just this ability:

> The whole must have succeeded admirably in creating in the minds of the poet's contemporaries the illusion of surveying a past, pagan but noble and fraught with a deep significance – a past that had depth and reach backward into a dark antiquity of sorrow.[4]

The second letter was written a week later to a fellow-author, Naomi Mitchison, and shows Tolkien putting quite a different kind of value on the labour of worldbuilding. Here, Tolkien talks about 'the *game* of inventing a country – an endless one, because even a committee of experts in different branches could not complete the overall picture' (emphasis in original).[5] He goes on to list those areas where he feels confident – for example, economics – and some where he is aware that his knowledge is sketchy, such as archaeology and metallurgy. In this letter, worldbuilding is an absorbing writerly challenge, rather than the precondition of a readerly pleasure. However, it is a challenge that many of Tolkien's readers have also undertaken, at least vicariously. As the abundance of Middle-earth guides, glossaries, dictionaries, atlases and encyclopaedias attests, Tolkien's stamina and attention to detail in creating Middle-earth have been rivalled only by those of his readers in learning about it. For these readers, both adults and children, his texts act not only as narratives but as gateways to a world. For some children and young adults especially, part of Middle-earth's attraction may lie in the opportunity it offers to gain expertise in a complex subject, beyond the reach of the adults in their own lives.

If depth and detail are two desirable aspects of an invented world as Tolkien conceived it, a third is consistency. As Humphrey Carpenter writes:

> Not content with writing a large and complex book, he felt he must ensure that every single detail fitted satisfactorily into the total pattern. Geography, chronology, and nomenclature all had to be entirely consistent.[6]

In the case of Middle-earth, the very abundance of detail made this degree of consistency difficult to sustain, as did the fact that the world had been developed over a period of decades, during which some later ideas inevitably came to contradict earlier ones. Long after *The Lord of the Rings* was published, Tolkien was busying himself with correcting inconsistencies in the text, many of them pointed out by readers.

In general, Tolkien dealt with problems of this kind in one of two ways. One was simply to amend the text as and when the opportunity arose. The appearance of the second edition of *The Lord of the Rings*, for example, gave him the opportunity to make numerous minor corrections of this sort. The second was to assume the persona (as Christopher Tolkien put it) of the 'translator and redactor'[7] of a complex manuscript tradition, written by different hands in different genres over a long period, and not all harmonious with each other. Christopher Tolkien set out this way of viewing Tolkien's oeuvre in the Foreword to the first of his major publications of Tolkien's work, *The Silmarillion* (1977):

> A complete consistency (either within the compass of *The Silmarillion* itself or between *The Silmarillion* and other published writings of my father's) is not to be looked for, and could only be achieved, if at all, at heavy and needless cost. Moreover, my father came to conceive *The Silmarillion* as a compilation, a compendious narrative, made long afterwards from sources of great diversity ... that had survived in agelong tradition.[8]

This was not entirely a literary device on Tolkien's part. Carpenter reports that Tolkien talked 'about his book not as a work of fiction but as a chronicle of actual events',[9] and Tolkien reported that for him, as for many writers, the act of creation was experienced subjectively as one of discovery: 'always I had the sense of recording what was already "there", somewhere: not of inventing'.[10] The adoption of the role of editor not only sorted well with Tolkien's professional expertise as a textual scholar, but also provided a neat way of 'saving the phenomena', allowing apparent inconsistencies to be redefined as discrepancies between manuscript traditions. Readers' experience of Middle-earth might thus not be entirely coherent at the level of text, but this need not diminish their sense of the world's underlying consistency.

It is instructive from this point of view to see how Tolkien handled what is probably his best known emendation: the change in the account of how Bilbo won the Ring from Gollum. In the 1937 edition of *The Hobbit*, written at a time when Tolkien had not yet realised the true nature of the Ring, Gollum is genuinely willing to give up his prize in return for Bilbo's victory in their riddle contest. With the second edition, of 1951, Tolkien altered the incident, to make it clear that Gollum had no such intention. Such a change was necessary if *The Hobbit* was to be consistent with the presentation of the Ring and of Gollum in *The Lord of the Rings*, in which the idea that Gollum might willingly relinquish his Precious is unthinkable.

Part of Tolkien's solution, then, was simply to alter the earlier text, and for most writers this would no doubt have been sufficient. Tolkien, however, also went to the trouble of accounting for this change within *The Lord of the Rings* itself. In that book, Bilbo is said to have initially told the earlier version of his adventure to his companions in an uncharacteristic (and, to Gandalf's mind, telling) display of dishonesty, so as to enhance his right to the Ring. In this way, Tolkien transformed a point of textual inconsistency into a psychologically significant demonstration of the Ring's insidious power over those who possess and are possessed by it. Not only that, but *The Lord of the Rings* also establishes the principle of an evolving manuscript tradition, in the form of Bilbo's written account of his own and Frodo's adventures (the latter being completed by Frodo himself) in a volume known to later generations as the Red Book of Westmarch. A passage towards the end of *The Return of the King* describes the book's title page, in which various titles are crossed out (including *There and Back Again*, the alternative name of *The Hobbit*), and a final one is written in Frodo's hand:

THE DOWNFALL
OF THE
LORD OF THE RINGS
AND THE
RETURN OF THE KING[11]

In his 'Note on the Shire Records' at the beginning of *The Fellowship of the Ring* Tolkien extends the story yet further, tracing the history of this volume's transmission, augmentation and alteration in succeeding generations, with the implication that it is the ultimate source and authority for his own telling of the story.

Middle-earth and the transition from *The Hobbit* to *The Lord of the Rings*

The transition from Bilbo's homely titles to Frodo's upper-case seriousness tells its own story about what was involved in Tolkien's development from *The Hobbit* to *The Lord of the Rings*. In part it represents a change of genre, from something akin to fairy-tale to something more like epic; but this is accompanied by a change of implied readership, from children to adults. How did the differences between the texts affect their representation of Middle-earth?

Tolkien was not entirely consistent in his accounts of *The Hobbit*'s relationship to Middle-earth. In a *New York Times Book Review* article in June 1955, Harvey Breit quotes him as stating (apparently in correction of a notion Breit had put to him) that his 'work did not "evolve" into a serious work. It started like that. The so-called "children's story" [*The Hobbit*] was a fragment, torn out of an already existing mythology.'[12] From this, it appears both that *The Hobbit* was part of a pre-existing mythology, and that Tolkien was reluctant to accept that it was, in any straightforward sense, a children's book. Writing later the same month to W. H. Auden, however, Tolkien appears to reverse both positions:

> *The Hobbit* was originally quite unconnected, though it inevitably got drawn into the circumference of the greater construction; and in the event modified it. It was unhappily really meant, as far as I was conscious, as a 'children's story', and … it has some of the sillinesses of manner caught unthinkingly from the kind of stuff I had had served to me …[13]

The contradictions between these statements can be largely accounted for by a consideration of their different contexts. In writing to Breit, Tolkien was concerned to correct the notions that Middle-earth had come into existence only with the writing of *The Hobbit*, and that *The Lord of the Rings* was no more than a *Hobbit* sequel that had got out of hand. In such a situation, it made sense to stress the pre-existence of the world informing both works. In writing to Auden, however, he was addressing an informed correspondent who was already aware of 'the greater construction' and would be in a position to sympathise with Tolkien's regret over some of the early choices made in writing *The Hobbit*, which had come to prove troublesome once that book was drawn into the orbit of Middle-earth.

By no means all those choices proved negative in their effect. The most significant was the invention of hobbits themselves, who came to take their place within the ecology and history of Middle-earth, much to its enrichment. The fact that they were not always a part of Tolkien's scheme is visible in *The Lord of the Rings* mainly in the tendency of elves (and even Sauron) to forget the existence of hobbits and the Shire – although narrative reasons for this neglect are also adduced. As for the 'sillinesses of manner' Tolkien mentions, these probably include *The Hobbit*'s occasionally whimsical narration, and the strong whiff of the twentieth century about Bilbo Baggins's bourgeois lifestyle and sensibility. Tolkien admitted to Mitchison that 'Some of the modernities found among them [hobbits] (I think especially of *umbrellas*) are probably, I think certainly, a mistake.'[14] In addition, *The Hobbit* refers to such exotic and/or modern items as coffee,[15] golf (p. 22) and tobacco (p. 37), only the last of which would reappear in *The Lord of the Rings*. (In the later book tobacco is more often referred to as 'pipe-weed', but Tolkien suggests that it is indeed a species of *Nicotiana*,[16] and Merry produces 'a bag full of tobacco' in *The Two Towers*.)[17] The earliest existing draft of the story (the so-called 'Pryftan Fragment') suggests that the story was at first still more tightly coupled to modern history and geography, referring as it does to the Hindu Kush, the Gobi Desert and China.[18] The first two editions of the book even featured a mention of 'policemen', although this was deleted in the Ballantine edition of 1966.[19]

These elements are difficult to reconcile with Tolkien's assertions, discussed below, that the settings of both books are Europe during an imaginary prehistory. The status of *The Hobbit* as a children's book does, however, provide one potential justification for this apparent inconsistency. As is well known, some of the creatures and characters in that book are referred to by different names from those used in *The Lord of the Rings*: orcs are goblins, Sauron is 'the Necromancer' (p. 31), Esgaroth is (usually) Lake-town. Such differences are indicative of *The Hobbit*'s younger implied readership, who might find goblins easier to comprehend than orcs. A similar argument can be applied to the book's exotics and anachronisms – that Tolkien uses more familiar terms in *The Hobbit* so as to render his world comprehensible.

This was precisely the principle invoked by T. H. White, for example, when he revised his 1939 children's book *The Sword in the Stone* for inclusion in the 1958 adult tetralogy *The Once and Future King* (a process that offers some suggestive points of comparison with Tolkien's own revisions). In *The Sword in the Stone*, White shows Sir Ector and his friend Sir Grummore (depicted as twentieth-century fox-hunting men in all but name) discussing over a glass of port whether to send Ector's son to Eton. In the revision, however, White adds the following gloss:

> It was not really Eton that he mentioned, for the College of Blessed Mary was not founded until 1440, but it was a place of the same sort. Also they were drinking Metheglyn, not Port, but by mentioning the modern wine it is easier to give you the feel.[20]

This device recalls the theological principle of accommodation – the doctrine that (even in Scripture) communication and comprehension may sometimes be served best by sacrificing a degree of accuracy. Tolkien nowhere invokes this principle explicitly, but as a reading strategy it offers a degree of mitigation for the damage his anachronisms otherwise do to the integrity of Middle-earth.

Middle-earth as a world independent of our own

In a recent discussion of Tolkien's influence, Edward James identifies Middle-earth's status as an independent world as one of its original contributions to the fantasy genre:

> Tolkien's greatest achievement ... in retrospect, was in normalizing the idea of a secondary world. Although [Tolkien] retains the hint that the

action of *LOTR* takes place in the prehistory of our own world, that is not sustained, and to all intents and purposes Middle-earth is a separate creation, operating totally outside the world of our experience. This has become so standard in modern fantasy that it is not easy to realize how unusual it was before Tolkien. ... After 1955 fantasy writers no longer had to explain away their worlds by framing them as dreams, or travellers' tales, or by providing them with any fictional link to our world at all.[21]

Here we must distinguish between the influence of Middle-earth on subsequent fictions, and the nature of the world as conceived by Tolkien himself. James is no doubt correct in saying that Tolkien's fiction has been read as exemplifying the principle of an independent world, and that a major part of its influence lies in its 'normalizing' of that idea, but is that how Tolkien thought of it? In fact, he was repeatedly at pains to say the opposite, stating, for example, that '"Middle-earth" ... is not a name of a never-never land without relation to the world we live in.'[22] How can such contradictory ideas of Middle-earth's nature co-exist?

Tolkien gives several different accounts of his world's origins and its relationship to our own. On occasion, he writes as if the world were begotten by his desire to invent languages, which necessitated a place for them to be spoken: 'the "stories" were made rather to provide a world for the languages than the reverse'.[23] This vision of Middle-earth as an artificial environment, a 'philological equivalent of CERN' in which linguistic particles could be made to spin and collide,[24] is probably not foremost in the experience of many readers, but it certainly reinforces the idea of that world as effectively separate from our own. More typically, however, Tolkien stresses the *connections* of Middle-earth to this world, and particularly to north-west Europe. He does this in three related ways, which we may label mythological, historical and geographical.

One purpose of Tolkien's work seems to have been to create, in Humphrey Carpenter's resounding phrase, 'a mythology for England'.[25] Where other European cultures had retained their native mythologies to a greater or lesser degree, that of the English had been virtually obliterated by the Norman Conquest, a fact that Tolkien publicly lamented even as an undergraduate: 'I would that we had more of it left – something of the same sort [as the Finnish *Kalavela*] that belonged to the English.'[26] In a letter of 1951 to Milton Waldman he described his wish to remedy the situation:

once upon a time (my crest has long since fallen) I had a mind to make a body of more or less connected legend, ranging from the large and cosmogonic, to the level of romantic fairy-story – the larger founded on the lesser in contact with the earth, the less drawing splendour from the vast backcloths – which I could dedicate simply to England; to my country.[27]

For all Tolkien's parenthetical self-deprecation, there is indeed a sense in which the legends and stories of Middle-earth constitute his attempt at an 'asterisk-mythology' (to adapt Tom Shippey's usage) – that is, a reconstruction of what an English mythology might have looked like had it survived.[28]

Tolkien had a painful sense of the injury done to his nation's psychic integrity by the loss of its mythology; but he also found in the sense of loss and irretrievable grandeur qualities that were aesthetically valuable in themselves. The *ubi sunt* trope – 'where are those that were before us?' – was prominent in the Old English poems he loved, such as *The Wanderer*, while *The Ruin*'s description of the remains of a vanished (in this case Roman) civilisation also haunts *The Lord of the Rings*, with its awareness of past Númenórean glories and of a future characterised by the melancholy dwindling of magic. This awareness is felt by the characters in *The Lord of the Rings*, but it models the reaction Tolkien envisaged in his own readers, and it is here that the mythological significance of Middle-earth is enhanced by a sense of its status as prehistory. 'Not we but those who come after will make the legends of our time,' Aragorn admonishes Eomer,[29] while Sam, waiting to die on the slopes of Mount Doom, looks forward to the songs that will be sung in his and Frodo's memory: 'Do you think they'll say: *Now comes the story of Nine-fingered Frodo and the Ring of Doom*? And then everyone will hush, like we did, when in Rivendell they told us the tale of Beren One-hand and the Great Jewel.'[30] Such speeches anticipate the modern readers of *The Lord of the Rings* as much as the future inhabitants of an elven hall, and in order for them to have their full effect, the setting of Middle-earth in a time of our own world's prehistory must be appreciated.

To Tolkien, mere temporal distance seems to have offered much the same quality of remoteness as the transition to another world does to many of his modern readers. For example, writing about a book set in the far distant future, H. G. Wells's *The Time Machine* (1895), Tolkien noted that the two species into which Wells supposes the human race to have evolved, the Eloi and Morlocks, 'live far away in an abyss of time so deep as to work an enchantment upon them; and if they are descended from ourselves, it may be remembered that an ancient English thinker once derived the *ylffe*, the very elves, through Cain from Adam'.[31] For Tolkien the chains of cause and effect that were his stock-in-trade as a philologist become attenuated over longer, less imaginable periods, so that the appeal of Wells's novella lies not in its exploration of an evolutionary hypothesis but rather in its ability to work as, in effect, a fairy-story. It is also notable that Tolkien's own forays into time-travel fiction, *The Lost Road* and *The Notion Club Papers*, involve characters experiencing such 'historical' events as the fall of Númenor.[32]

Finally, Middle-earth is related to our own world not only mytho-logically and historically but also geographically. As Christopher Tolkien puts it, in Tolkien's 'earliest writings the mythology was anchored in the ancient legendary history of England; and more than that, it was peculiarly associated with certain places in England'.[33] The specificity – not to say rigidity – of a vision that would fix Tol Eressëa as England, Kortirion as Warwick, and Tavrobel as the village of Great Haywood in Staffordshire did not survive into the published works,[34] but Tolkien never relinquished the sense that 'imaginatively this "history" is supposed to take place in a period of the actual Old World of this planet',[35] and as late as 1967 he saw this as far more than a vestige of a previous incarnation of his world:

> The action of the story takes place in the North-west of 'Middle-earth', equivalent in latitude to the coastlands of Europe and the north shores of the Mediterranean ... If Hobbiton and Rivendell are taken (as intended) to be at about the latitude of Oxford, then Minas Tirith, 600 miles south, is at about the latitude of Florence. The Mouths of Anduin and the ancient city of Pelargir are at about the latitude of ancient Troy.[36]

Tolkien was, of course, aware that the geography and geology of Middle-earth did not 'fit' the scientific evidence of our own world any more than its history fitted the available archaeology, but he suggested that the 'gap in time between the Fall of Barad-dûr and our Days is sufficient for "literary credibility", even for readers acquainted with what is known or surmised of "pre-history"'.[37] 'Literary cred-ibility' here means something like 'poetic licence', but if Tolkien's words betray an unusually latitudinous attitude for such a notorious stickler, they also indicate how tenaciously he was prepared to cling to his original conception of a vital link – geographical and temporal – between Middle-earth and his own homeland.

England bleeds through into Middle-earth at innumerable points, particularly in and around the Shire. Many have noted that Tolkien makes repeated use of English place names in his work, with a substan-tial number deriving from the countryside near Birmingham (where he grew up) and Oxford (where he lived as an adult). Diana Wynne Jones, for example, a former pupil, found in the road running from the Shire to Rivendell echoes of the prehistoric Ridgeway, as it passes through the chalk downland of Oxfordshire and beside the longbarrow known as Wayland's Smithy (a place for wights if ever there was one);[38] while Mathew Lyons, in *There and Back Again in the Footsteps of J. R. R. Tolkien* (2004), has devoted an entire book to exploring the various English locations that inspired Tolkien's writings.[39]

Conclusion: a tale of two readerships?

Tolkien's fiction appeals to a variety of tastes, including some that have come to seem almost contradictory. For certain readers, the sense of Middle-earth as a self-contained, independent, complex but theoretically *knowable* sub-creation is a major part of its attraction. It offers the enjoyment of a game or puzzle, the mastery of a technical subject, the knowledge of oneself as a member of an elite with its own distinctive vocabularies, jargons and even languages. All this goes with the sense of Middle-earth as a place apart, marked off from our reality by sharply-drawn boundaries, and Tolkien's unrivalled effort in creating a detailed and coherent world caters directly to this taste. Other readers (or the same readers in other moods) value Middle-earth as a place to which we are geographically and temporally connected, which we can hear echoed in familiar names and landscapes, and which lends an enchantment (sometimes melancholy) to the contemplation of our own world, presenting us with vistas of a deep past from which we are nevertheless irrevocably exiled.

In the context of the current volume it is notable that, while (as Edward James observes) Tolkien has been hugely influential on the development of independent fantasy worlds, that aspect of his work has had a significantly greater impact on adult than on children's fantasy, at least in the British Isles. While British children's books set in independent fantasy worlds certainly exist (recent examples include Angie Sage's Septimus Heape series [2005–present] and the Sebastian Darke books by Philip Caveney [2007–present]), they have never occupied the dominant place in the canon of children's fantasy that such works have enjoyed in fantasy for adults. In Britain and Ireland at least, it is the second aspect of Tolkien's appeal that has had the more profound influence. Specifically, Middle-earth may be said to have nourished and invigorated a tradition of mythological children's fantasy, set in this world and characterised by a fascination with the potent intersection of myth, place, and the deep past. That tradition did not begin with the appearance of *The Lord of the Rings*, but it enjoyed renewed strength in the years following its publication, flourishing in the hands of such writers as Alan Garner, William Mayne, Susan Cooper, John Gordon, Penelope Farmer, Pat O'Shea and (more recently) Kate Thompson and Catherine Fisher.

The distinction between fantasy set in our own world and that set elsewhere has tended to loom larger and sharper in the discourse of modern critics than in Tolkien's own writings, and in so far as this distinction is read retrospectively back into those writings it threatens to warp our understanding of their nature. The bias towards such readings begins with the tendency to interpret the term 'Secondary World' in 'On Fairy-Stories' as if it were synonymous with 'independent fantasy world', and continues with the view of Tolkien's world of Middle-earth as having at most only a vestigial relationship with our own. It has also obscured some of the ways in which *The Hobbit* and *The Lord of the Rings*, in particular, not only gave rise to the tradition of independent-world fiction now evoked by the epithet 'Tolkienian', but also fed directly into a tradition of this-worldly fantasy for children. Tolkien's legacy to children's literature within both these traditions has been immense, and their subsequent bifurcation should not prevent us from acknowledging the multifaceted nature of that achievement.

Notes

1. Strictly, Middle-earth is only one region of Tolkien's world, albeit the part where the majority of his fiction is set. The world as a whole he calls Arda, and the universe of which it is part is Eä. But 'Middle-earth' is frequently used loosely to refer to all these.
2. J. R. R. Tolkien, 'On Fairy-Stories' (1939, rev. 1964), in *The Monsters and the Critics and Other Essays* (London: HarperCollins, 1997): 109–61, at 132, 138–9, 146, 147.
3. J. R. R. Tolkien, *The Letters of J. R. R. Tolkien*, ed. Humphrey Carpenter, with Christopher Tolkien (London: HarperCollins, 2006): 185.
4. J. R. R. Tolkien, '*Beowulf*: the Monsters and the Critics', in *The Monsters and the Critics and Other Essays* (London: HarperCollins, 1997): 5–48, at 27.
5. Tolkien, *Letters*: 196.
6. Humphrey Carpenter, *J. R. R. Tolkien: A Biography* (London: Unwin, 1978): 198.
7. Christopher Tolkien, 'Introduction', in J. R. R. Tolkien, *Unfinished Tales* (London: HarperCollins, 1993): 1–14, at 3.
8. Christopher Tolkien, 'Foreword', in J. R. R. Tolkien, *The Silmarillion* (London: Unwin, 1979): 7–9, at 8.
9. Carpenter: 12.

10. Tolkien, *Letters*: 145.
11. J. R. R. Tolkien, *The Return of the King* (1955) (London: HarperCollins, 2007): 1344.
12. Harvey Breit, 'In and Out of Books', *New York Times Book Review*, 5 June 1955. Cited in Tolkien, *Letters*: 218.
13. Tolkien, *Letters*: 215.
14. Ibid.: 196.
15. J. R. R. Tolkien, *The Hobbit* (1937) (London: HarperCollins, 2006): 14.
16. J. R. R. Tolkien, *The Fellowship of the Ring* (1954) (London: HarperCollins, 2007): 10.
17. J. R. R. Tolkien, *The Two Towers* (1954) (London: HarperCollins, 2007): 733.
18. John Rateliff, *The History of the Hobbit* (London: HarperCollins, 2011): 9.
19. David Bratman, 'The Artistry of Omissions and Revisions in *The Lord of the Rings*', in *The Lord of the Rings 1954–2004: Scholarship in Honor of Richard E. Blackwelder*, ed. Wayne G. Hammond and Christina Scull (Milwaukee, WI: Marquette University Press, 2006): 113–38, at 121–2.
20. T. H. White, *The Once and Future King* (1958; London: Fontana, 1962): 8–9.
21. Edward James, 'Tolkien, Lewis and the Explosion of Genre Fantasy', in *The Cambridge Companion to Fantasy Literature*, ed. Edward James and Farah Mendlesohn (Cambridge: Cambridge University Press, 2012): 62–78, at 65.
22. Tolkien, *Letters*: 220.
23. Ibid.: 219.
24. Charles Butler, 'Holiday Work: On Writing for Children and for the Academy', *Children's Literature in Education*, 38 (2007): 163–72, at 165.
25. Carpenter: 67.
26. Cited in, ibid.: 67.
27. Tolkien, *Letters*: 144.
28. On the asterisk form in philology and elsewhere, see Tom Shippey, *The Road to Middle-Earth* (rev. edn) (London: George Allen & Unwin, 2005): 22–6, 42–4, 80.
29. Tolkien, *The Two Towers*: 565.
30. Tolkien, *Return of the King*: 1244–5.
31. Tolkien, 'On Fairy-Stories': 116–15.
32. See Tolkien's *The Lost Road* and *The Notion Club Papers*, published respectively in *The History of Middle-earth*, Vol. 5: *The Lost Road and Other Writings*, ed. Christopher Tolkien (London: Unwin, 1987), and Vol. 9: *Sauron Defeated*, ed. Christopher Tolkien (London: HarperCollins, 1992).
33. J. R. R. Tolkien, *The Book of Lost Tales, Part One* (1983), ed. Christopher Tolkien (London: Unwin, 1985): 22.
34. Ibid.: 24–2. See also John Rateliff, 'And All the Days of Her Life are Forgotten: *The Lord of the Rings* as Mythic Prehistory', in *The Lord of the Rings 1954–2004: Scholarship in Honor of Richard E. Blackwelder*, ed. Wayne G. Hammond and Christina Scull (Milwaukee, WI: Marquette University Press, 2006): 67–100, at 77–9.

35. Tolkien, *Letters*: 220.

36. Ibid.: 376.

37. Ibid.: 283.

38. Diana Wynne Jones, 'The Shape of the Narrative in *The Lord of the Rings*', in *J. R. R. Tolkien: This Far Land*, ed. Robert Giddings (London: Vision, 1983): 87–107, at 89. See also Peter Hunt, 'Landscapes and Journeys, Metaphors and Maps: The Distinctive Features of English Fantasy', *Children's Literature Association Quarterly*, 12 (1987): 11–14, at 11–12.

39. Mathew Lyons, *There and Back Again: in the Footsteps of J. R. R. Tolkien* (London: Cadogan Guides, 2004).

8

A Topoanalytical Reading of Landscapes in *The Lord of the Rings* and *The Hobbit*

Jane Suzanne Carroll

It is often assumed that Tolkien's fiction is inextricable from its medieval sources and influences. For Tom Shippey, 'Tolkien cannot be properly discussed without some considerable awareness of the ancient works and ancient work which he tried to revive.'[1] Shippey excludes the naive readers of Tolkien – children and adults both – who may not be aware of and have access to these ancient works but who may still 'intuit the echoes'[2] of these intertexts and enjoy the works. Furthermore, Shippey imposes a kind of hierarchy of sources to a reading of Tolkien's fiction, discounting the value of a familiarity with other kinds of texts, especially contemporary texts. Yet these texts, I argue, are equally important to our understanding of *The Hobbit* and *The Lord of the Rings*. Twentieth-century fiction provides an important source for the plot and atmosphere of these texts. For instance, there is no medieval correspondent for the episode in *The Hobbit* when the dwarves are captured by Elves and each put in separate cells. This episode recalls a similar event in John Masefield's *The Box of Delights* (1935) when Kay and his friends are imprisoned. By evoking Masefield, Tolkien hints to the reader that the dwarves – like Kay and his friends – will soon escape. Tolkien uses this kind of narrative intertextuality throughout *The Hobbit* and *The Lord of the Rings* and so caters to a different kind of reader and a different kind of reading experience. Thus, although *The Hobbit* was 'written for children'[3] and *The Lord of the Rings* was published for an adult audience, both address a dual readership.

This dual-address is negotiated through landscape. For Tolkien, landscape offers a 'fusion-point of imagination'[4] which integrates

121

text with intertext. He uses landscape as a metaphor in his discussions of intertextuality. In his essay 'On Fairy-Stories', he demonstrates the process by which literary ideas are passed 'from mind to mind' and absorbed into the cultural consciousness through a discussion of readers' responses to space:

> Literature works from mind to mind and is thus more progenitive. It is at once more universal and more poignantly particular. If it speaks of bread or wine or stone or tree, it appeals to the whole of these things, to their ideas; yet each hearer will give to them a peculiar personal embodiment in his imagination ... If a story says 'he climbed a hill and saw a river in the valley below,' the illustrator may catch, or nearly catch, his own vision of such a scene; but every hearer of the words will have his own picture, and it will be made out of all the hills and rivers and dales he has ever seen, but especially out of The Hill, The River, The Valley which were for him the first embodiment of the word.[5]

Here, Tolkien directly acknowledges this idea of a multi-layered, accumulative, and even shared idea of landscape which in turn hints at a multi-layered and accumulative experience of reading. Crucially, this experience is open to all readers – naive or knowing – as it enables reading on a personal level as well as on a highly referential one; this kind of reading allows for the 'peculiar personal embodiment [of the space] in [the reader's] imagination' but also speaks to the canonical texts and to the process by which such texts are integrated within the 'shared experience' of literature. Through landscape, Tolkien's fiction actively supports these two kinds of reading.

This essay explores the role of spatial–cultural intertexts in Tolkien's fiction by applying topoanalytical methodologies to the landscapes of *The Hobbit* and *The Lord of the Rings*. Treating Tolkien's vast and apparently complicated landscapes as constructs made up of component morphological elements, it is clear that Tolkien's landscapes conform to a series of topological commonplaces – topoi – which may be traced from the beginnings of Northern European literature right through to the twentieth century. Focusing on a single topos – the sanctuary – this essay explores the homes, halls, and strongholds of Tolkien's fiction, from the round, comfortable homes of the hobbits, to the cold and unwelcoming halls of Edoras. Landscapes are acknowledged as a major part of the great 'appeal'[6] of *The Hobbit* and its pseudo-sequel *The Lord of the Rings*, and Middle-earth is regarded as among 'the richest of fantasy landscapes'.[7] Tolkien was acutely aware of the significance of topography, and the wealth of landscape detail within his fiction and the rich cartography surrounding it lend

weight to this awareness. For Tolkien the motivation behind writing
The Hobbit and *The Lord of the Rings* was a realisation that England
had 'no stories of its own (bound up with its tongue and soil)'.[8] These
twin fixations – language and landscape – gave shape to the texts.
But whereas the influence of language, particularly through Tolkien's
philological games, invented languages, and word-coining, has been
the subject of much academic debate,[9] there is comparatively little
critical interest in the role of landscape in his fiction. Whereas many
critics, including Shippey, Jane Chance, Clive Tolley, and Stuart D.
Lee and Elizabeth Solopova, have demonstrated the narrative parallels
between Tolkien's work and medieval source texts, I argue that the
influence of Old English and Old Norse texts on Tolkien's writing
may be seen most clearly in the *landscapes* of Middle-earth. Beginning
with a discussion of these sources, this essay traces the significance of
landscape topoi in Tolkien's work and demonstrates how topoanalysis
offers a new way to read Tolkien's fiction, which not only lays bare
the influence of medieval literature on his work but also reveals the
influence of children's literature on Tolkien's conception of space.

   In spite of their apparent complexity, Tolkien's landscapes are
actually very ordinary and very limited. In topographical terms, *The
Hobbit* and *The Lord of the Rings* are almost identical: the fundamen-
tals of landscape are a constant. Both texts are shaped by the simple
home–away–home narrative pattern, characteristic of children's literature.[10] The narratives are strikingly similar: first a hobbit leaves his
comfortable underground home in Hobbiton then travels through
wild and dangerous countryside, through forests and mountains, aided
by friends. At one point in the narrative, there is a subterranean scene
where the allies are attacked and separated and later the hobbit and
his friends are captured by elves in a forest and are led blindfolded to
an elvish settlement. The company leave this settlement by means of
a river. Afterwards, the hobbit passes through a narrow, secret tunnel
which leads to a monster's stronghold, and finally returns to his home,
forever altered by the impact of his adventures. Summarising the two
texts' narratives in terms of topography rather than in terms of action
allows us to see just how similar they are. Viewed in terms of topoi –
of types of landscape which are pieced together in different ways to
produce apparently different results – the landscapes of Middle-earth
are largely predictable. The spaces Tolkien employs are limited too:
sanctuaries (including halls, houses and homesteads), green spaces
(which include forests and pleasances), roads and rivers (as both
always facilitate passage in the books), lapsed spaces (including underground spaces and ruins) and, finally, wastelands and wildernesses.

This morphological treatment of landscape – breaking the landscape down to its smallest meaningful pieces – offers a new approach to the landscapes of Middle-earth.

Like all fictional landscapes, Tolkien's settings derive meaning not merely from their placement in relationship to one another, but also from their intertextual relationship with other texts. The examination of topoi, conventional settings rather than particularised spaces,[11] enables a study of landscape which is at once diachronic – taking in the whole scope of Tolkien's fiction – and synchronic – allowing us to read the historical antecedents of Tolkien's landscapes. Combining the morphological separation of landscape into conventionalised topoi with an historicist examination of the origins and development of these conventions, topoanalysis allows us to understand Tolkien's land-scapes 'in the light of a continuous literary tradition'.[12] Tolkien readily engaged with this literary tradition, for it presented him with the means to create fuller, more vibrant landscapes. Marjorie Burns notes that:

> Tolkien wanted greater landscape drama in his Middle-earth. What he wanted, in fact, were settings and scenes that the Norse and Anglo-Saxons carried along with them to England within their mythologies: desolate reaches, vast rolling plains, and mountains of fire and ice ... topo-graphically speaking, Tolkien's Middle-earth includes North-western Europe and Scandinavia through a reconstruction that does not 'relate the shape of the mountains and landmasses to what geologists may say or surmise'.[13]

What Tolkien wanted, then, was not real landscapes, in terms of geology or geography, but the cultural ideas of landscape which have been created over time, layer upon layer, accumulated 'as mould accu-mulates in a forest, through the shedding of innumerable lives since the beginning of life'.[14] Such layers of story and cultural imagining are evident in Tolkien's work: just as many of the words in his invented languages ultimately have their origins in medieval languages, many of his landscapes have their roots in medieval texts. In his essay 'On Fairy-Stories', Tolkien directly acknowledges the existence of arche-typal – and therefore typical and even stereotypical – spaces which are at once 'universal' and 'particular'. These typical spaces, that Ernst Robert Curtius terms 'topoi',[15] are carried 'from mind to mind' through reference, intertext, and allusion. Through the use of topoi, Tolkien engages with the texts which represent the 'first embodiment' of these spaces in vernacular literature and connects his fiction with older literature, intertextually asserting a place for his work within canonical tradition. For Tolkien the 'first embodiment' of these topoi could be found in medieval literature.

Tolkien and medieval literature

The validity of medieval culture as a source for modern literature was established in the nineteenth century. Interest in medieval culture had grown in popularity in England through the work of writers such as Matthew Arnold and William Morris, artists such as John William Waterhouse, Dante Gabriel Rosetti, and John Ruskin, and architects such as Augustus Pugin. Although the revival in interest had long since peaked and passed by the time Tolkien was publishing his fiction, the influence of this nineteenth-century medievalism can be clearly detected in his work. Chance notes that, furthermore, Tolkien was also 'influenced by his own personal medievalism, his profession as a medi evalist, his relationships with other medievalists, and his own mytholo-gising in constructing his major fiction.'[16] To date, however, critical interest has focused on the narrative similarities between medieval literature and Tolkien's work: Chance reads *Farmer Giles of Ham* as a parody of *Sir Gawain and the Green Knight*[17] and Lee and Solopova demonstrate how specific passages in *The Lord of the Rings* are influenced by, and at times even borrowed from, medieval texts. The fight at Balin's tomb, for instance, is read as analogous with episodes from the *Fight at Finnsburg* and an episode from the chronicles known as *Cynewulf and Cyneheard*. Correspondences between characters are also commonly observed. Clive Tolley observes that the Rohirrim 'are, in fact, the Anglo-Saxons, as imagined and idealised by Tolkien'[18] and that the language they speak and the names they use are essentially Old English. Tolley also traces the association between Gríma Wormtongue and Unferth and between Éowyn and Wealhþeow.

While Chance, Tolley, and Lee and Solopova have demonstrated clear correspondences between medieval literature and those in Tolkien's fiction, I propose to shift the critical focus away from narrative and character and towards the influence of medieval texts on Tolkien's depictions of landscape. Medieval literature represents the first step in the chain which passes topoi 'from mind to mind'. These medieval landscapes offer the key to understanding the landscapes of Middle-earth. Focusing here on a single topos, the sanctuary, I will show how Tolkien mediates the influence of medieval literature and, in drawing on the topological features of earlier texts, invests his fictional landscapes with intertextual depth.

The sanctuary is among the earliest and most important topoi.[19] It is distinguished from other aspects of the landscape in three ways. Firstly, all sanctuaries are enclosed by clearly demarcated boundaries.[20] Secondly, although landscape is typically horizontal, the sanctuary topos rises up vertically, symbolically reaches towards the sacred space of the sky, inviting connotations of heaven, the mind, and ethereality (the inverse, whereby a site descends vertically, often creates an association with earth, with primal functions and physicality). Thirdly, the sanctuary encloses or protects an object – or a nexus of objects – which are 'vested with real and symbolic importance ... that compels notice and demands response'.[21] Halls and houses, especially those of anointed, and therefore sacred kings,[22] may be likened to sacred spaces. The shape of churches and cathedrals across Northern Europe reflects the hall-style dwelling which was most common in medieval times[23] and like the church, the hall is a 'metonym for the society centred in it'.[24] Given their social importance, it is appropriate that sanctuaries also become the narrative focus of many texts. In Old English and Old Norse literature, the physical form of the sanctuary dictates the narrative function of the space. With so much emphasis on the sanctuary's borders and limits, tension and action are generated when these boundaries are threatened or compromised: the occupants of the space must either defend the boundaries or allow the space to be overrun. This narrative pattern is repeated many times in medieval literature. *Beowulf*, for instance, is essentially the story of the desecration and reclamation of a hall, and its Norse analogues, Bodvarr Bjarki at the Court of King Hrolf, or Grettir's fight with Glám in the *Grettisaga*, also display the same narrative pattern. Structured around the defence mounted by a hero in the doorway of the building, these episodes involve the desecration and subsequent re-consecration of a sanctuary.

For Tolkien, *Beowulf* was 'the greatest of all surviving works of ancient English poetic art'[25] and the exemplar of medieval literature. The poem accounts for the most direct influence on his use of the sanctuary topos in his fiction. The first half of the poem centres on the great feast-hall, Heorot, and the Grendelkins' attacks upon it. Like all sanctuaries, Heorot has a strong vertical dimension. It is 'heah' – 'high' – and its horned roof reaches heavenwards. The poet describes the hall in terms of its limits and borders, emphasising the doorway, the threshold, the lintel and the walls. Grendel's attacks are presented as a breach of these boundaries:

> The door soon retreated
> The fire-forged bars fast, after his hand touched it,
> He threw it open, evil-minded. Then he was swollen
> In the mouth of the building.[26]

Grendel's attacks ruin the building, preventing Hroþgár from using it for its intended purpose as a gift-hall. Hroþgár and his people are forced to abandon the hall and, once they leave, it can no longer be sacralised by their presence. It is no longer safe or sacred: it is no longer a sanctuary. Beowulf's arrival signals a turning point: he defends the hall, defeats Grendel and, by pinning Grendel's severed arm to the lintel, reasserts the proper boundaries of the hall. Once the borders are re-established, Hroþgár and his people can reclaim the hall. Their reinstated presence re-consecrates the space.

Heorot is an antecedent for both the physical appearance and the narrative function of many of the homes and halls in Tolkien's fiction. The older text provides a set of tropes and commonplaces which Tolkien often draws upon in his descriptions of sanctuaries. Thus, although his writing is associated with rich detail, the description of Beowulf's hall in *The Hobbit* is sketchy and functional. Tolkien provides only enough description to allow the reader to form a mental picture or, rather, to be able to recall the embodiments of these spaces she may have encountered earlier through canonical literature. The gate to Beorn's house is 'high and broad', which indicates something of the size and scale of the structure and inside and also echoes the description of Heorot as 'heah'. Inside, Beorn's hall is 'quite dark' and the guests sit around trestle-tables on 'two low-seated benches', just as they do in *Beowulf* and *Bodvarr Bjarki*. Like the abandoned and sadly disused Heorot, Beorn's hall 'had not seen such a gathering for many a year'.[27] These topological parallels allow Tolkien to play a kind of narrative joke. The episode in Beorn's hall parodies the action of *Beowulf*: the hall is invaded by unwelcome forces but the reader knows that Gandalf, Bilbo and the Dwarves mean Beorn no harm. As soon as they leave, Beorn can re-establish the borders of his home and repel any further incursions.

The motif of the sanctuary under threat and the sanctuary re-consecrated is repeated many times throughout *The Lord of the Rings*. All of the sanctuaries of men and hobbits are attacked and over-run. The heroes' task is to defend, repair, and re-consecrate these spaces. This pattern dictates the narrative action at Helm's Deep, inside the mines of Moria, at Minas Tirith, and in the Shire itself during the final Scouring. At some points in the text, Tolkien deliberately isolates the narrative pattern from the topos. At Weathertop, for instance, Aragorn and the hobbits mount a useless defence against the Ring-wraiths. The topologically astute reader will note that Weathertop is not a proper sanctuary – it is not properly enclosed by boundaries and is not sacralised by or to any object or person. Weathertop is a grass-covered ruin; the grass blurs the limits of the building; rather than standing apart from the surrounding landscape, Weathertop blends right into it – again, Tolkien uses landscape to inform narrative. On other occasions, he inverts the narrative pattern by having the protagonists attack a stronghold. This happens, for example, at Isengard when the Ents and the hobbits march against Saruman. And while the houses of the Elves are over-run by time and are subsequently abandoned, they do not strictly follow the same topological patterning as other sanctuary spaces in *The Lord of the Rings*. This may be a way to indicate, through landscape, that the Elves are otherworldly and their homes, like the Elves themselves, do not conform to the norms of landscape depiction. These variations, inversions and subversions show Tolkien's awareness of the topos as well as his ability to adapt these landscape motifs.

His most obvious engagement with the sanctuary topos, and with Anglo-Saxon landscapes, comes in his representation of Meduseld. The topologically-alert reader, conscious of both text and intertext, will see Meduseld not simply as a building, but as the 'fusion-point' of Tolkien's imagination and his medieval sources. Shippey notes that 'the chapter "The King of the Golden Hall" is straightforwardly calqued on *Beowulf*.[28] Just as the Rohirrim are modelled on the Anglo-Saxons, Meduseld is clearly based on the halls of Anglo-Saxon literature: a long rectangle with pillars supporting a high, pitched roof. Like Heorot, Meduseld is first described in terms of its roof, which is a synecdoche for the hall as a whole. Meduseld is 'thatched with gold'[29] and this indicates the wealth and ornamental beauty of the rest of the structure. Tolley notes that in the passage where Aragorn, Gandalf and the others arrive at Edoras, 'it is clear that Tolkien paid homage to *Beowulf* in the detailed, but circumstantial, similarity of the arrival scenes'.[30] But Tolkien extrapolates the metaphor elegantly, allowing the setting of the scene, as well as the narrative action, to echo the earlier text:

> Inside it seemed dark and warm after the clear air upon the hill. The hall was long and wide and filled with shadows and half lights; mighty pillars upheld its lofty roof ... the travellers perceived that the floor was paved with stones of many hues; branching runes and strange devices intertwined beneath their feet, they saw now that the pillars were richly carved, gleaming dully with gold and half-seen colours.[31]

Meduseld is long and wide, just as its predecessor is 'long and broad'. The decorated floor recalls the 'fágne flór', the 'fretted floor', of Heorot and the gold inlaid mead-benches and carved pillars.[32] These formal elements serve to provide the informed reader with clues to the narrative function of Meduseld. In spite of the beauty of the hall, a reader familiar with medieval literature and with the role of the sanctuary topos will expect this hall to be, like Heorot, a place of fear and misery, a place where the inhabitants expect to be attacked at any moment. A reader familiar with the narrative action of *Beowulf* will assume that the hero and his companions will be challenged by a self-serving and cynical advisor, but whereas Unferth is merely sceptical of Beowulf's prowess, Wormtongue has made Théoden, and by extension all the Rohirrim, suspicious and fearful of all outsiders. Here, as in all sanctuaries, the hero's function is to re-consecrate the hall, to re-establish its boundaries, to defeat and expel the evil that threatens it, and thus to restore order and power to the king. At this point, Tolkien subverts the reader's expectations and, as Michael Kightley observes, the chapter focuses on Gandalf rather than Aragorn and it is the ancient wizard rather than the virile warrior who must take action.[33] Furthermore, whereas the majority of sanctuaries are threatened by external forces, Meduseld is threatened from within. The threat posed by Wormtongue is psychological and emotional and so, rather than engaging in physical combat, Gandalf uses words to persuade Théoden to give up his suspicion and to begin to fight against the power of Isengard. Gandalf restores Théoden's faith in his people and expels Wormtongue, and so re-consecrates the hall, enabling Théoden to take full control over the space once more.

There are, however, other sanctuaries in Middle-earth which do not seem to fit in with the established topos. Whereas Meduseld and Beorn's hall and the other great halls of Middle-earth, such as the throne-room at Gondor, bear the obvious influence of medieval literature and of medievalism, there are some spaces which are smaller, more personal, and more private such as the homes and houses of Hobbiton. Although the narrative pattern is unchanging, these spaces strike an entirely different tone from the stark majesty of the royal halls of Rohan and Gondor. It would appear that medieval intertexts were simply incongruous with the atmosphere Tolkien wanted for Hobbiton and a place that 'means comfort'.[34] In order to set the correct atmosphere for Hobbiton and for Bilbo and Frodo's home, Bag End, Tolkien cut a scion of a different branch of literature.

Tolkien and children's literature

Whereas the task of tracing an author's literary sources and antecedents can often be quite straightforward, Tolkien, 'like anyone who reads widely ... was exposed to many influences',[35] and these varied influences account for what contemporary reviewers felt was a somewhat inconsistent style. Peter Green criticised Tolkien's writing as 'veer[ing] from Pre-Raphelite to *Boy's Own Paper*'.[36] Whereas medieval literature was regarded as a suitable influence on a work of such magnitude and ambition written by an esteemed philologist and academic, the influence of later nineteenth- and early twentieth-century children's authors was considered somewhat inappropriate. Part of this may stem from Tolkien's own attitudes to the subject: whereas he had professional interests in philology and medieval antiquity and wore the influence of the medieval texts with pride, his interest in, and engagement with, contemporary children's literature is discussed almost apologetically. In a letter to W. H. Auden, Tolkien notes that *The Hobbit* 'was unhappily really meant, as far as I was conscious, as a "children's story" ... it has some of the silliness of manner caught unthinkingly from the kind of stuff I had served to me'.[37] Here, I suggest, there is a subtle note of untruth; for whatever Tolkien may have 'unthinkingly' absorbed from children's fiction, a great deal more was deliberately borrowed.

Whereas Green treats the 'Pre-Raphaelite' and the *Boy's Own Paper* as opposing ends of a literary spectrum, these two kinds of literary influence on Tolkien's work are actually quite closely linked. The surge of interest in medieval languages, literature, and culture in the late nineteenth century coincides with the first 'golden age' of children's literature, sometimes identified as 1860–1914. There are even indications that the rise of children's literature and the increasing interest in medievalism were linked. Ruth Bottigheimer suggests that medieval Norse material entered the Anglophone literary tradition through the publication of two texts for children: Keary's *Heroes of Asgard* (1857) and Webbe-Dasent's translation of the folktale collection *East O' the Sun and West O' the Moon* (1859).[38] Janet Fisher notes that 'the ethos and brotherhood' of these ancient heroic texts made them particularly popular as source-material for children's literature, particularly boys' adventure stories.[39] Tolkien's earliest encounters with medieval literature – particularly Old Norse literature – were mediated through such adventure stories. Andrew Lang's *Red Fairy Book* (1890), which contains the story of Sigmund and Fafnir, was a childhood favourite, and as a young boy he used Latin prize money to buy a copy of Wright's *Primer of the Gothic Language* and a copy of a William Morris novel.[40] Later, as a young scholar at Exeter College, Oxford, he used the money he won for the Skeat Prize in English to purchase more of Morris's books.[41] For Tolkien, at least, there was a clear overlap between his experience of late Victorian and early Edwardian children's literature and his early encounters with medieval texts, and he consciously, carefully and deliberately positioned and balanced his work between two literary extremes.

As with the borrowings from medieval literature, the references and borrowings from children's literature in Tolkien's work range from wry allusions to carefully crafted intertexts. *The Father Christmas Letters*, for instance, are peppered with references to Alison Uttley and E. Nesbit, particularly to *The House of Arden* (1908). Kenneth Grahame's languorous poetry-reading dragon in *Dream Days* (1898) is a clear forerunner of the smug, articulate Smaug. Christina Scull and Wayne G. Hammond note the similarities between E. Nesbit's Psammead from *Five Children and It* (1902) and *The Story of the Amulet* (1906) and the sand-dwelling wizard Psamathos Psamathides in *Roverandom* (1998).[42] Just as Winnie-the-Pooh feels 'a little eleven o'clockish', Roverandom feels 'tea-timeish'[43] and many of Tolkien's other characters, especially the hobbits, show a preoccupation with food which is normally reserved for characters in children's literature.[44] Thus, Tolkien integrates influences from children's literature seamlessly into books which show the heavy influence of medieval texts.

Whereas the influence of children's literature may be detected in Tolkien's characters and narrative, the clearest connection between Tolkien's novels and early twentieth-century children's literature lies in his landscapes. Take, for example, this passage from *The Fellowship of the Ring*:

> A golden afternoon of late sunshine lay warm and drowsy upon the hidden land between. In the midst of it there wound lazily a dark river of brown water, bordered with ancient willows … there was a warm and gentle breeze blowing softly … and the reeds were rustling, and the willow-boughs were creaking.[45]

The scene includes references to trees, sunshine, shade, flowing water, and a gentle breeze, elements which, for Curtius, characterise the classical *locus amoenus* and its northern equivalent, the pleasance. The nearest and most obvious intertext for this passage comes, not from classical poetry, but from children's literature. The 'golden afternoon' is a direct reference to Lewis Carroll's *Alice's Adventures in Wonderland* (1865) – a text which opens and closes with exactly this kind of drowsy, river-side scene.[46] Closer to Tolkien's own time, Grahame invoked a similarly sleepy pleasance in *The Wind in the Willows* (1908). Tolkien's reference to willow-trees in connection with the dark brown water has immediate associations with Grahame's text. Here, landscape is both the message and the medium through which it is expressed.

But why should Tolkien, the celebrated philologist, refer to *Alice's Adventures in Wonderland* when there are perfectly good examples of the pleasance in Northern European medieval literature to draw from? Moreover, as the form and narrative function of topoi remain stable over time and the topoi of children's literature share the same physical and symbolic characteristics as their medieval equivalents, Tolkien does not, and arguably cannot, use children's literature to access a different set of topoi. We must assume that these references are the result of a conscious, deliberate, and careful choice: Tolkien refers to children's books in this scene in order to change the tone and mood of the landscape. As John Stephens notes:

> Actual settings implicate attitude and ideology, because writers of fiction are rarely content to use the spatio-temporal dimension of setting merely as an authenticating element of narrative ... practically and traditionally the function of setting in fiction is to convey atmosphere, attitudes and values.[47]

Landscapes act as a conduit for the changing atmospheres of Middle-earth. Rather than the grim and elegiac tone of medieval heroic poetry,[48] this scene evokes subconscious associations of innocence and delight. The hobbits are, at this point, innocent, in that they are free from guilt and also free from knowledge about the true horrors of the warring world beyond the borders of the Shire. They are not children, but they are somewhat childlike in their size and in their outlook on the world.[49] Tolkien intertextually asserts the innocence of the hobbits many times in the early stages of *The Lord of the Rings*. The descriptions of their early adventures, before their encounters with the Black Riders and the Ring-wraiths – going further from home than ever, gorging themselves on stolen mushrooms – have more in common with Grahame's Mole and Ratty, and Beatrix Potter's Peter Rabbit, than with any medieval text. As the narrative draws the hobbits into darker, deeper, and older parts of the world, the references to children's texts give way to references to older 'deeper' literature, and the halls and homes of Eodoras and Minas Tirith have more in common with Norse saga and Old English heroic verse than with the gentle adventures of the Hundred Acre Wood.

Tolkien also draws on children's literature in some instances of the sanctuary topos, especially in his depiction of Bilbo's home Bag End. Although they may be sanctified by the presence of a king, the great halls of Anglo-Saxon and Old Norse literature are generally communal spaces. Here, in presenting a domestic space with a single, ordinary occupant, children's literature offers a more appropriate intertextual source. The subtitle of *The Hobbit*, 'There and Back Again', underlines the importance of the domestic space in this landscape of adventure and aligns *The Hobbit* with children's literature. Pauline Dewan notes that in children's literature, the home is 'the preeminent place of importance ... charged with great emotional significance as the focus of all that is most important'.[50] Also, as is common in children's literature, Bag End functions as a metaphorical extension of its occupant. The round, comfortable home is an apt environment for the round, comfortable, bourgeois hobbit.[51] As a true embodiment of the sanctuary topos, the home is sacred to, and sacralised by the presence of, an individual. Bag End is the centre of Bilbo's world and his movements are centrifugal rather than explicitly linear. Like Grahame's Mole, his thoughts turn towards home whenever he grows tired of his adventures. Thus, even though Bag End appears only at the beginning and end of the narrative its significance as the first, and perhaps even primary, topos in the text cannot be disputed. Appropriately, such an important space is afforded a rich description:

> It had a perfectly round door like a porthole, painted green, with a shiny yellow brass knob in the exact middle. The door opened into a tube-shaped hall like a tunnel: a very comfortable tunnel [...] with panelled walls, and floors tiled and carpeted, provided with polished chairs, [...] and many little round doors opened out of it [...] The best rooms were all on the left-hand side [with] deep-set round windows looking over his garden and meadows beyond, sloping down to the river.[52]

Bilbo's home is rather like other subterranean domestic spaces known from popular Edwardian children's literature. The very name of 'Bag End' has connotations of 'Mole End' in *The Wind in the Willows*, although the 'narrow, meagre dimensions'[53] of Mole's house are not a patch on Bilbo's round comfortable home. The little round doors and winding passages leading to pantries and cellars are similar to the construction of Mrs Tittlemouse's house in Potter's tale, which, like Bag End, is invaded by all sorts of unsavoury visitors which the owner is obliged to entertain.[54] Mrs Tittlemouse is justifiably irritated by the invasion, but the topologically alert reader will observe that Bilbo Baggins has no real grounds for complaint: the opening description of Bag End notes that it is unusually placed within the landscape, with views of gardens and farmland, it is close to both the road and the river and is, thus, perfectly situated at a confluence of topoi. While the arrival of the dwarves is sudden and therefore unexpected, it is also perfectly appropriate: Bag End is, topographically, a meeting point and the events of the narrative simply echo this.

Even though 'the poor little hobbit ... wondered what had happened, and what was going to happen',[55] the topological alignment of Bag End makes it clear what will happen. Bag End is a sanctuary: it is described in terms of its outer borders and liminal areas and it is clearly linked to Bilbo's personality. Bag End will certainly follow in the narrative patterning associated with the sanctuary topos: the borders of this space will be breached and Bilbo will either defend or surrender his home. Bilbo is unable to defend his space (he imagines hiding in the cellar rather than ordering everybody out), and he finds that once the building is full of dwarves and smoke-rings and dirty plates, it no longer properly reflects his personality. Bilbo repeatedly remarks that the Dwarves are in 'the wrong house'[56] but the Dwarves are not in error; rather it is the home and its owner that need to change.

Bag End is changed by the influx of visitors: the neat home is disordered, the cellars and pantries depleted, and even the furniture is misused as the dwarves make their beds on chairs and sofas. Bilbo also finds his personality inexorably altered over the course of the unexpected party: he becomes more 'Tookish'[57] and less like himself. By the morning, he has changed so much that Bag End is no longer sacred to him. Thus, Bilbo is faced with a choice: either he reasserts the borders of the space and reclaims it as his own, or he abandons it. Bilbo chooses the latter course. This kind of abandonment is common in children's literature; Dewan observes that 'if a home no longer reflects the self, the protagonist often leaves it'.[58] Whereas many characters leave their homes in search of a new and better place to live, Bilbo goes searching – however unwittingly – for a new personality that will match the disordered place that housed 'strange and sorcerous'[59] beings.

The effect of the children's literature intertexts in the depiction of Bag End is twofold. First, it allows Tolkien to invest Hobbiton – and the other parts of Middle-earth where appropriate – with something of the tone and mood of late nineteenth and early twentieth-century children's literature. By using different sets of intertexts for both kinds of space, Tolkien sets up an atmospheric distinction between the Shire and the world beyond. There is a certain comic value to some of the early scenes in *The Hobbit* and *The Lord of the Rings* which is totally out of key with the epic poetry of the Middle Ages. By using different intertexts, Tolkien successfully changes the tone and mood of the scenes while remaining faithful to traditional topological landscapes.

Second, it allows Tolkien to establish Hobbiton as a place separate from the wide world of adventure that lies beyond the borders of the Shire. Thus, both *The Hobbit* and *The Lord of the Rings* take on something of the dichotomous structure of the domestic fantasy even though they are technically set in a High Fantasy world. Hobbiton is a kind of primary world in which the characters are safe and secure. The protagonists' journeys – from innocence to experience, from childish security to a world of adult dangers – are presented as a kind of *bildungsroman*. The reader, familiar with the 'home–away–home' narrative pattern of children's books, is reassured that the hero will return home.

Conclusion

Middle-earth, like its creator, wilfully exhibits the influence of varied and multiple literary sources. Although the sanctuary is among the oldest of the canonically-established topoi, Tolkien does not always reach for the 'first embodiment' of the space in his creation of Middle-earth. By drawing on a range of influences, he seems to subtly alter the mood and tone of each invocation of the topos. Even though Meduseld and Bag End draw on the same topos and display formal and narrative similarities, each has a completely different atmosphere. Thus, Tolkien gives the impression of a varied and complex imaginative landscape rather than one which is obviously constructed out of tired stereotypes. It is clear that Tolkien does not merely reproduce the landscapes of older literature faithfully and unthinkingly. He engages with the topoi, adapts them, manipulates them, demonstrating a willingness 'to use old motifs and make them familiar once more'.[60] The landscapes of Middle-earth are part of a continuous tradition of which Tolkien seems acutely aware. The overlapping and intersecting references and intertexts embedded in the landscapes of Middle-earth enable the texts to cater for and appeal to a wide audience. Tolkien's fiction does not move 'from Pre-Raphelite to *Boy's Own Paper*'[61] but moves between them. This intertextual dance, I wish to suggest, allows Tolkien to negotiate a balance between apparently different kinds of literature and, more importantly, between two apparently different kinds of reader.

Notes

1. Tom Shippey, *J. R. R. Tolkien: Author of the Century* (London: HarperCollins, 2000): xxvii.
2. Christine Wilkie-Stibbs, 'Intertextuality and the Child Reader', in *Understanding Children's Literature: Key Essays from the Second Edition of*

the International Companion Encyclopedia of Children's Literature, ed. Peter Hunt (London and New York: Routledge, 2005): 168–79, at 175.

3. C. W Sullivan III, 'High Fantasy', in *International Companion Encyclopedia of Children's Literature*, ed. Peter Hunt (London and New York: Routledge, 1996): 300–10, at 305.

4. J. R. R Tolkien, '*Beowulf*: The Monsters and the Critics', in *The Monsters and the Critics and Other Essays* (1983; London: HarperCollins, 2008): 5–48, at 19.

5. J. R. R Tolkien, 'On Fairy-Stories', in *The Monsters and the Critics and Other Essays* (1983; London: HarperCollins, 2008): 109–61, at 159.

6. George Clark and Daniel Timmons, *J. R. R. Tolkien and His Literary Resonances: Views of Middle-earth* (Westport, CT: Greenwood Press, 2000): 196.

7. John R. Stilgoe, *Landscape and Images* (Charlottesville, VA: University of Virginia Press, 2005): 12.

8. Stuart D. Lee and Elizabeth Solopova, *The Keys of Middle Earth: Discovering Medieval Literature Through the Fiction of J. R. R. Tolkien* (Basingstoke: Palgrave Macmillan, 2005): 9.

9. See Tom Shippey, *The Road to Middle Earth* (London: HarperCollins 2005): 1–31, and Peter Gilliver, Jeremy Marshall and Peter Weiner, *The Ring of Words: Tolkien and the Oxford English Dictionary* (Oxford: Oxford University Press, 2006).

10. Perry Nodelman, *The Pleasures of Children's Literature* (London: Longman, 1992): 192.

11. Stephen Siddall, *Landscape and Literature* (Cambridge: Cambridge University Press, 2009): 40.

12. Ernst Robert Curtius, *European Literature and The Latin Middle Ages*, trans. Willard R. Trask (London and Henley: Routledge & Kegan Paul, 1953): 184.

13. J. R. R. Tolkien, *The Letters of J. R. R Tolkien*, ed. Humphrey Carpenter with Christopher Tolkien (London: HarperCollins, 1995): 220, and see Marjorie Burns, *Perilous Realms: Celtic and Norse in Tolkien's Middle-earth* (Toronto: University of Toronto Press, 2005): 26.

14. Jacquetta Hawkes, *A Land* (London: The Cresset Press, 1953): 4.

15. Curtius, *European Literature*.

16. Jane Chance (ed.), *Tolkien the Medievalist* (London and New York: Routledge, 2003): 4.

17. Jane Chance, *Tolkien's Art: A Mythology for England* (Bowling Green, KY: University of Kentucky Press, 2001): 129–30.

18. Clive Tolley, 'Is It Relevant? Old English Influence on *The Lord of the Rings*', in Richard North and Joe Allard (eds), *Beowulf and Other Stories: An Introduction to Old English, Old Icelandic, and Anglo-Norman Literatures* (London: Pearson, 2007): 38–62, at 41.

19. Edward S. Casey, *Getting Back Into Place: Toward a Renewed Understanding of the Place-World* (Indianapolis: Indiana University Press, 1993): 179.

20. Harold W. Turner, *From Temple to Meeting House: The Phenomenology and Theology of Places of Worship* (The Hague: Walter de Gruyter, 1979): 15.

21. Richard Kieckhefer, *Theology and Stone: Church Architecture from Byzantium to Berkeley* (Oxford: Oxford University Press, 2004): 63.

22. Sergio Bertelli and R. Burr Litchfield, *The King's Body: Sacred Rituals of Power in Medieval and Early Modern Europe* (Philadelphia: Pennsylvania State University Press, 2001): 22.

23. Sarah Hamilton and Andrew Spicer (eds), *Defining the Holy: Sacred Space in Medieval and Early Modern Europe* (Aldershot: Ashgate Publishing, 2005): 6.

24. Daniel Donoghue, *Old English Literature: A Short Introduction* (Oxford: Blackwell, 2004): 29.

25. J. R. R. Tolkien, 'On Translating *Beowulf*' in *The Monsters and the Critics and Other Essays* (London: HarperCollins, 2006): 49–72, at 49.

26. *Beowulf*, in F. R. Klaeber (ed.), *Beowulf and The Fight at Finnsburg* (Boston, MA: D. C. Heath, 1941), lines 721b–724a (my translation).

27. J. R. R. Tolkien, *The Hobbit* (1937; London: HarperCollins, 1998): 149.

28. Shippey, *The Road to Middle Earth*: 94.

29. J. R. R. Tolkien, *The Two Towers* (1954; London: HarperCollins, 1999): 129.

30. Tolley: 47.

31. Tolkien, *The Two Towers*: 136.

32. *Beowulf*, line 725.

33. Michael R. Kightley, 'Heorot or Meduseld? Tolkien's Use of *Beowulf* in "The King of the Golden Hall"', *Mythlore: A Journal of J. R. R. Tolkien, C. S. Lewis, Charles Williams and Mythopoeic Literature*, 24(3/4) (2006): 119–34, at 129–30.

34. Tolkien, *The Hobbit*: 11.

35. Lee and Solopova: 11.

36. Peter Green, 'Outbound by Air to an Inappropriate Ending', *The Daily Telegraph and Morning Post*, 27 August 1954: 8.

37. Tolkien, *Letters*: 215.

38. Ruth Bottigheimer, 'Fairy Tales and Folk-tales', in *International Companion Encyclopedia of Children's Literature*, ed. Peter Hunt (London and New York: Routledge, 1996): 152–65, at 155.

39. Janet Fisher, 'Historical Fiction', in *International Companion Encyclopedia of Children's Literature*, ed. Peter Hunt (London and New York: Routledge, 1996): 368–76, at 368.

40. Lee and Solopova: 7.

41. Chester N. Scoville, 'Pastoralia and Perfectibility in William Morris and J. R. R. Tolkien', in Jane Chance and Alfred K. Siewers (eds), *Tolkien's Modern Middle Ages* (London: Palgrave Macmillan, 2005): 93–103, at 94.

42. J. R. R. Tolkien, *Roverandom*, ed. Christina Scull and Wayne G. Hammond (London: HarperCollins, 2002): 94.

43. A. A. Milne, *The House at Pooh Corner* (1928; Boston, MA: E. P Dutton, 1956): 33.
44. Wendy R. Katz, 'Some Uses of Food in Children's Literature', *Children's Literature in Education*, 11(4) (1980): 192–9.
45. J. R. R. Tolkien, *The Fellowship of the Ring* (1954; London: HarperCollins, 1999): 152.
46. Lewis Carroll, *Alice's Adventures in Wonderland and Through the Looking Glass*, ed. Peter Hunt (Oxford: Oxford University Press, 2009): 9 and 109–11.
47. John Stephens, *Language and Ideology in Children's Fiction* (London: Longman, 1992): 209.
48. See Lee and Solopova: 135.
49. Chance, *Tolkien's Art*: 22–3.
50. Pauline Dewan, *The House as Setting, Symbol and Structural Motif in Children's Literature* (Lewiston, NY: The Edwin Mellen Press, 2004): 2–3.
51. Shippey, *The Road to Middle Earth*: xx.
52. Tolkien, *The Hobbit*: 11–12.
53. Kenneth Grahame, *The Wind in the Willows*, ed. Peter Hunt (Oxford: Oxford University Press, 2010): 54.
54. Beatrix Potter, *The Tale of Mrs Tittlemouse* (London: Warne, 1910).
55. Tolkien, *The Hobbit*: 21.
56. Ibid.: 32.
57. Ibid.: 28.
58. Dewan: 8.
59. Tolkien, *The Hobbit*: 25.
60. Shippey, *J. R. R. Tolkien Author of the Century*: 255.
61. Green, 'Outbound by Air': 8.

9

Tolkien and Trees

Shelley Saguaro and Deborah Cogan Thacker

The forest and the fairy tale

Our sense of the forest derives as much from the depictions we encounter in stories heard or read in childhood as from actual encounters, and the expectation of enchantment or the sense of threat with which fictional forests are endowed animates our 'readings' of actual forests. At first, it might appear that the trees and forests of Tolkien's Middle-earth are used primarily to stand for the natural world, in opposition to the unstoppable forces of modernity, but they are a multi-layered portrayal, with subtle links to fairy tale and folklore, and complex psychological symbolism. As Richard Hayman observes: 'Trees are important in Tolkien's work because they stand for attitudes to nature in general ... woods for Tolkien therefore offer temporary respite from the modern world, whether they are actual lived experience or the stuff of myth.'[1] It is only by tracing the representation of trees and forests from *The Hobbit* to *The Lord of the Rings*, that it is possible to see that Tolkien's 'attitude to nature' is central to both his particular use of fantasy, and his belief in the power of fantasy to imbue lived experience with meaning. For Tolkien, fantasy does not signify escape, but a deepening of understanding. In *Tree and Leaf* he claims that, '[t]he magic of Faerie is not an end in itself, its virtue is in its operations ... to hold communion with other living things'.

This sense of communion and 'the importance of imagined wonder'[2] is one of the factors that leads to the complex status of Tolkien's work in relation to children's literature, creating limits that Tolkien himself decries in *Smith of Wootton Major*, in which he attributes a sense of 'Faery' to imagination:

> This compound – of awareness of a limitless world outside our domestic parish; a love ... for the things in it; and a desire for wonder, marvels, both

139

perceived and conceived – this 'Faery' is as necessary for the health and complete functioning of the Human as is sunlight for physical life.[3]

However, the roots of what we recognise as children's literature, and particularly the importance of folk and fairy tales to the Romantic sensibility, provide a connection to an apprehension of nature as imbued with 'quasi-historical depth'[4]. Forests, perhaps most powerfully, retain this mythic sensibility. Historians and commentators on fairy tales, including Tolkien, recognise the power and duality of the forest trope, and the extent to which its use demonstrates the interconnectedness of the fantasy world and the real world.

The forest is an important trope in fairy stories. In *Fantasy, Myth and the Measure of Truth*, his study of the links between German Romanticism and the British fantasy tradition, William Gray claims that Tolkien's particular use of fantasy set in an alternative world reflects the importance of its connection with the real world derived from the earlier fairy tale tradition, especially in *The Hobbit*.[5] Roger Sale sees the forest as a recurring motif in fairy tales and lists many stories that involve the passage of a central character through the forest:

> [F]orests in fairy tales are so frequent, and their associations so obvious, that they come to seem a given, not unlike the opening chord in a piece of music that can be played loudly or softly, by this or that instrument or the ensemble. It is, thus, important, because the story could not proceed without it, but the last thing one needs to do is to ponder what it means, because what it means will be what is made of it. After each other change in the story, especially in the character of the person in the wood, the wood itself will become tinged slightly, but it will never be anything in itself other than a forest, a place where one is liable to become lost, a place where princes never live but woodcutters often do and witches or wolves.

He sees Tolkien (along with Bruno Bettelheim) as one of the key commentators on fairy tales, and he cites Tolkien's comment on 'The Juniper Tree' in *Tree and Leaf*, that 'such stories have now a mythical or total (unanalysable) effect ... we stand outside our time, outside Time itself maybe'.[6] As Tolkien put it in a letter:

> The theatre of my tale is this earth, the one in which we now live, but the historical period is imaginary. The essentials of that abiding place are all there ... so naturally it feels familiar even if a little glorified by the enchantment of distance in time.[7]

This quality, of being beyond interpretation, is found in the 'root stories' that influence Tolkien's work, particularly those of the Nordic and Germanic traditions. There is also a resemblance to his English forebears, particularly George MacDonald, which Tolkien acknowledged;[8] there are direct similarities, for instance, in the personification of the forest in MacDonald's *The Golden Key*, where Tangle 'began to feel as if all the trees were waiting for him, and had something they could not go on with till he came to them', and Bilbo's first encounter with Mirkwood.[9]

The characteristic that Tolkien appears to take from MacDonald and from the epic, myth and folklore to which he continually alludes, is the nature of the forest *as* forest − endowed with the qualities of the forest as it is experienced. The forest itself is not magical, and although it can take on allegorical readings, that is not its significance in relation to the story. Rather, it is the nature of forests themselves, for those familiar with them and the potential danger inherent in them (particularly for children), that is emphasised. Descriptions, brief though they are, do not portray the forest as enchanted. The darkness *is* the 'suffocating and uncanny darkness' that Bilbo experiences, the 'tangled boughs' that allow 'a slender beam of light' to 'slip through an opening in the leaves far above' and the 'eerie' sounds in the beech trees *are* all realistic portrayals of ancient woodlands of England − woodlands with which Tolkien was very familiar.[10]

Although many recent interpreters of fairy tales reject psychoanalytic readings in favour of a more materialist approach, Bruno Bettelheim's influence on our attempts to explain their effects cannot be ignored. For Bettelheim, the passage into the forest signifies a psychoanalytic space − a place separated from everyday experience in which to be lost is to be found. The uncanny sense of the forest waiting to do its work invites a reading that suggests the inevitability of such a journey:

> Since ancient times the near impenetrable forest in which we get lost has symbolised the dark, hidden, near-impenetrable world of our unconscious. If we have lost the framework which gave structure to our past life and must now find our way to become ourselves, and have entered this wilderness with an as yet undeveloped personality, when we succeed in finding our way out we shall emerge with a much more highly developed humanity.[11]

Jack Zipes, in his study of the Brothers Grimm, develops an alternative analysis of the distinctive quality of fictional forests in order to explain the importance of the forest in the Grimms' tales, in ways that echo Tolkien's own concerns for the loss of human apprehension of the natural world. Zipes suggests that in the Grimm Brothers' tales, 'the forest is rarely enchanted though enchantment takes place there. The forest *allows* for enchantment, for it is the place where society's conventions no longer hold true.'[12] This description is similar to Tolkien's depiction of Mirkwood in *The Hobbit*: it is the Wood-elves, who 'wandered in the great forests that grew tall in lands that are now lost',[13] who contribute the enchantment rather than the forest itself. Though elves are of the past and Tolkien appears to instruct his readers not to look for them any longer, his forest is indebted to those of earlier fairy tales, as an environment where enchantment and transformation can take place. Attributing the imaginative power of ancient forests to the sustenance of national identity and a memory of past unity, he quotes Wilhelm H. Riehl (1852): 'In the opinion of the German people the forest is the only great possession that has yet to be completely given away.'[14] This is a concern similar to Tolkien's own position. Paul Kocher emphasises the point that Middle-earth is supposed to be 'our own green and solid Earth at some quite remote epoch in the past'.[15] The world Tolkien portrays in *The Hobbit* and in *The Lord of the Rings* is a world in which the old forests remain, but have since been lost to us, as in the tales of the Brothers Grimm. This loss is a loss of wholeness that, Tolkien claims, once existed.

For Tolkien, the enchantment is already part of the nature of forests and trees, and in *The Hobbit*, it is quite clear that he has derived this sense from the history of fairy tales. In *Tree and Leaf*, Tolkien refers to his own childhood reading and throughout his letters he emphasises that the power of fantasy to stir the imagination is not an end in itself, but a way of accessing an earlier, primeval understanding of 'communion with other living things'. According to Kocher, for Tolkien, 'only fantasy can provide a recovery of knowledge of ourselves and the world around us'.[16]

'In all my works I take the part of trees as against all their enemies'[17]

Readers of Tolkien's work would know well, and by the fiction alone, that Tolkien was a lover of trees, for they abound. Further, many book covers on texts by or about Tolkien bear pictures of Tolkien himself, with trees: sitting against a tree or sitting among the twisted roots of an ancient tree-trunk.[18] The last photo taken of Tolkien, included in Humphrey Carpenter's biography, is of him standing companionably, next to one of his favourite trees (*Pinus nigra*) in the Botanic Gardens,

Oxford,[19] with his right hand pressed flat against the surface of its gnarled bark. The HarperCollins edition of *Tree and Leaf* has on its cover a drawing by Tolkien of an elaborate, fanciful tree, 'The Tree of Amallion'. From *The Hobbit* through 'Leaf by Niggle' and *The Lord of the Rings* to *The Silmarillion*, Tolkien represents extraordinary trees and creates tree-related beings, such as the tree-herder Ents, or the even more tree-like but still mobile former Ents, the Huorns. As Tolkien himself explains in a letter of June 1955 to his American publisher, Houghton Mifflin, 'I am (obviously) much in love with plants and above all trees and always have been; and find human maltreatment of them as hard to bear as some find ill treatment of animals.'[20] His son Michael acknowledged a related personal legacy and the inspiration for an artistic one:

> From my father I inherited an almost obsessive love for trees: as a small boy I witnessed mass tree-felling for the convenience of the internal combustion engine. I regarded this as the wanton murder of living beings ... My father listened seriously to my angry comments and when I asked him to make up a tale in which the trees took revenge on the machine-lovers, he said, I will write you one.[21]

As a lover of trees, Tolkien could also offer detailed and obviously closely observed descriptions of them in all his writings. His letters, particularly to his son Christopher, contain descriptions such as:

> The poplars are now leafless except for one top spray; but it is still a green and leafy October-end down here. At no time do birches look so beautiful; their skin snow-white in the pale yellow sun, and their remaining leaves shining fallow-gold.

or

> ... the silver light of spring on flower and leaf. Leaves are out: the white-grey of the quince, the grey-green of young apple, the full green of hawthorn, the tassels of flower even on the sluggard poplars.

and

> The rime was yesterday even thicker and more fantastic ... breathtakingly beautiful: trees like motionless fountains of white branching spray against a golden light and, high overhead, a pale translucent blue.[22]

These find their fictive and fantastical correlatives in *The Lord of the Rings*; there is a close relation between the fantasy elements and the

vividness of Tolkien's apprehension of the trees he encountered daily.
Thus, the trees of magical Lothlorien are described as scintillatingly
as the trees Tolkien observed outside his window.[23]

The mythical *mallorn*, whose seed like a 'little silver nut', a gift from
Galadriel, is carried by Sam back to the Shire,[24] where he plants it
in the Party Field, where once stood the tree that had witnessed so
much hobbit history, including Bilbo's farewell speech. As it grows, a
symbol of recovery after great tribulation, it is resplendent with silver
and gold: 'the only *mallorn* west of the Mountains and east of the Sea,
and one of the finest in the world'.[25] Tolkien sees *all* trees in ways
that are out-of-the ordinary; a short-hand term might be 'magical',
and so the transposition to fairy stories and fantasy is not a huge leap.

Tolkien also 'deploys' trees for their symbolic value, signifiers,
when healthy, of hope and regeneration (and in this he is not alone,
drawing as he does on a long tradition of legendary trees). Tolkien's
'Introductory Note' to *Tree and Leaf*, first published in 1964 and at
the time bringing together, 'On Fairy-Stories' and 'Leaf by Niggle',
states: 'though one is an "essay" and the other "a story", they are
related: by the symbols of Tree and Leaf' and by both touching in
different ways on what is called, in the essay, 'sub-creation'.[26] Paul
Kocher further addresses the figurative aspects of 'tree' and 'leaf' and
finds that Tolkien's 'tree' stands sometimes for that same whole body
of Tolkien writing, but more often for the living, growing tradition
of fairy stories in general, which the essay 'On Fairy-Stories' calls the
'Tree of Tales'.[27]

Tolkien refers to his short story 'Leaf by Niggle' in a letter to his
aunt Jane Neave, refuting that it should be seen as an 'allegory', and
preferring that it should be seen as 'mythical', because its main character, Niggle, 'is meant to be a real mixed-quality *person* and not an
'allegory' of any single vice or virtue'.[28] (Tolkien insists on the same
complexity for trees.) The tale is about an artist, whose topic is 'tree'
and 'leaf', and whose life work *is*, and is *emblemised by*, a Tree. Although
he is a painter, Niggle's favoured subject has much in common with
Tolkien's, as do the vistas his work generates, evocative as they are of
landscapes in the long narrative of *The Lord of the Rings*:

> He was the sort of painter who can paint leaves better than trees ...
> Yet he wanted to paint a whole tree, with all of its leaves in the same
> style, and all of them different ... Then all around the Tree, and behind it,
> through the gaps in the leaves and boughs, a country began to open out;
> and there were glimpses of a forest marching over a land, and of moun-
> tains tipped with snow.[29]

Tolkien explained that the story related to a time when 'I was anxious about my own internal Tree, *The Lord of the Rings*. It was growing out of hand, and revealing endless new vistas – and I wanted to finish it, but the world was threatening.'[30] Niggle's own artistic labours always fall short, not least because of the interruptions and irritation caused by his neighbour, Parish. After illness, and a strange period of inter-rogation and journeying, he arrives in a place where he is confronted by 'the Tree, his Tree, finished. If you could say that of a Tree that was alive.'[31] The estimation that 'the Tree was finished, though not finished with' is a reflection of Niggle's understanding that the Tree is not his project alone. At this stage, Niggle also realises that Parish, the philistine neighbour he has only seen as disruptive, has had a contribution to make to the style he considers most distinctively his own. The conclusion of the story shows how simultaneously impor-tant and insignificant is Niggle's own contribution to the Great Tree; most important of all is that the Tree lives and continues to put forth 'leaves'. The remnant of Niggle's picture is eventually lost to view 'in his old country', stored in a dusty museum and then forgotten. Such individual obscurity, however, belies the ongoing life of 'the Tree' to which an important contribution has nevertheless been made. Of his own Tree, Tolkien acknowledged that it 'grows like a seed in the dark out of the leaf mould of the mind: out of all that has been seen or thought or read, that has long ago been forgotten, descending into the deeps'.[32] In *Tree and Leaf* he encouraged overcoming the depressed and depressing view: 'Who can design a new leaf?' His answer, couched, of course, in arboreal terms, is also a plea for the 'recovery fairy stories help us to make':

> Each leaf, of oak and ash and thorn, is a unique embodiment of the pattern, and for some *eye*, this very year may be *the* embodiment, the first ever seen and recognised, though oaks have put forth leaves for countless generations …[33]

The Hobbit

While trees and forests are central to Tolkien's own conception of living in the world, it is in the act of creation that they signify most profoundly and it is in his fictional world that he most effectively 'passes on' this apprehension. Through fantasy, Tolkien can be seen to attempt to awaken his readers to the powerful and emblematic significance of trees and forests – to *see* them as he does. The quality of forests as 'tinged', but only ever a forest, is certainly familiar to a

reading of the forest in *The Hobbit*, and in part explains the workings
of Tolkien's use of fantasy. By alluding to this 'unanalysable' effect in a
book for children, Tolkien relies on a recognition of forests encountered earlier in both fictional and actual terms, but also embeds a sense
of them that can be taken to later reading, and perhaps, particularly,
to *The Lord of the Rings*.

The importance of 'imagined wonder'[34] is embedded in Tolkien's
treatment of the forest in *The Hobbit*, most often classified, because of
its straightforward plotting and narrative voice, as a book for children.
Tolkien himself looked back critically on its tone, but, for those who
read *The Hobbit* as an introduction to the story of Middle-earth, this
ability to engage with the 'imagined wonder' of his world is central
to Tolkien's lasting attraction. Not only does his method of blending
the mythic with actual experience use the forest as a site of enchantment and adventure, but he also portrays the forest in such a way as
to embody *real* forests rather than to translate them into something
fantastical.

In fact, there are few forests in *The Hobbit* and very few mentions
of individual trees – certainly nothing that matches those in *The Lord
of the Rings* – but they are crucial to the functioning of what could
be considered a classical quest narrative, and provide an intimation
of encounters in Tolkien's later work. We are in the same world:
Middle-earth, at once a land of mythic status and a reminder of a
possible primeval past of our own world. So that, while Tolkien's
representations of the forest serve a narrative function similar to those
in fairy tales, they also recall the qualities of forest-ness that are familiar and realistic. Mirkwood, in particular, serves as a testing ground for
the central character and provides the place for a rite of passage. It is
in the forest that Bilbo discovers his 'true' character and recognises the
role he will need to perform. His passage from innocence, particularly
in terms of self-knowledge, to awareness, is played out through his
adventure in Mirkwood, made more significant by the fact that once
he has performed his function as the burglar, he no longer has to pass
through the forest, but can travel around it during his journey home.
However, on the outward journey, as is the case with many fairy tales,
there is little choice for him but to go through the forest, for going
round it would take too long – they must, according to Gandalf, go
through 'if you want to get to the other side'. It might be possible to
consider his encounter with Mirkwood, this 'dark', 'forbidding' and
'uncanny' forest, in Bettelheim's terms, for even Gandalf's remarks:
'keep your spirits up, hope for the best, and with a tremendous slice
of luck you *may* come out one day ...' seem to be echoed in *The Uses*

of Enchantment,[35] at once recognising the need to confront one's fears in order to allow the ego to come into being and teasing the reader with the possibility of failure.

Yet it is not enough to interpret this 'unanalysable' aspect of the forest as merely a fairy-tale motif representing a symbolic space, although its place in Bilbo's adventures suggests a symbolic function. Mirkwood, like many such places in children's books and fairy tales, is significant because it is a place which differentiates between those who *know* it and those who do not. An innocent here, Bilbo is warned about the dangers of the forest by those who are familiar with its codes, such as Gandalf and Beorn. Like Mole, in *The Wind in the Willows*, overcome by a sense of being watched and later admonished by Ratty, who explains that it is necessary to 'know' the codes of the Wild Wood, Bilbo is endangered precisely because he ignores the rules and warnings, although his endangerment is required for the acquisition of the necessary self-knowledge to succeed in his task. Bilbo's innocence in relation to the dangers of the forest is emphasised by his childlike stature, while those who issue the warnings, Beorn and Gandalf, are represented as adult and knowledgeable. As Bilbo approaches the woods where Beorn lives, his size, and therefore his position in relation to the forest, is emphasised: 'At times they were pushing through a sea of bracken with tall fronds rising right above the hobbit's head, at times they were marching along quiet as quiet over a floor of pine needles, and all the while the forest-gloom got heavier and the forest-silence deeper.'[36]

Bilbo's reluctance to enter Mirkwood is due in large part to the warnings of Beorn, who is *of* the forest. His home reflects his sense of belonging to that world and even his stature is described in striking contrast to the hobbit's childlike smallness. This helps to emphasise the knowledge of, and power over, whatever the forest signifies, for Beorn's home resembles a forest, though a controlled version of it: 'the pillars of the house standing tall behind them and dark at the top like the trees of the forest'. Whereas the darkness at the top of Beorn's hall is compared to the forest, the company are surrounded by 'the light of dancing flames', suggesting warmth and safety in contrast to the encounters yet to come. It is only as Bilbo approaches Mirkwood that the foreboding caused by Beorn's warnings, like those of Little Red Riding Hood's mother – not to stray from the path – come into force. The reliance on his child readers' familiarity with fairy-tale forests imbues Tolkien's version with an uncanny quality, and as the party approaches Mirkwood, the personification of the forest serves to accentuate both a sense of enchantment and its malign presence: 'They could see the forest coming to see them, or waiting for them like a black and frowning wall before them.' In particular, when Bilbo steps alone into the forest, it seems 'very secret'; 'a sort of "watching and waiting feeling"', he said to himself'.[37] His own 'reading' of the forest echoes the anthropomorphic quality of not only fictional forests already known to readers of fairy tales, and, as suggested, George MacDonald's *The Golden Key*, but an experience of actual encounters with forests as beings, as living entities, creating a feeling that is full of foreboding. In this way, Tolkien can already be seen to pull away from the kind of anthropomorphism he rejected in others, just as he later resists confining the meaning of the forest to allegory or symbolism.

Bilbo's foray into Mirkwood, like those of characters who enter the forests of the fairy tales of the Brothers Grimm, changes him and, more importantly, allows him to recognise that transformation. His experiences in Mirkwood – being led off the path by the Wood-elves, and battling the spiders in the treetops – allow him to discover his inherent bravery and cleverness. He has faced a test of character and redefined himself, by passing through the forest.

The Lord of the Rings

Whereas, in *The Hobbit*, 'the forest' is predominantly typological and, perhaps, rather functional in terms of its symbolic resonance, forests and trees in *The Lord of the Rings* are much more complex. Although children 'from about 10 onwards' do read and become caught up in the trilogy, Tolkien expressed the view that it was 'rather a pity, really' as it 'was not written for them'. Rather, his aim was to write for 'any one who enjoyed a long exciting story', the kind of narrative he himself enjoyed, addressed expressly and directly to those who could 'understand adult language'.[38] Tolkien objected to fairy stories that are 'carefully pruned' in a false and romantic estimation of what is suitable for children: 'if a fairy story as a kind is worth reading at all it is worthy to be written for and read by adults'.[39]

Trees in the later narrative are not anthropomorphised, neither are they static but rather, carefully differentiated: 'as different from one another as trees from trees ... as different as one tree is from another of the same name but quite different growth and history; as different as one tree-kind from another, as birch from beech, oak from fir'.[40] Rather than passive objects, they are seen as complex living subjects, who respond to other subjects living in a particular environment. In

The Lord of the Rings, we see trees and forests which have, largely, fallen out of positive inter-relationship with other living beings:

> Lothlórien is beautiful because there the trees are loved; elsewhere forests are represented as awakening to consciousness of *themselves*. The Old Forest was hostile to two-legged creatures because of the memory of many injuries. Fangorn Forest was old and beautiful, but at the time of the story tense with hostility because it was threatened by a machine-loving enemy. Mirkwood had fallen under the dominion of a Power that hated all living things but was restored to beauty and became Greenwood the Great before the end of the story.[41]

The restoration of relationship is one of the themes of the long saga.

In Tolkien's view, fairy stories are able to represent 'profounder wishes: such as the desire to converse with other living things ... and the magical understanding of their proper speech'.[42] This is not, however, simply to represent humanised attributes in an anthropocentric setting. Michael Perlman notes in *The Power of Trees: The Reforesting of the Soul*, the frequent and 'myriad forms of human–tree parallels', but such 'analogy never implies a full and literal identity of humans and trees'. Rather, 'neither the parallels or differences ... can be consistently avoided or reconciled'. This is 'a tension ... basic to the world's tree stories'.[43] Where there is a tendency to anthropomorphise trees, it is due to a lack of thorough understanding and intimacy. Perlman also cites Michael Pollan, who claims in *Second Nature: A Gardener's Education*, that a gardener's familiarity with trees would highlight the differences between species, and would militate against Romantic and naïve identification. Pollan further differentiates between 'a humanised tree' and an 'ensouled' one, adding that someone who prunes trees, removing limbs and lopping growth for the tree's sake, would certainly develop 'a more complicated and less anthropomorphic understanding of how, and where, a tree lives'.[44] In all his descriptions of trees, one would be hard-pressed to find Tolkien privileging human characteristics, although they are certainly represented as having 'emotional' responses and survival strategies.

Fundamentally, for good or ill, trees change (as do Ents and Entwives, Huorns, hobbits, humans and all other beings). The Ents, once 'asleep' and silent, were 'woken up by Elves'. Ents and Entwives separate because their 'hearts did not go on growing in the same way', and the Huorns, once Ents, have grown more tree-like, and angry and 'queer'.[45] 'Trees may 'go bad' as in the Old Forest; Elves may turn into Orcs, noted Tolkien in a long explanatory letter.[46] At times and in some cases, trees and forests are welcoming and benign, actively helping the Hobbits, providing bowers of safety and fuelling camp-fires with off-cast limbs. At other times, however, woods such as the Old Forest are malign, or have become so. The Old Forest is terrifying by reputation and, once entered, actively unwelcoming. It is in the Old Forest and by the active malevolence of Old Man Willow that the travellers are variously nearly drowned or nearly consumed by and suffocated in the rotten heart of a tree. Tragedy is only averted by Tom Bombadil's intervention, and he later offers an explanation for the behaviour of Old Man Willow, but it is also important to note that trees are not without their own inherent peculiarities, prejudices and flaws:

> Tom's words laid bare the hearts of trees and their thoughts, which were often dark and strange and filled with a hatred of things that go free upon the earth, gnawing, biting, breaking, hacking, burning: destroyers and usurpers. ... The countless years had filled them with pride and rooted wisdom, and with malice. But none was more dangerous than the Great Willow: his heart was rotten, but his strength was green; and he was cunning, and a master of winds, and his song and thought ran through the woods on both sides of the river. His grey thirsty spirit drew power out of the earth and spread like fine root-threads in the ground, and invisible twig fingers in the air, till it had under its dominion nearly all the trees of the Forest from the Hedge to the Downs.[47]

Critics have puzzled over the meaning of Tolkien's depiction of such a malevolent tree as Old Man Willow. It sits uneasily with the view of Tolkien as a 'tree-hugging' environmentalist and *The Lord of the Rings* as an iconic book for the Green Movement. Old Man Willow can be seen as rare and aberrant, but Tolkien refuses to patronise trees (or any creature) by making them one-dimensional, or less subject to the post-Fall corruption and conflict that threatens all living beings. Tolkien also makes clear that when trees suffer injury, they can become hostile. Contrary to simplistic expectations, hobbits are among those who have harmed trees. The skirmish over the planting of the Hedge involved trees moving nearer to it; in retaliation and to secure their boundary, the hobbits 'cut down hundreds of trees' and made 'a great bonfire in the Forest'.[48] Eventually, Hobbits and trees negotiate a wide boundary and an uneasy peace, with mutual fear and resentment. Perhaps it is Tom Bombadil who is the exemplar of a right relation to trees and the living world; he has an acceptance of their variety and rightful co-existence. Bombadil is the polar opposite of those who, like Saruman, cannot resist 'plotting to become a

Power', who have 'mind[s] of metal and wheels' and who care not 'for growing things, except as far as they serve him for a moment'.[49]

'The suffering tree is the epitome of universal pain'[50]

In 1953, Tolkien wrote to his long-term friend Father Robert Murray (who had presciently noted that critics might have difficulty evaluating *The Lord of the Rings*: 'they will not have a pigeon-hole neatly labelled for it'), affirming the book's positive religious aspect: '*The Lord of the Rings* is of course a fundamentally religious and Catholic work; unconsciously so at first, but consciously in the revision. That is why I have not put in, or have cut out, practically all references to anything like religion, to cults or practices, in the imaginary world. For the religious element is absorbed into the story and the symbolism.'[51] There is a passage in another letter, where Tolkien uses a familiar image to represent his particular faith: a tree. In a long letter to his son Michael in 1967/8, Tolkien contrasted the 'protestant' 'search backwards' with the dynamism ('likened to a plant') of the Catholic church, and the arboricultural skill and familiarity required of those who tend it:

> 'my church' was not intended by Our Lord to be static or remain in perpetual childhood; but to be a living organism (likened to a plant), which develops and changes in externals by the interaction of its bequeathed divine life and history – the particular circumstances of the world into which it is set. There is no resemblance between 'the mustard seed' and the full-grown tree. For those living in the days of its branching growth, the Tree is the thing, for the history of a living thing is part of its life, and the history of a divine thing is sacred. The wise know it began with a seed, but it is vain to try and dig it up, for it no longer exists, and the virtues and powers that it had now reside in the Tree. Very good: but in husbandry the authorities, the keepers of the Tree, must look after it according to such wisdom as they suggest, prune it, remove cankers, get rid of parasites and so forth. (With trepidation knowing how little their knowledge of growth is!) But they will certainly do harm if they are obsessed with going back to the seed or even the first youth of the plant when it was (they imagine) pretty and unafflicted by evils.[52]

Explicit mention of his faith is made by Tolkien in the Notes to the essay 'On Fairy-Stories' – a somewhat surprising turn. Having claimed, more familiarly, that 'successful Fantasy can … be explained as a sudden glimpse of the underlying truth or reality', he continues: 'The Gospels contain a fairy-story, or a story of a larger kind which embraces all the essence of fairy-stories,' and introduces his own

neologism: 'Eucatastrophe' or 'good destruction'; 'among the marvels
is the greatest and most complete conceivable eucatastrophe ... The
Birth of Christ is the eucatastrophe of Man's history: ... the story
begins and ends in joy.'[53] In his own 'sub-creation', *The Lord of the
Rings*, a similar restoration of joy is accomplished, and represented, in
deliberately religious language and imagery, by 'a scion of the Eldest
of Trees', which will replace the withered White Tree in the courtyard
of Minis Tirith. In this passage, all the features already discussed in this
essay come together: trees, creation (art), fairy stories, and religion:

> Then Aragorn turned ... out of the very edge of the snow there sprang
> a sapling tree no more than three foot high. Already it had put forth
> young leaves long and shapely, dark above and silver beneath, and upon
> its slender crown it bore a small cluster of flowers whose white petals
> shone like the sunlit snow. ...
>
> And Gandalf coming looked at it, and said: 'Verily this is a sapling of
> the line of Nimloth the fair, and that was a seedling of Galathilion, and
> that a fruit of Telperion of many names, Eldest of Trees. Who shall say
> how it comes here in the appointed hour? But this is an ancient hallow,
> and ere the kings failed or the Tree withered in the court, a fruit must
> have been set here. For it is said that, although the fruit of the Tree comes
> seldom to ripeness, yet the life within may then lie sleeping through
> many long years, and none can foretell the time when it will awake. ...
>
> And Aragorn planted the new tree in the court by the fountain, and
> swiftly and gladly it began to grow, and when the month of June entered
> it was laden with blossom.
>
> 'The sign has been given,' said Aragorn, 'and the day is not far off.' And
> he set watchmen upon the walls.[54]

Tolkien concludes his essay 'On Fairy-Stories' with the claim that
'Story, fantasy, still go on, and should go on' and that the Christian
'may now, perhaps, fairly dare to guess that in Fantasy he may actually
assist in the effoliation and multiple enrichment of creation'.[55] The
now-familiar metaphor of effoliation (producing leaves) combines
with the metonym of 'the Tree' standing for all creation. The bibli-
cal and religious connotations of Tolkien's work — and, in particular,
his late work — are explicit only intermittently: in his letters and
in the coda to the essay on fantasy, sub-creation and fairy stories.
Throughout all of his work, and with increasing complexity, Tolkien
attempts to express the profound meaning of trees as expressed variously in religious traditions, myth, saga and legend. Verging on the
pagan, and identified with by those who would identify themselves
as more pagan than religious, Tolkien's tree- and forest-love seems at

first to stand in opposition to the Church, which was suspicious of the pagan vestiges that continued 'to haunt the conservative woodlands' with their 'age-old demons, fairies, and nature spirits'. Robert Pogue Harrison notes both the various enjoinders in the Old Testament to destroy the gentile's ritualised sacred groves with prohibitions, such as 'Thou shalt not plant thee a grove of trees near unto the altar of the Lord our God' (Deuteronomy 16:21), and yet the persistence of 'certain elements of pagan culture':

> If certain elements of pagan culture survived the Christian revolution in covert forms ... it was thanks in part to the fact that Christian imperialism did not take it upon itself to burn down the forests in a frenzy of religious fervour ... Fortunately for the forests, and for the ancient folklore they fostered and perpetuated, the Christians did not organize crusades ... which serves to remind us that, when forests are destroyed ... a preserve of cultural memory also disappears.[56]

Of course, the Old and New Testaments both contain their tree references, from the Old Testament Tree of Knowledge to the Tree of Life in Revelation 22: 'and the leaves of the tree of life are for the healing of the nations' (22:2). In the Christian tradition, Christ is crucified on a tree of death (dead tree) and then, eucatastrophically, becomes the Tree of Life.

Tolkien brings all these elements together, including his very personal view that a tree is a beautiful, albeit fallen, aspect of creation, and his knowledge of legend, saga and fairy story, of which, he claims, the Christian Gospel is a prime example. Perhaps this is why Tolkien insisted that *The Lord of the Rings* was not written for children, for the eucatastrophic stories he tells contain both the most dreadful possibilities (death) and the most joyful elements: creation; sub-creation; re-creation.

Notes

1. Richard Hayman, *Trees: Woodlands and Western Civilization* (London: Palgrave Macmillan, 2003): 202.
2. J. R. R. Tolkien, *Tree and Leaf* (1964; London: HarperCollins, 2001): 13, 19.
3. J. R. R. Tolkien, *Smith of Wootton Major* (1967; London: HarperCollins, 2005): 10.
4. William Gray, *Fantasy, Myth and the Measure of Truth* (London: Palgrave Macmillan 2009): 68.
5. Ibid.: 69.

6. Roger Sale, 'Fairy Tales', *The Hudson Review*, 30(3) (Autumn 1977): 372–94, at 382, and see Tolkien, *Tree and Leaf*: 32–3.

7. J. R. R. Tolkien, *The Letters of J. R. R. Tolkien*, ed. Humphrey Carpenter with Christopher Tolkien (1981; London: HarperCollins, 2006): 318.

8. See 'Tolkien's Green Time: Environmental Themes in *The Lord of the Rings*', in G. Bassham and E. Bronson (eds), *The Lord of the Rings and Philosophy* (Chicago, IL: Open Court, 2003): 150–64.

9. George MacDonald, *The Golden Key and Other Stories* (1867; Tring: Lion, 1980): 2.

10. J. R. R. Tolkien, *The Hobbit* (1937; London: Houghton Mifflin, 1984): 130.

11. Bruno Bettelheim, *The Uses of Enchantment* (London: Penguin, 1991): 94.

12. Jack Zipes, *The Brothers Grimm: From Enchanted Forests to the Modern World* (London: Routledge, 1988): 45.

13. Tolkien, *The Hobbit*: 154.

14. Zipes: 60.

15. Paul Kocher, *Master of Middle-earth: The achievement of J. R. R. Tolkien* (London: Thames and Hudson, 1972): 3.

16. Ibid.: 11.

17. Tolkien, *Letters*: 419.

18. Kocher; photograph by Snowdon.

19. Humphrey Carpenter, *Tolkien: A Biography* (London: Houghton Mifflin, 1997).

20. Tolkien, *Letters*: 220.

21. Cited in Michael Perlman, *The Power of Trees: The Reforesting of the Soul* (London: Spring Publications, 1994): 175.

22. Tolkien, *Letters*: 63, 73, 107.

23. See, for example, J. R. R. Tolkien, *The Fellowship of the Ring* (London: Allen & Unwin, 1966): 434.

24. Ibid.: 374.

25. J. R. R. Tolkien, *The Return of the King* (London: Allen & Unwin, 1966): 375.

26. Tolkien, *Tree and Leaf*: v.

27. Kocher: 162.

28. Tolkien, *Letters*: 297, 321, 321.

29. Tolkien, *Tree and Leaf*: 94.

30. Tolkien, *Letters*: 321.

31. Tolkien, *Tree and Leaf*: 109.

32. Cited in Carpenter, *Tolkien: A Biography*: 126.

33. Tolkien, *Tree and Leaf*: 56, 57.

34. Ibid.: 19.

35. Tolkien, *The Hobbit*: 127, and see Bettelheim: 94.

36. Ibid.: 91.

37. Ibid.: 117, 124, 126.

38. Tolkien, *Letters*: 429, 297.

39. Tolkien, *Tree and Leaf*: 45.
40. J. R. R. Tolkien, *The Two Towers* (London: Allen & Unwin, 1966): 83.
41. Tolkien, *Letters*: 419–20.
42. Tolkien, *Tree and Leaf*: 66.
43. Perlman: 3.
44. Michael Pollan, *Second Nature: A Gardener's Education* (London: Grove Press, 1991): 88.
45. Tolkien, *The Two Towers*: 109, 287.
46. To Rhona Beare, unsent draft continuation of a letter; Tolkien, *Letters*: 277.
47. Ibid.: 180–81.
48. Tolkien, *The Two Towers*: 156.
49. Ibid.: 77.
50. Gaston Bachelard, cited in Perlman: 127.
51. Tolkien, *Letters*: 172.
52. Ibid.: 394.
53. Tolkien, *Tree and Leaf*: 71, 72.
54. J. R. R. Tolkien, *The Two Towers* (London: HarperCollins, [1981], 2006): 72.
55. Tolkien, *Tree and Leaf*: 73.
56. Robert Pogue Harrison, *Forests: The Shadow of Civilization* (Chicago, IL: University of Chicago Press, 1992): 62.

10

From Illustration to Film: Visual Narratives and Target Audiences

Kate Harvey

The afterlife of Tolkien's *The Hobbit* and *The Lord of the Rings* has been composed primarily of adaptations and embellishments set firmly in specific visual media, and this essay will consider the ways in which these adaptations address their target audiences through visual narrative. The analysis is divided into four sections: illustrated editions, focusing on Alan Lee's illustrations for *The Lord of the Rings* (1991) and *The Hobbit* (1997);[1] cinema animation – Ralph Bakshi's animated adaptation of the first half of *The Lord of the Rings* (1979);[2] computer graphics – *Hobbit* computer game released by Beam Software in 1982, and the graphic novel, in particular David Wenzel and Charles Dixon's adaptation of *The Hobbit* (1991), illustrated by David Wenzel;[3] and mainstream cinematic adaptations – Peter Jackson's film trilogy (2001–3).[4] This essay is not concerned with cataloguing the changes made to Tolkien's novels in adaptation, as this has been amply addressed elsewhere, particularly in relation to Peter Jackson's films.[5] The focus instead is on the methods used by adapters to address specific audiences through a range of visual media. As we shall see, in each of these adaptations, the visual narrative conveys assumptions about the age and level of sophistication of the reader or viewer. Illustration and animation are widely assumed to appeal primarily to young children, graphic novels and computer games overtly target pre-teen males, while large budget films, like Peter Jackson's, attempt to cast their net as widely as possible, in the hope of being seen as 'family films'. The visual styles of the adaptations discussed here have occasionally proven difficult to categorise, as they are in constant dialogue with each other, with each text carrying visual traces of its predecessors, ranging from unintentional allusions to deliberate homages. For example, Wenzel, Dixon and Deming's graphic novel *Hobbit* contains images that are near-exact reproductions of Tolkien's own illustrations for the earliest editions of *The Hobbit*. The positions of Alan Lee and John Howe as artistic consultants on Peter Jackson's films mean that there is a great deal of crossover, visually, between these films and the editions of Tolkien's novels illustrated by Lee and Howe. Meanwhile, Jackson himself deliberately replicated some of the shots in Ralph Bakshi's film as a homage to his cinematic predecessor. Additionally, each of the adaptations discussed in this essay addresses Tolkien's own view of the novels as speculative histories, rather than works of fantasy.

Illustrated editions

A number of artists have produced illustrations of Tolkien's works since their initial publication, with varying degrees of success; this section will focus on the editions illustrated by Alan Lee, partly because his are the most well-known, but also because it is difficult to look at Lee's illustrations now without seeing them through the lens of his work on Peter Jackson's films. However, it is necessary to bear in mind that Lee's illustrations are produced with an eye to a fundamentally different audience than is his work on the films, and that the production of an illustrated edition of a canonical work carries with it a distinct set of assumptions about the implied reader. Of course, Tolkien himself had produced a great deal of artwork for early editions of *The Hobbit*, which was later repackaged for calendars, postcards, and other memorabilia. Indeed, though I am in part concerned with the dialogic relationship between the imagery in the various visual adaptations of the novels, it is also worth pointing out that one set of images has been replicated almost without alteration in every single adaptation discussed here: Tolkien's maps of Middle-earth. This points to another common thread – namely, the emphasis on setting and location. Over half of Lee's colour plates (29 out of 50) for *The Lord of the Rings* depict specific settings, and the remaining 21 plates all have a strong sense of location within the world of Middle-earth.

Because illustration is associated with a young readership, such illustrated editions tend to be marketed to children and placed in children's sections of libraries and bookstores. Or it is perhaps more accurate to say that they are marketed as gift editions, to parents and older relatives eager to pass on their love of Middle-earth to their offspring in an ostensibly accessible format. In this respect, editions such as Lee's have a great deal in common with illustrated editions of the works of Shakespeare or of 'classic' fairy tales, in which illustrations are used to clarify, rather than complement, the text. Unlike adaptations in other media, an illustrated edition keeps the text intact, enabling it to be advertised as 'complete', 'unabridged', or 'authoritative'. This means that although some Tolkien-lovers may be wary of presenting an abridged or adapted version to their children, illustrated editions such as Lee's can be seen as a 'safe' format through which to introduce young readers to beloved literary classics. Lee's illustrated edition of *The Hobbit* seems even more pointedly to be aimed at younger children: it includes proportionately more colour plates than its three-volume sequel, as well as black-and-white drawings at the start of each chapter and interspersed throughout the text. Furthermore, the content of the illustrations includes a smaller proportion of depictions of locations and landscapes, focusing more frequently on characters and action scenes.

Cinema animation

Several critics have commented on the surge in popularity of *The Lord of the Rings* in the late 1960s; Frieda Riggs is among those who speculate that the novel's 'use of fantasy to represent the conflict between good and evil coalesced with a particular consciousness, one which was becoming aware of social inequality and injustice',[6] and Riggs and others have drawn parallels between the hobbits' pipe-smoking and various popular mind-altering substances.[7] Ralph Bakshi's film has not found favour with Tolkien enthusiasts, who have been disappointed with the adaptation of the novel into what they perceive as a more simplistic, childlike medium, or with fellow animators, who have regarded Bakshi's use of the rotoscoping technique, in which live-action footage is traced and converted frame-by-frame into animation, as something of a betrayal to animation as an art form. John Canemaker's remarks are typical:

> [i]n its heavy reliance on traced-over live action footage, the film displays an unbelievable distrust in the medium of animation. Bakshi shot the entire film in live action first and then a staff of 'tracers' (they do not even deserve the designation of animators) worked over the footage.[8]

Riggs notes that this animation technique is in keeping with Bakshi's vision for the film:

> The choice of subject for his film was a criticism of the status quo, an attempt to play a part in altering the reactionary nature of the pre-1960s society. In his own field, he needed to wrest the ring from the Disney-dominated world of animation and throw it into the fire; and he did this

by reinventing an old technique – rotoscoping – and using it in a new and personal way.[9]

Part of the problem may have been with the assumptions made about the age and level of sophistication of the stereotypical viewer of animated film. There is therefore a tension present in Bakshi's project from the outset, in that while animation is traditionally viewed as a medium designed to appeal to young children, Bakshi himself is known as the animator 'who turned a child's medium into something more serious and ambitious' with 'adult' animations like *Fritz the Cat* (1972) and *Heavy Traffic* (1973).[10] Indeed, many of the characters resemble cartoon archetypes – Aragorn is made to resemble a He-Man-style action hero, while Galadriel is figured as a fairy-godmother type. Additionally, the medium of animation itself, although it seems appropriate to a fantasy story at first glance, in fact serves to distance the viewer from the story and limit identification with the characters. This can be seen from the opening sequence, in which voice-over narration tells the history of Sauron and the rings of power over a stylised shadow play, which traces the ring's journey from its forging to the beginning of *Lord of the Rings*. Although the voice-over warns the viewer of the dangers of the ring and Sauron's power, the shadow play reinforces the idea of the story as just that, a legend to be played out in dumb show, in contrast to Tolkien's insistence on foregrounding the story as history rather than fiction. Perhaps this is because, in contrast to Tolkien's historical view of his work, animation as a narrative medium has been assumed to go hand in hand with stories which involve fantasy, magic, and transformation. Animator John Halas claims that

> [t]he purest form of visual expression is where the least physical restrictions exist, in animated film. Drawn film can break away completely from physical nature and devote itself to free expression in the purest pictorial terms. Animation also has the advantage that it is not chained to the optical eye of the photographic camera, which automatically reflects reality. It can penetrate easily to examine the physical world, and can visualise the invisible.[11]

In keeping with this philosophy, Stan Hayward's article 'Scriptwriting for Animation' specifically instructs would-be animators not to 'make images conform to the laws of a real physical world'.[12] Bakshi's film capitalises on this in the sequences involving magic, such as Bilbo and then Frodo putting on the ring and becoming invisible, Gandalf's battle with the Balrog or Galadriel's description of herself as an imposing Queen. Each of these instances in the animated film is potentially alienating to the viewer, drawing attention to the medium itself and placing the viewer at a remove from the story.

Similarly, the idea that Bakshi's team did no more than trace the live-action frames is misleading, as changes are inevitably made in the process of conversion, so that the finished product is something of a hybrid: not quite animation but not quite live action either. However, Canemaker's last claim is partially correct, as Bakshi made a point of hiring painters rather than professional animators to convert the live-action footage into an animated film. Bakshi has defended his choice of medium, claiming, 'The Lord of the Rings ... is not a comic book. It is realistic. But it wouldn't be believable either in live action with people dressed up in Orc suits, or as a standard cartoon.'[13] The question of 'believability' is one that seems to be at the heart of visual adaptations of Tolkien's Middle-earth, and a great deal of the negative response to Bakshi's film has revolved around its lack of realism. The desire to attribute realism to an animated film is surprising, and is perhaps partly a result of the use of live-action footage, which may have led some to believe (mistakenly) that realism was Bakshi's primary goal. Paul Gray writes:

> The live actor-models flicker like ghosts behind a thin wash of colour, and the viewer feels an urge to apply a damp cloth and see what is really going on ... This technique turns Frodo, the wizard Gandalf and the other main characters into simplified humans. Their personalities do not come from within but from behind, and they rarely seem anything other than what they are: acrylic images superimposed on something more real.[14]

However, film theorists have long noted that the distinction between live-action and animated cinema is not as clear-cut as it may seem. Discussing the tensions inherent in animated film, Yuri M. Lotman observes:

> In our cultural perception a photograph is a substitute for nature and as such we ascribe to it an identity with the object ... If motion naturally harmonises with [the] essential naturalness of a photograph then, by the same token, it conflicts with the artificiality of a drawn or painted image.[15]

Rotoscoping is one of the many ways in which animation can be made to simulate live-action filmmaking, and vice-versa.[16] In a sense, then, Bakshi's film has a somewhat ambiguous status: not quite animation, but not quite live action, and likewise not quite a children's film but not quite a film for adults either.

This extends to the content of the film as well as its form. In many ways, the film seems designed for a child audience. The four hobbits are figured as children, presumably in order to give the implied child viewer a set of characters with whom to identify. Throughout the film they are both guided and contained by the parental figures of Gandalf and Aragorn. When Gandalf explains to Frodo that the ring must be destroyed, he gives little by way of a reason, except to tell Frodo that the Ring is evil and corrupts its wearer, at which point Frodo gasps and brings his hands to his face. The screenplay also has Gandalf orchestrating even the smallest details of Frodo's journey, instructing him even on the particulars of what to tell his neighbours so as to arouse less suspicion. The hobbits constantly experience a withholding of information on the part of the designated authority figures like Gandalf, Aragorn, and Elrond. When Frodo and Sam are joined by Merry and Pippin, the four hobbits are shown skipping down a path, playing musical instruments and singing, apparently blissfully unaware of any impending danger; when they meet Aragorn in Bree he argues with the landlord over the proper course of action, but the hobbits do not seem to have any say in the decision and are given very little agency. Throughout the journey they are shown to be entirely dependent on the more 'adult' characters. When Frodo awakens in Rivendell, Gandalf chastises him like a disappointed father for his behaviour since they last met. The implication here is that the grown-ups will be handling things from now on.

Frodo is shown maturing as the film goes on, and in this respect it conforms to a traditional coming-of-age narrative. As we shall see, a similar narrative logic governs Peter Jackson's films. There is also a diminished sense of actual peril in Bakshi's presentation of potentially distressing images. For example, the hobbits' first encounter with the Black Riders is accompanied by light-hearted music so that there is never any real doubt as to the outcome. However, the film ends on a note of uncertainty, which is somewhat unsettling. The theatrical release ended with the voice-over narrator inviting viewers to return to the cinema to see the conclusion of the story. However, once it became clear that the second part would not be made, the video release replaced this teaser with an assurance that good has triumphed over evil, which directly contradicts what the viewer has just seen.

Computer graphics and the graphic novel

While the primary focus of this section is on Wenzel, Dixon and Deming's graphic novel, Beam Software's 1982 PC game is also worth mentioning, as they seem to target similar audiences. It is curious that both of these are adaptations of *The Hobbit* and not *The Lord of the Rings* (although Beam Software did follow up with the less successful two-part *Lord of the Rings* game, released in 1986 and 1987), and this suggests that their creators have similar perceptions about the tastes of their target audience of pre-teen boys. This is in keeping with the idea that *The Lord of the Rings* is a book for adults while *The Hobbit* is a children's book. However, it is worth noting that Dixon, Deming and Wenzel's graphic novel has more in common with graphic novel and comic book adaptations of canonical literature than it does with original graphic novels aimed at this demographic, in that it is presented as an 'introduction' from which the reader will eventually graduate to the 'real' text. This can be seen in the language of the promotional material on the back cover, which boasts, 'Illustrated in full colour throughout, and accompanied by the carefully abridged text of the original novel, this handsome authorised edition will introduce new generations to a magical masterpiece – and be treasured by Hobbit fans of all ages, everywhere.'[17] The privileging of the 'original novel', which has been 'carefully abridged' and 'authorised', implies that the graphic novel is designed on the one hand to inspire the 'new generation' to read Tolkien's novel and on the other not to offend those who are already 'Hobbit fans'. Crucially, it is not anticipated, as it was with Jackson's and (perhaps to a lesser extent) Bakshi's films, that the adaptation will be read as a stand-alone text, or appeal to readers who have no interest in the source text. This suggests that although Dixon, Deming and Wenzel are adapting Tolkien's supposedly more child-friendly text, there is an implicit assumption being made about Tolkien's own place in the canon.

Both the computer game and the graphic novel call for a greater degree of interaction with the text on the part of the reader than do their verbal counterparts. The computer game is frequently cited as among the first examples of what has become known as 'emergent gameplay', in that non-player characters have independent personalities and interact with each other in ways that are not predictable and can alter the outcome of the game for the player, creating seemingly infinite in-game scenarios and encouraging repeat plays. Developer Veronika Megler explains,

> it was not deterministic, and the game played differently every time you played it … Literally, the player had a turn, then each animal had a turn, and the animals just 'played' the game themselves according to their character profile, which included interacting with each other. In essence, the

animals would do to each other anything that they could do to or with you. So we would constantly have animals interacting in ways that had never been progammed or envisioned ... For a while, we had terrible trouble with all the animals showing up in one location and then killing each other before you got there.[18]

The game is designed to play out in real time, so that the narrative continues even when the player is not physically present. A parallel can therefore be drawn between the comparative level of sophistication of the game and the conventions of the graphic novel and comic book, which, Charles Hatfield observes, 'are not mere visual displays that encourage inert spectatorship but rather texts that require a reader's active engagement and collaboration in making meaning'.[19] The narrative properties of both the graphic novel and the computer game therefore require a sophisticated and specialised skill set to read them, despite perceptions of the medium as being somehow easy or simplified.

A persistent problem in graphic novel and comic book adaptations of works which are designated literary classics is that of translating the text from an almost exclusively verbal medium to one which is predominantly visual. There seems to be a need among adapters to fit as much of the source text as possible onto each page, despite the fact that graphic novels communicate their meanings more effectively when they are told with a minimum of words, as the visual narrative should be sufficient to convey relevant story and character information. This wordiness is not surprising, as adapters tend to approach their projects as fans, and therefore want to include as much of the writing they admire as possible. However, the result is frequently large blocks of text, either in speech bubbles or in narrative captions, which leave little room for visual storytelling. Additionally, so much information is packed into the text blocks that the images can appear redundant. For example, in Wenzel, Dixon and Deming's adaptation, the first page is devoted to Tolkien's opening description of hobbits, in five panels. The first two panels feature establishing images of The Hill and of Bilbo's hole, the next two a medium and then a close-up of Bilbo, sitting outside and smoking his pipe, and the last depicts Bilbo startled at Gandalf's arrival (although Gandalf is neither mentioned nor shown until the following page). However, the majority of the space in each panel is given over to text boxes, each of which features a different segment of Tolkien's opening paragraphs including, in the third panel, his physical description of hobbits:

What is a hobbit?
    I suppose hobbits need some description nowadays, since they have become rare and shy of the Big People, as they call us.

> They are a little people, smaller than dwarves. They are inclined to
> be fat in the stomach; they dress in bright colours and wear no shoes,
> because their feet grow natural leathery soles and thick warm brown
> hair.[20]

Admirable as this passage may be, it is entirely redundant when positioned opposite an image of Bilbo, which allows the reader to see
that hobbits are small and fat, that they dress in bright colours, and
that they have thick hair on their feet in place of shoes. There are
other instances where the images inadequately address the gaps in the
verbal narrative, perhaps a result of insufficient collaboration between
adapter and artist. For example, when Bilbo successfully steals Smaug's
golden cup, we are told that Smaug's 'rage passes description'.[21] This
line seems to be an invitation for the visual narrative to convey what
the verbal narrative cannot, yet the accompanying picture only depicts
Smaug's head and neck, with fire coming out of his mouth. Another
instance where words are relied upon to convey information that
could perhaps be better expressed visually occurs in Bilbo's prophetic
dream just before the group's first encounter with the goblins. Two
texts boxes explain:

> He dreamed that a crack in the wall at the back of the cave got bigger
> and bigger, and opened wider and wider, and he was very afraid but
> could not call out or do anything but lie and look.
>   Then he dreamed that the floor of the cave was giving way, and he was
> slipping – beginning to fall down, goodness knows where to.[22]

Dixon and Deming provide an abridged version of Tolkien's verbal
description of the dream, while Wenzel's images accompanying
these words depict Bilbo sleeping, and then falling; in other words,
the images fail to live up to the possibilities offered by the text and
therefore appear redundant. The sequence, like the graphic novel as
a whole, is disproportionately balanced toward text, when the dream
sequence would seem to be the ideal place to give full scope to an
artist's imagination.

Mainstream cinema

It should be clear at this point that the best-known visual adaptation
of *The Lord of the Rings* to date, Peter Jackson's film trilogy, cannot
be seen as a stand-alone event, as it consistently draws on what came
before. Despite having some reservations about the adaptation itself,

Victoria Gaydosik concludes that Jackson's films confirm, rather than erode, Tolkien's status:

> Tolkien wanted to create an original mythology, and to the extent that myths are the stories that keep being told and retold and adapted to new techniques of telling, I think that Peter Jackson's adaptation of Tolkien's masterwork stands as a testimony to the novel's enduring value while also helping to guarantee its survival and extending its influence to new generations of enthusiasts.[23]

Thus Jackson's film can in many ways be seen as a visual palimpsest of everything that came before it. An avid admirer of Bakshi's (Jackson reportedly saw Bakshi's film before he had read Tolkien's novels),[24] Jackson pays homage to his predecessor in several recreated shots, perhaps most noticeably in the image of the four hobbits hiding in the roots of a tree to escape the Nazgul. In addition, as discussed above, concept artists Lee and Howe, who are largely responsible for the 'look' of the films, have also produced what is perhaps the most well-known artwork inspired by the novel; both were hand-picked by Jackson to work on the film because he admired their artwork.[25] Kristin Thompson and others have commented on the 'fairly common reaction among readers, who often claimed that the film had captured their own mental images of Middle-earth';[26] it should not come as a surprise that the design of the film should adhere so closely to the Middle-earth imagined by readers when the film's concept artists had themselves 'given countless readers concrete notions of what Middle-earth looked like'.[27]

While the graphic novel and computer game adaptations were aimed at an audience consisting of pre-teen boys, the ideal audience of Jackson's films included children and adults, as well as Tolkien fans and those who had never read the novels. As such, the films speak to the then newly-identified genre of 'crossover' films, as film producers apparently discovered a new way of marketing fantasy films as appealing both to adults and to children. (This is not to suggest that films with crossover appeal did not exist previously; rather that such films had hitherto rarely been recognised to be marketable as such.)

The films capitalise on what Geoff Lealand has termed 'the "inheritance" factor: the desire of many parents to pass on their enthusiasm for Tolkien's heady mixture of fantasy and repudiation of modernity to their offspring'.[28] There is a paradox here: while Thompson asserts, 'The fact that *Rings* attracted many adults and won many Oscars, however, should not obscure that it was of necessity aimed primarily at a teenage and young adult audience,'[29] Lealand notes that 'very little child-related merchandising has accompanied the films, in contrast with the Harry Potter films', concluding that the heavy merchandising often cited as targeting children is in fact aimed at 'adults who like to collect and acquire'.[30] This lack of consensus among critics suggests that the films were in fact courting a dual audience. Despite the popularity of Jackson's films over a range of ages and levels of experience, the fantasy genre remains associated with a young audience, and the word 'childish' is thrown around as a descriptor, usually with pejorative connotations. Thompson's comments are telling in this respect; while her criticism of the films is largely positive, she still contrasts the film's prestigious award nominations with its appeal to young adults, implying on some level that prestige and a young audience are not natural companions. Additionally, many of Jackson's detractors include some pejorative reference to the films as childish, simplistic, or naïve, frequently coupled with implications that the story has been 'dumbed down' in order to achieve its mass appeal, which reveal more about the prejudices of the commenters than they do about the films themselves. David Bratman, for example, relates an anecdote from author Michael Swanwick, in which the latter describes reading the novels to his nine-year-old son and realising 'that the story the boy was hearing was not the same as the one he was reading. To the boy, it was just an exciting adventure story, but to the man it was ever so much more.'[31] Bratman concludes, 'Peter Jackson has a nine-year-old's understanding of Tolkien. I expect more than that.'[32] Not only is 'a nine-year-old's understanding of Tolkien' assumed to be insufficient and of less value than that of an adult, but the idea that a nine-year-old audience should be addressed at all is presented as a disappointment. This is symptomatic of a wider failure of most of the scholarship surrounding these films to view them on their own terms.

The question then becomes, what can the film medium add to the story that other media cannot accomplish, and what strategies do the films use to address its hoped-for 'crossover' audience? Thompson argues for seeing the films not as imperfect translations of an 'original', but 'as a very elaborate sort of illustration of the book',[33] and indeed the aspect of the films that is consistently praised, even by their detractors, is their visual style. Indeed, the film has become a prime example of what David Bordwell has termed 'world-building',[34] which is closely related to Tolkien's own term, 'sub-creation', which has become a staple of the vocabulary of the fantasy genre. Tolkien writes that a sub-creator

> makes a Secondary World that your mind can enter. Inside it, what he relates is 'true': it accords with the laws of that world. You therefore

believe in it, while you are, as it were, inside. The moment disbelief arises, the spell is broken; the magic, or rather, the art, has failed.[35]

For Jackson's team, if the Middle-earth onscreen did not ring true or conform to readers' expectations, the film would have been considered to have failed.

In addition to pointing out the differences between book and film, another favourite practice of critics has been detailing the great lengths to which the design team went to ensure a fully realised, complete Middle-earth, including individually hand-crafted props in a variety of sizes depending on which characters were to handle them, down to the thickness of the fabric.[36] Jackson also put a great deal of effort into the creatures that would inhabit his Middle-earth, which can of course be traced to his background directing horror films. However, Jackson's ground-breaking use of computer graphics in manufacturing these creatures also points to another similarity between the projects of Jackson and Bakshi, in that the film is in the end a hybrid of animation and live-action. Indeed, the films' award-winning use of performance-capture technology to create the character of Gollum is directly analogous to Bakshi's widely condemned use of rotoscoping, in that both processes involve converting the performance of a live actor into an animated character in order to attain a higher degree of realism in the character's movements.

Thompson has pointed out how Jackson's film 'mixes conventions of several popular genres into its overarching fantasy structures' in order to speak to a wide range of cinemagoers,[37] while Lealand suggests that Jackson's hobbits, like Bakshi's, are more childlike than their literary counterparts and 'by default, represent ideas of children and childhood in the films'.[38] Lealand suggests that this enables the film to address a younger audience than it might otherwise, by treating Frodo and Sam's journey as a coming-of-age narrative:

> Life within the Shire, as Jackson portrays it, is a prolonged state of childhood and innocence and immediate gratification, perpetually sunny days where evil is unknown and the outside world a mystery to be avoided. In many ways, Frodo and Sam's physically fraught journey from the Shire to Mount Doom is their journey from childhood (and, indeed, childishness) to adulthood.[39]

Indeed, an implicit parallel is drawn between the relative size of the hobbits and their childlike innocence from the opening of Jackson's *Fellowship of the Ring*. After the prologue, heavy with foreboding, detailing the history of the ring and the last alliance of men and elves, which ends with Galadriel's voice-over lament that the lessons of history have been forgotten and her prediction that hobbits will shape the future, the tone shifts and we are introduced to life in the Shire, which has gone on seemingly untouched by and oblivious to the conflicts in the outside world. This is reinforced by the hobbits' small stature, as the first Shire scene in the theatrical release depicts Frodo greeting Gandalf in a manner that suggests a son welcoming his father home: Frodo runs up to Gandalf, gives him a big hug, and questions him about his travels. Visually, a combination of camera tricks, body doubles, and forced perspective draws attention to the differences in their size. Jackson's use of forced perspective in the hobbit scenes is not seamless, but rather, deliberately designed to draw attention to the difference in height between the hobbits and the other characters. This is particularly apparent in Gandalf's appearances in Bag End, in which the spectacle of the tall wizard in a space designed for a hobbit is drawn out to comic effect as he is repeatedly shown stooping, knocking things over, and bumping his head on beams and doorframes.

Although, at the time of writing, Jackson's three-part version of *The Hobbit* has yet to be released, it is worth noting for the purposes of this essay that the promotional material so far has likewise seemed to target a double audience. The first official trailer is a similar contrast between the idyllic Shire and the dark and threatening world outside, and includes a sequence of visual gags and pratfalls involving the dwarves which seems to target young viewers. It also courts a somewhat knowing audience, inviting the viewer to recognise the film's relationship to the earlier trilogy, presenting a series of recognisable names and faces with shots of Ian Holm (Old Bilbo), Ian McKellan (Gandalf), Cate Blanchett (Galadriel), and Andy Serkis (Gollum). Indeed, the cast seems to have been designed to include as many familiar faces as possible, regardless of whether or not the character appears in Tolkien's novel, including Elijah Wood (Frodo), Orlando Bloom (Legolas), Hugo Weaving (Elrond), Christopher Lee (Saruman), and fan favourite Bret McKenzie (Lindir, aka 'Figwit').[40] In addition to the obvious financial motivations, this decision was also made, presumably, to enhance the sense of continuity between the two sets of films, situating the three *Hobbit* films firmly within the world of Jackson's *Lord of the Rings* trilogy. Furthermore, viewers are encouraged to recognise Martin Freeman (Young Bilbo) in terms of his previous roles; the trailer opens with Bilbo protesting that he is not the type to seek out adventure, connecting the character to Freeman's other reluctant adventurers, such as Arthur Dent (in *The*

Hitchhiker's Guide to the Galaxy, 2005) and Dr Watson (in *Sherlock*, 2010). The film's status as a prequel creates an interesting dynamic in the trailer, as a great deal of weight is given to Gollum and to the finding of the ring, seeming to promise that the two films will have resonances beyond the 'there-and-back-again' adventure of the story's source material.

Thomas Leitch and others have discussed the problems inherent in judging adaptations in terms of fidelity to their source material; Leitch concludes:

> it should be clear now that fidelity itself, even as a goal, is the exception to the norm of variously unfaithful adaptations. Instead of constantly seeking answers to the question, 'Why are so many adaptations unfaithful to perfectly good sources?' adaptation studies would be better advised to ask the question, 'Why does this particular adaptation aim to be faithful?'[41]

As John Stephens and Robyn McCallum have pointed out, when it comes to adaptations of canonical texts for a child audience, it is precisely at the point of infidelity that it becomes clear how retold stories 'serve to initiate children into aspects of a social heritage, transmitting many of a culture's central values and assumptions and a body of shared allusions and experiences'.[42] Indeed, the visual medium chosen for adaptation has significant implications in terms of who the implied reader is and how this reader is addressed. Adapters can reproduce these assumptions about the consumer of a particular medium, or they can subvert them. The advent of Web 2.0 and 'meme' culture has inspired a range of user-generated content on sites such as Youtube, Tumblr, and Memebase, most of which incorporate images from Jackson's film. These are essentially adaptations of an adaptation, in which specific moments are broken down and reassembled into new creations. One popular 'meme' has been Boromir's line 'One does not simply walk into Mordor', which is adapted as a caption and used to make a cultural reference ('One does not simply warp into Mordor'; 'One does not silly walk into Mordor') or to provide commentary on a range of subjects ('One does not simply sue the Oatmeal'; 'One does not simply ask girls what they're thinking'; 'One does not simply stop procrastinating'). On Youtube, there are creatively edited techno mixes of Sam and Gollum's argument over potatoes, Legolas's 'They're taking the hobbits to Isengard', and Gandalf's 'You shall not pass',[43] as well as a wealth of re-edits, parodies, animations, and amateur reviews. In light of these online reconfigurations, it is interesting to speculate about the direction in which visual adaptations of Tolkien's work might be going.

However, it is perhaps inappropriate even to read these as versions of Tolkien; rather, Jackson's creations are being used as intertextual cultural referents. Fans of Tolkien's novels and of Jackson's films have come to refer to themselves as 'book-firsters' or 'film-firsters', depending on how they first came to the stories, and this egalitarian view of adaptation and source may be an indication of the reference points of the next generation of Tolkien adapters. Adaptation of Tolkien is still a relatively young genre compared with the long tradition of adapting classic or canonical texts for different audiences, and it remains to be seen what will happen when those adapting Tolkien for young readers are further removed from his original readership.

Notes

1. J. R. R. Tolkien, *The Lord of the Rings*, illus. Alan Lee (London: HarperCollins, 1991); *The Hobbit*, illus. Alan Lee (London: HarperCollins, 1997).
2. Ralph Bakshi (dir.), *The Lord of the Rings* (United Artists, 1978).
3. Charles Dixon and Sean Deming, *The Hobbit; or, There and Back Again*, illus. David Wenzel (London: HarperCollins, 1991).
4. Peter Jackson (dir.), *The Fellowship of the Ring* (New Line, 2001); *The Two Towers* (New Line, 2002); *The Return of the King* (New Line, 2003).
5. Janet Brennan Croft (ed.), *Tolkien on Film: Essays on Peter Jackson's 'The Lord of the Rings'* (Altadena, CA: The Mythopoeic Press, 2004). See also Tom Shippey, 'From Page to Screen: J. R. R. Tolkien and Jackson', *World Literature Today*, 77 (2003): 69–72, and 'Another Road to Middle Earth: Jackson's Movie Trilogy', in *Roots and Branches: Selected Papers on Tolkien by Tom Shippey* ([n.p.]: Walking Tree, 2007): 365–86; John D. Rateliff, 'Two Kinds of Absence: Elision and Exclusion in Peter Jackson's *The Lord of the Rings*', in *Picturing Tolkien: Essays on Peter Jackson's 'The Lord of the Rings' Film Trilogy*, ed. Janice M. Bogstad and Philip E. Kaveny (Jefferson, NC, and London: McFarland, 2011): 54–69.
6. Frieda Riggs, 'The Infinite Quest: Husserl, Bakshi, the Rotoscope and the Ring', in *The Illusion of Life II: More Essays on Animation*, ed. Alan Cholodenko (Sydney: Power Publications, 2007): 243–71, at 248.
7. Paul Gray, 'Frodo Moves', *Time*, 20 November 1978: 98; Rateliff, 'Two Kinds of Absence': 56; Kristin Thompson, *The Frodo Franchise: 'The Lord of the Rings' and Modern Hollywood* (Berkeley: University of California Press, 2007): 7.
8. Quoted in Riggs: 253.
9. Ibid.: 250.
10. James Craig Holte, 'Ethnicity and the Popular Imagination: Ralph Bakshi and the American Dream', *Melus*, 8 (1981): 106.
11. John Halas, 'Introduction', in *Visual Scripting*, ed. John Halas (London: Focal Press, 1976): 6–10, at 8.

12. Stan Hayward, 'Scriptwriting for Animation: The Basic Approach', in *Visual Scripting*, ed. John Halas (London: Focal Press, 1976): 21–30, at 27.
13. Quoted in Aljean Harmetz, 'Bakshi Journeys to Middle Earth to Animate "Lord of the Rings"', *New York Times*, 8 November 1978: C17.
14. Gray: 98.
15. Yuri M. Lotman, 'On the Language of Animated Cartoons', trans. Ruth Sobel, in *Film Theory and General Semiotics*, ed. L. M. O'Toole and Ann Shukman, Russian Poetics in Translation (Oxford: [n. pub.], 1981): 36–9, at 36–7.
16. For a fuller theoretical discussion of the relationship of animation to live-action cinema, see Edward Small and Eugene Levinson, 'Toward a Theory of Animation', *The Velvet Light Trap: Review of Cinema*, 24 (1989): 67–74.
17. Dixon and Deming: back cover.
18. Quoted in 'The Hobbit and His Lady', *L'avventura è l'avventura*, www.avventuretestuali.com/interviste/megler-eng.
19. Charles Hatfield, *Alternative Comics: An Emerging Literature* (Jackson: University of Mississippi Press, 2005): 33.
20. Dixon and Deming: 1.
21. Ibid.: 102.
22. Ibid.: 32.
23. Victoria Gaydosik, '"Crimes against the Book"? The Transformation of Tolkien's Arwen from Page to Screen and the Abandonment of the Psyche Archetype', in Janet Brennan Croft (ed.), *Tolkien on Film: Essays on Peter Jackson's 'The Lord of the Rings'* (Altadena, CA: The Mythopoeic Press, 2004): 215–30, at: 229.
24. Rateliff: 58.
25. Thompson, *The Frodo Franchise*: 86–7.
26. Ibid.: 88.
27. Ibid.: 87.
28. Geoff Lealand, '*The Return of the King* and the Child Audience', in *Studying the Event Film: 'The Lord of the Rings'*, ed. Harriet Margolis, Sean Cubitt, Barry King and Thierry Jutel (Manchester: Manchester University Press, 2008): 65–73, at 69.
29. Thompson: 53–4.
30. Lealand: 70.
31. David Bratman, 'Summa Jacksonica: A Reply to Defenses of Peter Jackson's *The Lord of the Rings* Films, after St. Thomas Aquinas', in Janet Brennan Croft (ed.), *Tolkien on Film: Essays on Peter Jackson's 'The Lord of the Rings'* (Altadena, CA: The Mythopoeic Press, 2004): 27–62, at 31.
32. Ibid.
33. Kristin Thompson, 'Gollum Talks to Himself: Problems and Solutions in Peter Jackson's *The Lord of the Rings*', in *Picturing Tolkien: Essays on Peter Jackson's 'The Lord of the Rings' Film Trilogy*, ed. Janice M. Bogstad and Philip E. Kaveny (Jefferson, NC, and London: McFarland, 2011): 25–45, at 26.
34. See David Bordwell, *The Way Hollywood Tells It* (Berkeley: University of California Press, 2006): 58–9.

35. J. R. R. Tolkien, 'On Fairy-stories', quoted in Sharin Schroeder, "'It's Alive!" Tolkien's Monster on the Screen', in *Picturing Tolkien: Essays on Peter Jackson's 'The Lord of the Rings' Film Trilogy*, ed. Janice M. Bogstad and Philip E. Kaveny (Jefferson, NC, and London: McFarland, 2011): 116–38, at 132.

36. See especially, Thompson, *The Frodo Franchise*, and Harriet Margolis, Sean Cubitt, Barry King, and Thierry Jutel (eds), *Studying the Event Film: 'The Lord of the Rings'* (Manchester: Manchester University Press, 2008).

37. Thompson: 57.

38. Lealand: 67.

39. Ibid: 68.

40. 'The Hobbit: An Unexpected Journey (2012): Full Cast and Crew', *The Internet Movie Database*, www.imdb.com/title/tt0903624/fullcredits#cast (accessed 29 July 2012).

41. Thomas Leitch, *Film Adaptation and its Discontents: From 'Gone with the Wind' to 'The Passion of the Christ'* (Baltimore, MD: Johns Hopkins University Press, 2007): 127.

42. John Stephens and Robyn McCallum, *Retelling Stories, Framing Cultures: Traditional Stories and Metanarratives in Children's Literature* (New York: Garland, 1998): 3.

43. 'Lord of the rings "Potatoes" Remix', www.youtube.com/watch?v=PXYOzdbep4o (accessed 29 July 2012); 'They're taking the hobbits to Isengard (Original), www.youtube.com/watch?v=nXbCw1U61FU (accessed 29 July 2012); 'YOU SHALL NOT PASS!!!! Techno Remix', www.youtube.com/watch?v=32kN5r-YZFY&feature=fvwrel (accessed 29 July 2012).

Further Reading

Tolkien is at once the 'author of the twentieth century' and a cult figure, and as such, his work has attracted a remarkable range of commentary. Much of the early 'criticism' was praise and defence: as Brian Rosebury put it, 'there is an appearance of industrial production about this steady output of favourably disposed commentaries'. On the other hand, 'the predominant response [until recently] to Tolkien in the academic world has not been hostility. It has been bemused silence' (Brian Rosebury, *Tolkien. A Cultural Phenomenon* (Basingstoke: Palgrave Macmillan, 2003) pp. 2–3).

Some of the earlier books of criticism may be relatively difficult to obtain, but they contain interesting and perceptive papers:

Neil D. Isaacs and Rose A. Zimbardo (eds), *Tolkien and the Critics: Essays on J. R. R. Tolkien's* The Lord of the Rings (Notre Dame, IN: University of Notre Dame Press, 1968), includes Roger Sale's, 'Tolkien and Frodo Baggins' (pp. 247–88) and Edmund Fuller's, 'The Lord of the Hobbits': J. R. R. Tolkien' (pp. 17–39), both pioneering approaches to the books. Other notable articles are Rose Zimbardo's 'Moral Vision in *The Lord of the Rings*' (pp. 100–8), which suggests that Sam can resist the ring because he is a gardener: 'In Sam's dream of power we are given a flash of comic insight into man's moral dilemma' (p. 108); and R. J. Reilly's 'Tolkien and the Fairy Story' (pp. 128–50), which sums up the early critical attacks on Tolkien – such as that by Edmund Wilson: '… certain people … have a lifelong appetite for juvenile trash' [Edmund Wilson, 'Oo, Those Awful Orcs!' *Nation*, CLXXXII (April 14, 1956), pp. 312–314] (p. 133).

Isaacs and Zimbardo later edited *Tolkien: New Critical Perspectives* (Lexington: University Press of Kentucky, 1981), a well-balanced collection. Probably the most interesting essay for children's literature scholars is Lois Kuznets's, 'Tolkien and the Rhetoric of Childhood' (pp. 150–62), in which she argues that Tolkien employs a 'rhetoric of childhood' highly influenced by Carroll, MacDonald, and Grahame, and points out that the seasons of Tolkien's books can be 'specifically equated with developmental cycles' (p. 151).

Paul Kocher's *Master of Middle-Earth: The Achievement of J. R. R. Tolkien* (Harmondsworth: Penguin, 1974) is one of the earliest book-length treatments, and although its untheorised critical approach may seem dated, it remains readable and incisive.

Also worthwhile:

Robert Giddings (ed.), *J. R. R. Tolkien: This Far Land* (London: Vision Press, 1983); an assured collection, including the urbane Fred Inglis's, 'Gentility and Powerlessness: Tolkien and the New Class' (pp. 23–41).

David Harvey, *The Song of Middle Earth: J. R. R. Tolkien's Themes, Symbols and Myths* (London: George Allen & Unwin, 1983); an example of a now unfashionable mode of criticism that takes the created world as real.

On Tolkien's life

Humphrey Carpenter, *J. R. R. Tolkien: A Biography* (1978; London: HarperCollins, 2002). This definitive biography draws upon Tolkien's writing, private papers, and interviews. It offers a useful background but, since Carpenter rarely names his sources for specific quotations and facts, scholars will usually need to search out the original sources on their own.

J. R. R. Tolkien, *The Letters of J. R. R. Tolkien*, edited by Humphrey Carpenter with Christopher Tolkien (London: HarperCollins, 1981). This indispensable selection of Tolkien's personal letters gives insight into his correspondence with his family, friends, publishers, colleagues, fellow writers, and fans. The earliest letters included are from 1914, while he was still an undergraduate, and the last letter in the collection was written four days before his death. The volume includes notes and a detailed index.

Also:

John Garth, *Tolkien and the Great War: The Threshold to Middle-earth* (London: HarperCollins, reissue, 2011).

Humphrey Carpenter, *The Inklings, C. S. Lewis, J. R. R. Tolkien, Charles Williams, and their Friends* (London: George Allen & Unwin, 1978).

On Tolkien's work

Tolkien may well be unrivalled for the 'comprehensive' reference works devoted to him. Every possible (it might seem) cultural and literary reference in his books is tracked in J. E. A. Taylor's *The Complete Tolkien Companion*, 3rd edn (London: Pan, 2002). But that book's 736 pages pale beside the nearly 1000 pages of Wayne G. Hammond and Christina Scull's *The Lord of the Rings: A Reader's Companion* (London: HarperCollins, 2008), which is in its turn dwarfed by the 2304 pages of Hammond and Scull's *The J. R. R. Tolkien Companion*, 2 vols (London: HarperCollins, 2006).

Possibly the two essential books on Tolkien are Brian Rosebury's *Tolkien: A Cultural Phenomenon* (Basingstoke: Palgrave Macmillan, 2003), which is particularly strong on the critical debate surrounding Tolkien, and Tom Shippey's *The Road to Middle-earth* (1982; London: HarperCollins, 2005). This is a scholarly but accessible study of the literary roots of Tolkien's invented languages and stories. Drawing upon medieval literature and philology, Shippey explores Tolkien's sources before turning to a discussion of *The Silmarillion*, *Unfinished Tales*, and *The History of Middle-earth*, and he points out the gulf that sometimes exists between Tolkien's scholarship and that of his critics.

The ideas are developed and brought into the context of contemporary fantasy in Tom Shippey's *J. R. R. Tolkien: Author of the Century* (London: HarperCollins, new edn, 2010).

Brian Rosebury's 'basic kit' of essential books (Rosebury, p. 221) for Tolkien scholars includes Tolkien's *The Monsters and the Critics and Other*

Essays, ed. Christopher Tolkien (London: HarperCollins, 2006). The seven essays in this volume provide useful insights into Tolkien's academic interests as a medievalist and philologist. 'On Fairy-Stories' offers insight into his thinking about fairy-stories, fantasy, and childhood, and will be useful for any student of *The Hobbit* and *The Lord of the Rings*. It also includes his essay '*Beowulf:* The Monsters and the Critics', which transformed studies of the Anglo-Saxon poem and brought its fantastical elements to critical attention, and an essay on the Arthurian poem *Sir Gawain and the Green Knight*, among others.

In the past decade or so, there have been many specialist studies, to which an excellent guide is Michael D. C. Drout (ed.), *The J. R. R. Tolkien Encyclopedia: Scholarship and Critical Assessment* (New York and London: Routledge, 2007). The list of specialist studies could be extended almost indefinitely; some examples:

Dimitra Fimi, *Tolkien, Race and Cultural History: From Fairies to Hobbits* (Basingstoke: Palgrave Macmillan, 2010); looks at the relationship of Tolkien's mythology to his life and cultural background.

Verlyn Flieger, *Splintered Light: Logos and Language in Tolkien's World* (Bowling Green: Kent State University Press, rev. edn, 2002); Tolkien in his cultural context.

Christopher Garbowski, *Recovery and Transcendence for the Contemporary Mythmaker: The Spiritual Dimension in the Works of J. R. R. Tolkien* (Lublin: Maria Curie-Sklodowska University Press, 2000); psychological and existential discussion of Tolkien and the nature of myth.

William H. Green, *The Hobbit: Journey into Maturity* (New York: Twayne, 1995); a very readable exploration of the psychology of the novel.

Thomas Honegger, *Reconsidering Tolkien* (Zurich: Walking Tree Press, 2005); a serious collection based on an ESSE conference, covering linguistics, medievalism, mythic space, archetypes, shadow as a motif, historical contexts, and a comparison of Tolkien's work with that of poets of the First World War.

Richard Purtill, *J. R. R. Tolkien: Myth, Morality and Religion* (San Francisco: Ignatus Press, 2003); discusses the relationships between *The Lord of the Rings*, Science Fiction, heroism, and different aspects of human nature. A sample: 'The Elves are the artistic, scientific part of humanity, the Hobbits are the home-loving, family-loving, comfort-loving part of human nature' (pp. 72–3).

And two slightly eccentric outings:

Patrick Curry, *Defending Middle-Earth, Tolkien: Myth and Modernity* (London: HarperCollins, 1997); a highly readable, if curiously reactionary, polemic, arguing that *The Lord of the Rings* addresses 'the most important conflict of our time – the struggle of community, nature and spirit against ... state-power, capital and technology'.

Karen Haber (ed.), *Meditations on Middle-Earth* (New York: St Martin's, 2001), is a rich, laid-back collection of essays by popular writers and artists including Terry Pratchett and Ursula K. Le Guin, on when they first encountered *The Lord of the Rings*.

On fantasy in general

This is such a rich field that newcomers might wish to begin with two accomplished overviews:

Farah Mendlesohn and Edward James, *A Short History of Fantasy* (London: Middlesex University Press, 2009).
Edward James and Farah Mendlesohn (eds), *The Cambridge Companion to Fantasy Literature* (Cambridge: Cambridge University Press, 2012).

Two more specialised key texts are:

Brian Attebery's *Strategies of Fantasy* (Bloomington, IN: Indiana University Press, 1992), which argues that fantasy is a viable and important movement in postmodern literature. Attebery defines the genre as a 'fuzzy set' based around Tolkien's *The Lord of the Rings* (rather than delineated by generic boundaries), and draws upon critical theory in his discussions of other fantasy authors. These include some who write for children, such as Ursula K. Le Guin and Diana Wynne Jones.
Farah Mendlesohn's *Rhetorics of Fantasy* (Middletown, CT: Wesleyan University Press, 2008) suggests a classification of fantasy based on four categories: portal-quest, immersive, intrusive, and liminal. Drawing upon works by over 100 authors (including a number of children's fantasy authors), Mendlesohn considers the relationship between style and the category of fantasy in which a text is written.

See also:

Brian Attebery, *The Fantasy Tradition in American Literature: From Irving to Le Guin* (Bloomington, IN: Indiana University Press, 1982).
Kathryn Hume, *Fantasy and Mimesis: Responses to Reality in Western Literature* (New York: Methuen, 1984).
Ursula K. Le Guin, *The Language of the Night: Essays on Fantasy and Science Fiction*, rev edn (New York: HarperCollins, 1992).
C. N. Manlove, *Modern Fantasy: Five Studies* (Cambridge: Cambridge University Press, 1975).
Richard Mathews, *Fantasy: The Liberation of Imagination* (London: Routledge, 2002).
David Pringle (ed.), *The Ultimate Encyclopedia of Fantasy* (London: Carlton, 2006).

On fantasy and children's literature

This is another wide field, and many examples can be found in the *Newcastle Check-List of Books on Children's Literature* at www.ncl.ac.uk/elll/assets/documents/A-Bibliography4.pdf (accessed 29 July 2012).

A good place to start would be C. S Lewis's *Of Other Worlds: Essays and Stories*, ed. Walter Hooper (San Diego: Harcourt, 2002). This accessible collection includes several of Lewis's essays on children, story, and the fantastic. This includes the piece 'On Three Ways of Writing for Children', which will be particularly useful for students of children's fantasy literature and Lewis's Narnia books.

A representative selection of other books:

Matthew Dickerson and David O'Hara, *From Homer to Harry Potter: A Handbook of Myth and Fantasy* (Grand Rapids, MI: Brazos Press, 2006).

Elliott Gose, *Mere Creatures: A Study of Modern Fantasy Tales for Children* (Toronto: University of Toronto Press, 1988).

William Gray, *Death and Fantasy: Essays on Philip Pullman, C. S. Lewis, George MacDonald and R. L. Stevenson* (Newcastle: Cambridge Scholars Press, 2008).

William Gray, *Fantasy, Myth and the Measure of Truth: Tales of Pullman, Lewis, Tolkien, MacDonald and Hoffman* (London: Palgrave Macmillan, 2008).

Peter Hunt and Millicent Lenz, *Alternative Worlds in Fantasy Fiction* (London and New York: Continuum, 2001).

Ruth Nadelman Lynn, *Fantasy Literature for Children and Young Adults: An Annotated Bibliography*, 4th edn (New York: Bowker, 1995).

Colin Manlove, *From Alice to Harry Potter: Children's Fantasy in England* (Christchurch: Cybereditions, 2003).

Nikkianne Moody and Clare Horrocks (eds), *Children's Fantasy Fiction: Debates for the 21st Century* (Liverpool: Association for Research in Popular Fictions, 2005).

On myth

An introductory sampling of texts that discuss or illustrate the background to Tolkien's mythology might include:

Theodore M. Andersson, *The Icelandic Family Saga* (Cambridge, MA: Harvard University Press, 1967).

Henry Adams Bellows, *The Prose Edda* (New York: Biblo and Tannen, 1969).

Kath Filmer-Davies, *Fantasy Fiction and Welsh Myth* (Basingstoke: Palgrave Macmillan, 1996).

Gwyn Jones and Thomas Jones (ed. and trans.), *The Mabinogion* (1949; London: Dent, 1989).

Stephen A. Mitchell, *Heroic Sagas and Ballads* (Ithaca, NY: Cornell University Press, 1991).

John D. Niles, Beowulf: *The Poem and Its Tradition* (Cambridge, MA: Harvard University Press, 1983).

Snorri Sturluson, *The Poetic Edda: Tales from Norse Mythology*, trans. Jean I. Young (Berkeley: University of California Press, 1954).

C. W. Sullivan III, *Welsh Celtic Myth in Modern Fantasy* (Westport, CT: Greenwood, 1989).

John Tucker (ed.), *Sagas of the Icelanders* (New York: Garland, 1989).

On-line materials

To venture into the extent of materials of every kind available on the internet is probably unwise. A sampling of sites that contain various kinds of critical material might be:

- the Tolkien Society: www.tolkiensociety.org/index.html (accessed 29 July 2012), which has archive resources and reading packs
- http://tolkiengateway.net/wiki/Main_Page (accessed 29 July 2012), a wiki site with over 10,000 articles
- www.tolkienlibrary.com/news/tolkiennews.htm (accessed 29 July 2012)
- www.theonering.net (accessed 29 July 2012), a very sophisticated fan site.

Index